Jimmy Carter

Jimmy Carter

Citizen of the South

Kaye Lanning Minchew

Published in association with Georgia Humanities

The University of Georgia Press ATHENS

This publication is made possible in part through a grant from the Bradley Hale Fund for Southern Studies

© 2021 by the University of Georgia Press
Athens, Georgia 30602
www.ugapress.org
All rights reserved

Designed by Erin Kirk
Set in New Caledonia
Printed and bound by Versa Press

The paper in this book meets the guidelines for permanence and durability of the Committee on Production Guidelines for Book Longevity of the Council on Library Resources.

Most University of Georgia Press titles are available from popular e-book vendors.

Printed in the United States of America
25 24 23 22 21 C 5 4 3 2 1

Library of Congress Cataloging-in-Publication Data

Names: Minchew, Kaye Lanning, author.
Title: Jimmy Carter : citizen of the South / Kaye Lanning
    Minchew.
Other titles: Citizen of the South
Description: Athens : The University of Georgia Press,
    [2021] | Includes bibliographical references and index.
Identifiers: LCCN 2020042469 | ISBN 9780820357409
    (hardback)
Subjects: LCSH: Carter, Jimmy, 1924– | Carter, Jimmy, 1924–
    —Family. | Plains (Ga.)—Biography. | Plains (Ga.)—
    Social life and customs—20th century. | Ex-presidents—
    United States—Biography. | Presidents—United States—
    Biography. | Governors—Georgia—Biography.
Classification: LCC E873 .M56 2021 | DDC 973.926092
    [B]—dc23
LC record available at https://lccn.loc.gov/2020042469

CONTENTS

ACKNOWLEDGMENTS

Jimmy Carter, Citizen of the South had its start on a beautiful Saturday during Memorial Day weekend, 2016. I had the first public signing for my book *A President in Our Midst: Franklin Delano Roosevelt in Georgia* at the Little White House in Warm Springs. Family and friends joined me there, including my husband Greg, college roommate Robin Riley Chandler, and friend Ken Thomas. Arden Williams of Georgia Humanities came as did her son, Danny Williams. I signed books in the breezeway at the entrance. During a quiet moment, the idea of doing a similar book, which relied on archival photographs and oral histories to tell the story of another Georgia president, came to me. Jimmy Carter spoke in Warm Springs several times, including in September 1976 when he stood in front of the Little White House and officially kicked off his fall campaign.

I am indebted to many people for their support. Jamil Zainaldin, director emeritus of Georgia Humanities, Kevin Shirley of the LaGrange College History Department, and Sheryl Vogt of the Russell Library at UGA have been particularly encouraging. Pat Allen, Nate Holly, Lisa Bayer, and Jon Davies of the University of Georgia Press have been tremendously helpful and supportive. Steven H. Hochman of the Carter Center generously answered questions and reviewed text. Archivists and librarians at LaGrange College, the Jimmy Carter Presidential Library and Museum, the Stuart A. Rose Library at Emory University, the Russell Library and Hargrett Special Collections at the University of Georgia, Georgia Tech Special Collections, Special Collections at Georgia State University, the Atlanta History Center, Mercer University, Georgia Southwestern State University, and the Troup County Archives provided assistance. Particularly helpful have been Tony Clark and Sara Mitchell at the Carter

Library, Jill Severn at the Russell Library, and Charlene Baxter and Arthur Robinson at LaGrange College. Chris Olson Becker at the Carter Center and Bryan Thomas at Habitat for Humanity International generously responded to numerous requests. Anastatia Sims, Mary Ann Wilson, and Harriet Keith offered much assistance.

I so appreciate the support of Lanning and Minchew family members and close friends who have shared the excitement and stress of the project. Special thanks for continuing encouragement from my husband Greg Minchew, who has done so many different things to make this book possible. Thank you all.

Jimmy Carter

INTRODUCTION

In a few days, I will lay down my official responsibilities in this office—to take up once more the only title in our democracy superior to that of president, the title of citizen.

With the words above, Jimmy Carter, the thirty-ninth president of the United States, began his farewell address to the nation. That night, January 14, 1981, six days before Ronald Reagan took office, many expected Jimmy and Rosalynn Carter to disappear into the sunset, only to be heard from on occasional anniversaries. Indeed, the Carters themselves did not know what the future held for them. He had spent most of the last twenty years running for office and serving the people of Georgia and the United States. Decades later, many people agree that he is one of the best former presidents ever and that he used the office of presidency as a stepping-stone to even greater things.

Georgia and the South nurtured Jimmy Carter, provided a place for him to heal after election defeats in 1966 and 1980, and offered a base for him to grow and move in directions he never expected. The importance of the red clay in his veins and the southern drawl in his voice cannot be overstated, as they combined with his character as a principled man throughout his life. He has used the South for his purposes when entering politics and has given back to Georgia and the South. Carter has been both a witness and an important participant in Georgia's transformation from the Jim Crow years to the post–civil rights era as he helped the South and the nation transition from the days of segregation to modern times.

THIS UNLIKELY MAN who became president of the United States called rural southwest Georgia home. Downtown Plains and Wise Sanitarium appear as iconic symbols of rural America in the early twentieth century. Both Jimmy and Rosalynn grew up in tiny Plains, which had a population of about 651 people in 1980.[1] For most of the twentieth century there had been few clues that one of the citizens walking the streets would one day become the president. In 1905, Plains looked like many small rural towns across the country. The economic livelihood of most residents depended on agriculture and serving farmers from the surrounding area. The dust of south Georgia came into town from fields and unpaved streets for several more decades. Rosalynn remembered that "dust was a prominent part of our life. Billows of red dust engulfed us every time a car passed or the wind blew. The only paved road in town was the main highway that went to Americus. . . . The dust would . . . seep into the house. There was no way to keep it out."[2]

Though the Carters lived in rural southwest Georgia, miles from the nearest big cities, the eldest child of Lillian and Earl Carter drew his first breath at Wise Sanitarium, making him the first U.S. president to be born in a hospital. Earl worked as a businessman, farmer, and politician while Lillian served as a nurse who cared for many in the community. She received her training at Grady Hospital in Atlanta and at the hospital in Plains, operated by the three Wise doctors. When the time came for her to deliver her firstborn, the sanitarium had an open room, and Dr. Sam Wise urged her to have her baby there instead of at the Carter home. The doctor thought that if she delivered at the hospital, she would be able to return to work more quickly.[3] That building now serves as a skilled nursing facility for Lillian Carter Health and Rehabilitation.

Plains, Ga. — Home of President Jimmy Carter in 1905

The Carter family had been in Georgia since the 1770s and in southwest Georgia since the early 1850s. Lillian's family, the Gordys, also arrived in southwest Georgia by the 1830s, when they settled in nearby Chattahoochee County.[4] Railroads first reached Sumter County in 1854. Thirty years later, the Americus, Preston, and Lumpkin Railroad opened. By 1889, this became the Savannah, Americus, and Montgomery Railroad, thus giving the SAM name to the line. Railroads provided the main system of transportation in those days and helped move crops, especially cotton, peaches, and watermelon, to markets in Macon, Savannah, and elsewhere. Passengers also used the railroads. The new community of Plains became the first city in Sumter County to get its start because of the rail line.

Located in a flat area, the city originally had the name "the Plains of Dura" after a place mentioned in the Old Testament. People from neighboring communities moved to Plains to be close to the railroad; however, railroad reorganizations and the coming of the automobile took their toll on rail lines. In the twentieth century, as farmers began to use trucks more often to ship their produce, Plains gradually became less of a commercial center for this part of Sumter County and southwest Georgia.

The Gordy and Carter families fostered the development of Jimmy, sisters Gloria and Ruth, and younger brother Billy. Rosalynn Smith, three years younger than Jimmy, grew up three miles from him. She and Ruth were good friends grow-ing up, and Rosalynn periodically spent nights at the Carter home.[5] During their earliest years, the Carter and Smith chil-dren had ample time to explore the town and countryside.

Jimmy Carter spent his first four years in Plains before his family moved to the nearby farming community of Archery. The younger members of the Carter family spent much of their days with the children of tenant farmers who lived on family property. African American boys comprised most of the young Jimmy's playmates. Only gradually did he realize that blacks and whites received different treatment in stores, theaters, and schools. Indeed, Earl and Lillian even treated blacks differently from each other. For instance, in the 1930s, his mother welcomed at least one African American into their home through the front door: Alvan Johnson, the northern-educated son of their prominent neighbor, Bishop William Decker Johnson. Bishop Johnson served the nearby St. Mark African Methodist Episcopal (AME) Church. He also opened and operated a school for black youths, the Johnson Home Industrial College, which started in 1912.[6] Earl Carter quietly left the house rather than show that he approved of blacks, including Alvan or his father, using any door other than the one in the rear of the house.[7] Jimmy Carter later said that his "mother was always, for those days, quite liberal on the race issue. She was the most liberal white person that I ever knew."[8] Segregation and the pretense of "separate but equal" would remain the law of the land in the Deep South for several more decades.

THE PLAINS COMMUNITY indoctrinated Jimmy and Rosalynn in its southern norms and traditions. Their social lives generally revolved around school and church. The Carters attended Plains Baptist, while Plains Methodist included the Smith family on its rolls. Plains Baptist Church provided an ongoing religious base for Jimmy until he and Rosalynn decided to join Maranatha Baptist Church on January 25, 1981, following a dispute over integration at Plains Baptist.[9] Teachers at Plains High School, including Miss Julia Coleman and Y. T. Sheffield, recognized Jimmy's intelligence and abilities and encouraged him. The teachers had great influence in helping shape Jimmy and Rosalynn's lives, promoting the American dream of working hard and having a life better and maybe easier than their parents had. Rosalynn remembered Miss Coleman saying, "Any schoolboy, even one of ours, might grow up to be president of the United States."[10]

CARTER ATTENDED GEORGIA SOUTHWESTERN COLLEGE in Americus and the Georgia School of Technology before graduating from the U.S. Naval Academy in June 1946.[11] Rosalynn also attended Georgia Southwestern. They married in July 1946. He planned to make the navy his career until his father got ill and died in 1953. Jimmy realized the important role his father played in the community, and after much personal debate he decided that they should move their sons back to Plains and take over the family peanut business.[12] Jimmy soon became involved in all aspects of the business, including producing and selling seed peanuts. He accepted appointment to the Sumter County Board of Education and joined the Lions Club, where he served as club president and district governor. He and Rosalynn soon had busy family, professional, and social lives in Plains and Sumter County.

Earl Carter had served a few months in the Georgia legislature in 1953 before becoming ill with cancer, so the thought that Jimmy might one day serve in the legislature had surely crossed their minds. In 1962, Jimmy first sought election by entering the race for Georgia State Senate. Georgia laws had changed earlier that year, eliminating the county unit system. That system had been in place since 1917 and allowed rural counties to control Georgia elections. Candidates had to focus on winning counties rather than winning the popular vote.

Carter lost the 1962 primary election due to voter fraud by the Quitman County political machine: 117 people voted in alphabetical order and 163 more votes were cast than actual people who voted. Dead people also voted in that election. Joe Hurst, a longtime political boss, orchestrated the fraud. Carter decided to fight the injustice. He had to quickly find people who could help his cause. Through family members he met Atlanta attorney Charles Kirbo, who assisted with the legal challenges. Kirbo became a lifelong advisor and friend. Carter also found an interested reporter, John Pennington, a writer for the *Atlanta Journal* who investigated the case and exposed the fraud to a statewide audience. Courts in south Georgia ended up overturning the results. Carter won that seat in the general election and served two terms as a state senator.[13]

Carter never actively took part in the civil rights protests of the Sixties even though Martin Luther King Jr. and others fought segregation in November 1961 in Albany, Georgia, less than forty miles from Plains. Carter, a businessman and family man, chose to stay away from the struggles, though he refused to join the White Citizens' Council in Plains in the 1960s even when their members threatened to boycott the Carter peanut business. He also actively sought to have his church admit black members.

Four years in the Georgia Senate generated increasing political ambitions in Jimmy Carter as he set his sights on other offices. He initially planned to seek the congressional seat for southwest Georgia in 1966, a seat he would have likely won, but changed his mind and ran for governor. This tumultuous time of political and social change in the United States involved civil rights and affected most aspects of life. The Peach State had begun a painful transition from Jim Crow rule to civil rights for all. During that election, Carter tended to be neither liberal nor conservative. Indeed, he described himself as "conservative, moderate, liberal and middle-of-the-road. . . . I believe I am a more complicated person than that."[14] He ran a unity campaign but did not openly support segregation or racial reform.

His major campaign activity consisted of shaking hands with as many people as he or family members could reach. He hoped his hard work would make up for his lack of name recognition beyond the Sumter and Webster County areas. Georgia residents and journalists asked questions like "Jimmy Who?"[15] Carter lost in the Democratic primary to Lester Maddox, a strong segregationist. Though the experience was painful and depressing, Carter matured as a politician during the 1966 race and learned much that would help him in his 1970 and 1976 campaigns.

He ran for governor again in 1970 with a better election organization and more modern techniques, including relying more on polling data and printed graphics. He campaigned heavily across the state. That year, he positioned himself as more conservative than he had in 1966. He appealed to people who had voted for George Wallace, the segregationist from Alabama, in his 1968 presidential run by seeking out the segregationist vote. Under Georgia laws at the time, Maddox could not succeed himself as governor and instead ran for lieutenant governor. Candidate Carter declared Lester Maddox to be "the essence of the Democratic Party" and added that he was "proud" to be on the ticket with him. Carter also joined Wallace in opposing court-ordered busing of public-school students to achieve integration.[16] Carter ran a very negative race by portraying former governor Carl Sanders as a liberal candidate closely linked to the national Democratic Party. Longtime Georgia political leader Zell Miller called this one of the roughest gubernatorial campaigns in Georgia history.[17]

Recognizing that many Georgia voters had trouble accepting the racial changes of the 1960s, Carter employed different positions on racial matters at different times in that campaign. His political pragmatism helped him win the election. He then took an unexpected stance during his inaugural address as governor on January 12, 1971. He proclaimed, "I say to you quite frankly the time for racial discrimination is over. . . . We who are strong or in positions of leadership must realize that the responsibility for making correct decisions in the future is ours."[18] He then proceeded to govern according to what he considered to be right for the people of the state.

The 1960s and early 1970s proved to be traumatic years for Americans. U.S. participation in the Vietnam War generated much dissension as servicemen came home from Southeast Asia to boos and jeers. Then five men connected to the Nixon reelection committee broke into Democratic headquarters in the Watergate Hotel in Washington, D.C., in June 1972.

Members of the Nixon administration denied all involvement with the crime. The following year, the Senate Watergate hearings started and in November 1973 Nixon famously declared "I am not a crook" during a national televised broadcast. Nixon resigned from office on August 9, 1974, before being impeached by the House of Representatives. During these years, many Americans lost faith in the presidency and other elected offices.[19]

Midway through his term as governor, Carter began to seriously consider seeking the highest office in the land. He had come to appreciate that the United States needed a leader of high moral character and he realized that he could lead as well as or better than other people seeking election. His keen political instincts also led him to believe that the political climate of the mid-1970s could give him a chance of being elected despite the fact that most people outside of his home state had never heard of him. He officially announced his intentions on December 12, 1974. This surprised many Georgians, while he and his supporters worked hard to gain name recognition and support.

Carter beat out many Democratic contenders to become the party nominee. He then defeated Gerald Ford to become president. People appreciated his pledge of honesty and his moral character during those post-Watergate days. Jimmy Carter won election as an outsider who would not lie to the public and would be an honorable president. He became one of the first presidential candidates ever to make his religious beliefs part of his campaign. Martin Luther King Sr. ("Daddy King") supported Carter, helping assure the national election for the Democrat.

People from Georgia were some of the closest advisors and supporters of the Carters. The Peanut Brigade, volunteers from Georgia who went to New Hampshire, Iowa, and elsewhere, helped Carter win the Democratic nomination in 1975. The "Georgia Mafia," as it was named by the press, included a tight group of aides who worked with Governor Carter plus others who joined the administration in Washington. The men had little if any national political experience before going to the White House. The group included his chief of staff Hamilton Jordan and press secretary Jody Powell at its core plus congressional liaison Frank Moore, budget director Bert Lance, communications director Gerald Rafshoon, domestic policy advisor Stuart Eizenstat, appointments secretary Phil Wise, and White House counsel Robert Lipshutz.[20] Other southerners, like George Wallace, proved to be both friends and foes at various times.

People from the South strongly supported Carter. In the 1976 general election, all the southern states except Virginia went for Carter, helping propel him to a win over Gerald Ford. When he took office in January 1977, Carter became the first person elected to the presidency from the Deep South since 1848. He overcame much to get elected, including a decades-old bias against residents of the former Confederate states. The Carters arrived in Washington, D.C., to much fanfare in 1977. Following the inauguration, the Carter family got out of their limousine and walked down Pennsylvania Avenue during the parade. They symbolically showed the world that they were going to be closer to the American people than his predecessors, Gerald Ford and especially Richard Nixon, had been.

WHILE IN OFFICE, Carter had several major successes, especially in the foreign policy arena. Achievements included the Camp David Accords, the Panama Canal treaties, a peace treaty between Egypt and Israel, the SALT II treaty with the Soviet Union, and establishing diplomatic relations with the People's Republic of China. On the domestic side, the Carter administration established a major energy program with the new Department of Energy, major environmental and conservation measures, and a renewed focus on education. Many negatives impacted the administration, though, especially the stagnant economy, including high unemployment and inflation that hurt many of Carter's supporters.[21] Then, Iranian students took sixty-six American citizens hostage in Tehran and held fifty-two of them for fourteen months. The eyes of the nation focused on that horror for most of the last year of his administration.

Always a hard campaigner before, Carter spent relatively little time in 1980 actively seeking reelection. By November 4, 1980, the American people wanted a change. Major supporters from the 1976 race, including Christians who left the Democratic Party to join the Moral Majority, voted against giving Carter a second term in office. Ronald Reagan won the 1980 election overwhelmingly as Americans selected the former Hollywood actor and rejected the continued leadership of the former peanut farmer.

The Carters, especially Jimmy, had little time to think about their future. On the morning of November 5, he did what he had done after most of his elections and spent time with Rosalynn and close friend Charles Kirbo. Already depressed by the vote, the Carters heard more unwelcome news: the family faced a bleak financial future. The family peanut warehouse business had been placed in a blind trust after the 1976 election. Jimmy's younger brother and business partner Billy had mostly neglected the business when he began spending his time at the gas station that he bought in Plains in the early 1970s and pursuing other career options, including acting. Large accounting and legal fees had eaten into profits. Kirbo recommended selling the business as soon as possible and, within months of the election defeat, the Carter peanut business, which had been in the family for decades, had been sold.

Before the 1980 election, Jimmy and Rosalynn had never discussed what they would do if Carter lost the election. Rosalynn and Jimmy soon left for Camp David to recuperate and rest from the stressful election. "At first—for just a few hours—we considered living in Atlanta, but soon agreed that we should go to our own home in Plains, try to pay our debts, and spend a while getting our financial affairs in shape."[22] By November 11 the Carters had returned to the White House as reality began to sink in. As Jimmy said, "Rosalynn seemed seriously depressed. I tried to cheer her up by talking about our home in Plains . . . and what it would mean to be free from campaigning or serving in public office for the first time in almost twenty years."[23] A few months later, he told *Parade* magazine that he had been "involuntarily retired" from the presidency.[24]

Despite the election loss, Carter had a busy lame-duck session. During the transition period Carter quickly realized that people do not respond to a leader on his way out the same way they did before, but he, Vice President Walter Mondale, and others in the administration continued to pursue their legislative agenda. Congress worked hard as both parties came together to pass some much-needed legislation. The Superfund legislation offers one example, establishing a system of insurance premiums charged to the chemical industry to clean toxic waste sites. Also, the Alaska National Interest Lands Conservation Act became official with a presidential signing on December 2, 1980, providing protection for over 150 million acres of land in our northernmost state.[25]

At the White House, many friends and family members came to visit while they still had the opportunity. The Carters also took time out during the lame-duck weeks to attend the Sugar Bowl in New Orleans on January 1, 1981. They watched the University of Georgia football team defeat Notre Dame 17–10 and win the national championship. In that famed game, Herschel Walker ran for 150 yards and received the Most Valuable Player award. Georgia governor George Busbee, Griffin Bell, Bert Lance, and almost two hundred other Georgians, White House aides, and members of the press joined Carter in his suite at the stadium. Georgia fans went wild after the game and concerned security guards had to get the president safely out of the Louisiana Superdome.[26] Following the game, Carter made no comments about the results but he waved his red and black shakers and left the game happy.

JIMMY CARTER TOOK A LAST TRIP TO CAMP DAVID aboard the Marine One helicopter on January 16, 1981. He spent most of these days trying to gain freedom for the fifty-two American diplomats and citizens being held hostage in Iran. Freeing the hostages remained the number-one goal of the administration, just as their freedom had been every day since the crisis started on November 4, 1979. In his last two weeks in office, Carter and his staff worked on the Iranian deal almost full time. By Tuesday morning, January 20, 1981, Carter had slept very little in forty-eight hours. Negotiations focused around a complicated plan to return over $12 million in Iranian funds in exchange for the hostages flying out of the country. Plans, hopes, and goals for his second term as president had evaporated, but Carter had limited time to reflect on his exit from the White House or on personal matters because of his focus on the hostage crisis.

At noon on January 20, 1981, Ronald Reagan became president and Jimmy and Rosalynn boarded Air Force One to fly home. Longtime friends and other visitors, including the lieutenant governor of Georgia, gathered in Plains to greet their former leader. Heavy rains added to the somber mood. Maxine Reese, who had helped run the Carter campaign in Plains, remembered that "everything that had ever happened here—every outside gathering, every fundraiser, anything that we ever had—the weather was good. . . . But when Jimmy came home to stay, it rained. And the whole street was full of umbrellas; it was just a sea of umbrellas." A huge covered-dish dinner had been organized and large crowds filled the small town despite the weather.[27]

By late January the Carters had transitioned into a new-normal lifestyle. They both wrote what would become best-selling books: Rosalynn penned *First Lady from Plains* while Carter wrote *Keeping Faith: Memoirs of a President*. During 1981 and 1982 the Carters developed a general template that would guide them through the next decades of their very busy lives. At fifty-six, Carter was a relatively young former president. Longtime friend Betty Pope had assured him that the Lord had bigger and better plans for Jimmy in this world.[28] In January 1981 the Carters felt certain they still had productive years ahead of them.

Carter could not totally withdraw from the public eye. He and Rosalynn agreed that they did not want to start another company after the sale of the family peanut business unless they needed to supplement their family income. Thanks to the success of their memoirs, his stipend as a former president, and their simple lifestyle, they did not return to peanut farming or running a peanut warehouse. He had one more official function to perform, though, as a former president.[29] Under the Presidential Libraries Act, the twenty-five million documents, letters, files, and memorabilia of the administration belonged to him and he had to oversee their care and storage for the coming years. He deeded the materials to the United States and the Carters began to raise the funds needed to assure the permanent preservation of these papers. This task would take a great amount of effort and work.

Back in Plains, they also had to focus on daughter Amy and her schooling. Amy was nine years old when she arrived at the White House and she had spent a third of her life in Washington, D.C. Leaving friends had to be traumatic for the young teenager. Amy joined her parents in Plains and attended Sumter County public schools since Plains High School had closed in 1981. She later enrolled at Woodward Academy, a college preparatory school in Atlanta. She no longer had to grow up in the public eye.

Within weeks of his leaving office, Carter accepted an appointment as university distinguished professor at Emory University.[30] Before this, the Great Park area just east of downtown Atlanta had been recommended as a possible location for the Carter Presidential Library, on land owned by the state. Once he decided to work at Emory, Carter opted to build the library there in Atlanta, the capital of Georgia and one of the most populous cities in the South. A short while later, Carter awoke in the middle of the night with an idea.

He wanted to develop more than just a library and archives. He envisioned something like Camp David where he and others could work to resolve and prevent conflicts. He soon affiliated the Carter Center with Emory University. During this time, a major fight occurred in Atlanta with Carter at its center. The Georgia Department of Transportation wanted a four-lane "Presidential Parkway" to lead to the Carter Center and library. The route would go near historic Atlanta neighborhoods, including the Druid Hills area next to Emory.

Some of the protestors included Emory faculty and staff members who feared future encroachment into the neighborhoods. In the end, DOT and Carter accepted a smaller road to the Carter property.[31] Carter soon started fundraising for the library and Carter Center.

Since its construction, the Carter Center has provided an opportunity for Carter to do much of what he does best. The nongovernmental organization advances peace and health around the world and addresses issues of public policy. The institute has always had an action agenda and looks for measurable results. In 2002, Carter received the Nobel Peace Prize for helping bring about the Camp David Accords between Israel and Egypt and, more importantly, the extensive work he had done after his time in office to advance international peace and human rights.[32]

DURING HIS EARLY post-presidency years Jimmy Carter also returned to his longtime love of teaching Sunday school, this time at the relatively new Maranatha Baptist Church in Plains, a calling he would continue to follow for four more decades. He and Rosalynn also became the best-known volunteers with Habitat for Humanity, a global nonprofit housing organization which started in Americus. The Carters got involved with the group between 1982 and 1983 and have continued to be dedicated Habitat volunteers. Since 1984 they have given a week each year to Habitat, helping build homes for needy people in Plains, elsewhere in Georgia and the South, and across the world. They have joined over 103,000 other volunteers in fourteen countries to help build, renovate, and repair over 4,331 homes.[33]

Except for his time in the navy and the White House, Carter has spent his life in Georgia. He has worked and traveled throughout the world but, time and again, Carter has returned to Georgia and the South for time to reflect, enjoy, recuperate, and relax. Plains has provided an important anchor throughout his life, while other Georgia places like the coast and the mountains have been important vacation sites.

Jimmy and Rosalynn Carter have continued to rely on this southern base in their activities since leaving the presidency in 1981. Jimmy Carter knew that he had helped restore respect to the presidency after the resignation of Richard Nixon in August 1974. He had been an honorable man who worked diligently to extend peace and human rights around the world. He had worked hard for the American people and had told them the truth. After he and Rosalynn returned to their tiny hometown of Plains, the people of Georgia and the South welcomed them with open arms and supported their activities. Carter has redefined what it means to be an active and exemplary former president, showing the world how a moral leader can act while proudly wearing the title of citizen of the South.

CHAPTER 1

Early Years

PLAINS, GEORGIA, AND THE SOUTH have played important roles in the life and development of Jimmy Carter, his parents, and their families. Like so many Georgians in the late nineteenth and twentieth centuries, Earl Carter staunchly supported the Democratic party and embodied the ideals of a self-made man in a poor region of the country. Earl bought a farm, started businesses, and expected his sons and daughters to help while he also quietly looked after the laborers and sharecroppers on his farm and other people in need. Lillian Carter defied the female stereotypes of the day and spent most of her life working outside the home. She had a strong independent streak and continued to work outside the home even after the birth of her children. Lillian and Earl thus gave Jimmy and his siblings both a traditional and a forward-thinking upbringing. Teachers in the Plains schools and church leaders further enforced ideas of working and studying hard and always representing your family in the best possible light. Falling in love with and marrying a hometown girl—who Lillian Carter had helped deliver—offers further evidence of Carter's traditional values.

Part of the fascination with Jimmy Carter lies with his early life. His is an authentic story of the Deep South, where a modest agricultural economy combined with the challenges of social equity and human rights. The story is also one of people in a backcountry rural area working daily to overcome the challenges of the Great Depression. Race, gender, class, and politics all played important roles in the development and upbringing of Carter.

Lillian and James Earl Carter welcomed their first child and oldest son into the world on October 1, 1924. Their ancestors, including the Carter and Gordy families, had been in south Georgia for almost a century before his birth. The families had been farmers and merchants. Lillian and Earl

Carter married in 1923 and a few years later moved two and a half miles away to a farm in the Archery community on the border of rural Sumter and Webster Counties. Earl Carter farmed and ran a store, very traditional male roles for the time. Lillian, however, always worked outside the home, during a time when few married women worked. As a registered nurse she assisted Dr. Sam Wise and helped deliver many Plains babies. An independent thinker, she and Earl had four children, Jimmy, Gloria, Ruth, and Billy. Carter has said that "there was no doubt that my father was the dominant person in our family, although mother was a strong-willed woman and really blossomed forth much more after my father's death in 1953."[1]

ANNIE MAE HOLLIS, the cook for the Carter family, sits with Ruth on her lap while Gloria Carter sits beside them. Jimmy Carter, Fred Foster, and Rembert Forrest are gathered behind Annie Mae.

In the South during much of the twentieth century, white families often had African American household help. These women generally served as cooks, cleaners, nurses, and nannies who kept households running smoothly. Since Lillian frequently worked outside the house, the Carter family employed others to assist at home. Two black women proved to be among the most important adults in the young life of Jimmy Carter: Rachel Clark and Annie Mae Hollis helped raise Jimmy, his brother, and sisters.

Rachel Clark and her husband Jack lived on the Carter property in Archery. Jimmy would sometimes spend the night at their home and the Clarks taught him much about farm life. Miss Hollis also cared for the Carter children when they lived in the country. After Jimmy went to college, Hollis married and moved to Albany. She came back to Plains in the 1950s at the request of Lillian Carter. Carter later lovingly recalled, "I will never forget that when my father breathed his last breath on July 22, 1953, Annie Mae [Hollis] Rhodes was holding him in her arms."[2]

THE CARTERS MOVED TO ARCHERY in the late 1920s. Jimmy lived there from age four until he went to college. Life revolved around the Seaboard Air Line Railroad maintenance crew. When the family arrived, the simple farmhouse lacked most modern conveniences, including running water, indoor plumbing, and electricity. White sand surrounded the home. Carter remembers, "We had to sweep frequently to remove fowl and animal droppings and leaves from our . . . trees. Most of our brush brooms were made of small saplings or limbs of dogwood, which were resilient and long lasting."[3] Earl Carter sold the property in 1949.

Activities on the Carter farm focused on family, neighbors, the land, and crops. Aside from his sisters Ruth and Gloria, Jimmy Carter had mostly African American playmates. Carter has reflected that "all my neighbors and my playmates growing up were black." He added, "We had a very close and intimate family life. The whole growing up experience was focused around my mother and father and my two sisters.

Billy was much younger than I was—he came along thirteen years after I did."[4] Twenty-seven families called Archery home, with only two of the families, the Carters and the Watsons, being white. Edward Watson served as section foreman for the Seaboard Railroad.[5]

Despite their living in the country, much of life during these formative years centered around Plains, where the Carter children attended school and church. Jimmy Carter later reflected on that time. "It was a pleasant life and we were very attentive to the proprieties of Plains. We never failed to be at Sunday school on time. Daddy was a teacher and we stayed for church. Plains Baptist was a half-time church then. Plains Methodist was a half-time church and we would alternate back and forth on occasion because they never had services on the same Sunday. The school was a very central point for social events as was the church. . . . We had a very stable life and an isolated life but a pleasant life."[6]

EARL, ALONG WITH THREE OF HIS CHILDREN,
Gloria, Ruth and Jimmy, stands in a doorway in the early 1930s.

Rural electrification officially began on August 11, 1938, during an afternoon program in Barnesville, Georgia, less than ninety miles north of the Carter farm in Archery. President Franklin Delano Roosevelt spoke to a crowd of fifty thousand or so at the stadium at Gordon Military College. Cities and towns had had electricity for years but homes and stores in rural areas relied on candles, kerosene lanterns, and batteries for light and power. The Rural Electrification Administration, one of the New Deal programs designed to fight the Great Depression, brought electricity to rural areas across the United States. The Carter farm had power later that year and Earl Carter made sure the home had electric lights in each room plus an electric refrigerator and stove.[7] Earl Carter entered the political arena for the first time when he began serving on the board of the Sumter Electric Membership Corporation.

Carter has spoken often about getting electricity. He noted that "an almost unbelievable change took place in our lives when electricity came to the farm. The continuing burden of pumping water, sawing wood, building fires in the cooking stove, filling lamps with kerosene, and closing the day's activity with the coming of night . . . all these things changed dramatically."[8] He fondly recalls getting electricity, saying in an interview, "Daddy really became active in politics and outside affairs only after REA came and I've told a lot of people . . . that the greatest day in my life was not being inaugurated President, it wasn't even marrying Rosalynn. It was when they turned the electricity on at our farm because that totally transformed our lifestyle."[9]

JIMMY CARTER HAS TALKED ABOUT THE HOLIDAYS, especially Christmas, in several of his books. Generally, family members received simple presents. He looks back at his seventh Christmas with special fondness. He had the measles and could not leave the house. He had wanted a pony but did not expect to receive one. His parents came in his room and suggested Santa Claus might have left him something outside. He opened a bedroom window and a pony stood in the yard. "I have never been more excited in my life and of course then for years, I rode my pony, whom I called Lady. . . . It really was one of the transformative moments of my boyhood."[10]

Even a present had to earn its keep. As Carter writes in *An Hour before Daylight*, "Daddy believed that everything on the farm should pay its own way, even a pony, so we took her at proper intervals to spend a few days to breed" with a pony belonging to a friend. The pony had some offspring. "It was a big event when her colts came, but a sad day when they were sold, for as much as $25."[11]

EARL CARTER served as a first lieutenant in the army during World War I. Jimmy and his generation grew up during the Depression and then served in World War II and the Korean War. Here, Jimmy and his dog Bozo paused long enough for someone to take a photograph. When out of school and not helping on the farm, he participated in a variety of activities. He went fishing or swimming in the nearby Flint River and played baseball and other games with African American children.

Like so many young people of the day, he also frequently went hunting. He first learned to use firearms at age five or six. His father instructed him about guns and Jack Clark helped him train dogs for quail hunting. During the twentieth century, south Georgia farms gained a reputation for fine quail hunting. Even during the worst of the Depression, families everywhere had dogs. Carter has remembered, "Except for transient day laborers, I don't remember any farm family that didn't own at least one hound dog and a single-barrel shotgun. . . . My only claim to fame concerning dogs was that I happened to own the best squirrel-hunter in the Plains community. My heart still picks up a beat when I look at the old photographs of me and Bozo, a Boston bulldog. He was a constant playmate of mine from the time he was a little puppy, and everyone was surprised that a dog of this non-sporting breed developed superb hunting instincts."[12]

YOUNG JIMMY CARTER attended a camp sponsored by the Future Farmers of America. He made good grades and wanted to go to the Naval Academy in Annapolis, even though his father had served in the U.S. Army. His uncle Tom Gordy, his mother's younger brother, joined the navy in the 1930s. "Tom would send me souvenirs from China and he would write me letters. . . . He was really a hero for me."[13] Jimmy remembers always wanting to go to college but knew his family could not afford tuition, so the Naval Academy provided a way to get a free education. "From the time I was five years old, I would always say that someday I would be going to Annapolis, and would become a naval officer."[14] As a child of the Depression, Carter felt the Naval Academy offered him his only real chance to attend college. He said, "All the way through high school, I was hoping and praying, literally praying, that I might get an appointment to Annapolis." At that time, getting into the military academies required political connections. His father supported Stephen Pace of Americus, who served in Congress from 1937 to 1951. After several years of trying, Jimmy eventually received his appointment to the Naval Academy.[15]

Carter recalled years later, "It's not easy for me to understand now why Daddy supported this unswerving commitment to such a distant dream. But perhaps the reasons were the obvious ones: the unattractive nature of farming in those years . . . or just a stubborn determination to reach a long-standing goal."[16] In reality, Earl and Lillian Carter lived in a farming community, but they owned property and had tenants, plus she worked as a nurse. Alton Carter, uncle of Jimmy, sent his two sons to the University of Georgia.

It seems likely that Earl Carter would have found a way to send his son to college if the appointment to the Naval Academy had not materialized.[17] Jimmy did attend Georgia Southwestern and Georgia Tech before going to Annapolis.

EARL CARTER OPERATED A COMMISSARY on the farm in Archery where workers and customers could gather. Jimmy, Gloria, and Ruth all spent time working in the store. Earl Carter showed his entrepreneurial side at the store. They sold cured ham and other farm products, including Plains-made syrup.[18] Earl had a major influence on Jimmy. In a 1988 interview, Jimmy recalled that "Daddy was a very aggressive, competent farmer. We had a wide range of agricultural productions from our farm, basically cotton and peanuts as the cash crop. We also planted corn and other grains and we had a wide range of animal products that we produced." He added, "I guess my father shaped my life more than anyone else as far as work habits and ambitions were concerned." Like many southerners at that time, Earl Carter did not go to college. He attended school through the tenth grade and his son remembers him as being a brilliant businessman.[19]

Young Jimmy showed signs of being a successful entrepreneur himself. He started selling boiled peanuts on the streets of Plains at age five. As soon as the nuts started to mature in the fields, he would pull up vines, pick off the peanuts, and soak them overnight in salty water. Then in the early morning, he boiled them. Green peanuts had to be cooked in water that had enough salt without being too salty.[20] He filled paper sacks and then took the bags to town by walking or riding his bicycle. He had regular customers and sold to salesmen and other visitors. He knew a group of men, some of whom had suffered injuries while serving in World War I, who would make jokes at his expense. He got to know the people and activities of Plains while making these sales.[21] Carter wrote about this southern delicacy in *Why Not the Best?*: "Boiled peanuts, incidentally, should be considered one of the great gifts of God to mankind—but only when done in proper fashion."[22]

As a high school student, Carter took his peanut savings, added money he made buying and selling bales of cotton, and bought five rental houses. He and later his father collected rent each month. He owned the houses for about five years. Carter would later recall, "So that was my first business venture in the commodities market. I came out pretty well in that."[23]

JIMMY CARTER ONCE HAD A SCHOOL ASSIGNMENT to dress as a character in literature and he picked Huck Finn from the classic novel by Mark Twain, complete with the straw hat and fishing pole. Miss Julia Coleman gave her class this assignment at Plains High School. Carter recalled that "outside of my mother and father, I think that one person that affected my life more in the future was Miss Julia Coleman, who was superintendent of our school. She was an extraordinary teacher. . . . She would identify students who had some special interest or abilities and concentrate on those students with extra assignments. . . . She was always challenging me to read classical books and to learn about great painters. And she had on occasion symphonies and operas that she would play for us. . . . So Miss Julia Coleman expanded my life in a cultural sense as a child far beyond what would ordinarily be expected in a very isolated rural community."[24] Miss Coleman encouraged the teachers at Plains High to promote reading for all students. They also regularly participated in debates and spelling contests. At major events later in his life, Carter honored Miss Coleman by repeating one of her quotes: "We must adjust to the changing times and still hold to unchanging principles."[25]

For Carter, the school proved to be "the center of our lives, not only for students but also for the adults. This was the only place that people could meet in Plains in a nondenominational way. Otherwise, you met in your own church." He also noted that the county library provided him with his first official public service job. "My first job in the county was on the Sumter County Library Board. I still have my library card, number 5. And we set up a travelling library, the bookmobile. . . . It would come out to Plains and stop in the grove . . . I think twice a week. And anybody in town could come and check out books from the bookmobile. And if you wanted a particular book, you could order it, and three or four days later they would bring it out to you."[26] Bookmobiles have played important roles in rural counties for several decades.

THE TWENTY-SIX MEMBERS of the Plains High School Class of 1941 gathered before graduation. Jimmy Carter squats on the right in the front row.

These young men and women made up what Tom Brokaw would later call the "Greatest Generation." They grew up during the hardships of the Great Depression and then they fought in World War II or supported war efforts on the home front. These students graduated after eleven years in school. Georgia added the twelfth grade when the state adopted a new constitution in 1945.[27] Carter should have been the valedictorian but lost the position after he and other senior boys left school on April Fool's Day and went to Americus. Carter received zeros for that day and became the salutatorian instead. He later became the only class member to earn a college degree.[28]

Jimmy attended all eleven grades in Plains. His sisters Gloria and Ruth graduated from Plains High in 1943 and 1946, while his brother Billy was a member of the class of 1955. During high school, living on a farm impacted his ability to play sports. His father expected him to help with planting during the spring, so he did not have the option of playing baseball, his favorite sport. Instead he played basketball because the few winter-time farm chores left plenty of free hours. Though the shortest member on the team, he moved quickly and played on a team that relied on fast breaks. Whenever he could, Carter also played tennis, either on the court at the Carter farm or in town. He continued this hobby for decades and would play in the occasional baseball or softball game.

ELEANOR ROSALYNN SMITH and Jimmy Carter seem to have always known each other, but he does not remember noticing her until a visit home while attending the Naval Academy. Miss Lillian had helped deliver Rosalynn three years after she gave birth to Jimmy. The families lived next door to each other before the Carters moved to Archery.[29] Her father, Wilburn Edgar Smith, operated the first garage for motor machines in rural Sumter County. Her mother, Allethea "Allie" Smith, had attended college and received a normal (or teaching) diploma, relatively rare for the time in south Georgia. When Rosalynn turned thirteen, her father became ill and Miss Lillian helped nurse him and gave him shots. He died of leukemia. Her grandmother died the following year. As the eldest of four, Rosalynn remembers, "At age thirteen or fourteen, my life really changed. I had to assume a lot of responsibility because my mother depended on me to help her with the smaller children. . . . But looking back, I didn't help her nearly as much as I should have. She had to go to work."[30]

During their school years, Rosalynn became best friends with Ruth Carter. She visited the Carter home periodically and knew of Jimmy. Though they lived close to each other, they had very different upbringings. He played with African American children and spent a lot of time hunting and fishing. Living in town, she mostly played with the children of townspeople. She has noted, "I grew up in Plains and Jimmy always teased me about being a city girl because he lived out in the country."[31]

JIMMY CARTER LOOKED VERY YOUTHFUL in the Georgia Tech yearbook in 1943 and in the navy.

After he graduated from Plains High, Carter attended Georgia Southwestern College in nearby Americus for a year, where he lived in the dormitory. In 1942 he received his much-desired appointment to the U.S. Naval Academy, though with a one-year deferral. He had the assurance of admission if he met the entrance requirements.[32] He attended the Georgia School of Technology that year and took engineering, math, and science classes so that he would be "as well qualified as possible."[33] Being in college in the midst of World War II meant attending classes with other students involved in the military. Carter joined the Naval Reserve Officers Training Corps at Tech and wore a uniform to campus one day a week. He recalls that the year proved to be a "very exciting experience for me because my life's ambition was to be in the navy and a professional officer. . . . It was serious business in the war years and extremely competitive."[34] The Tech yearbook for 1943 paid tribute "to the honored sons of Tech who have given their lives in World War II in order that the 'American Way of Life' shall not perish from the face of the earth."[35]

During this time, Rosalynn graduated from Plains High in 1944. Her father had made a dying wish that his four children attend college but she knew that funds for her schooling were limited. Like Jimmy, she decided to attend Georgia Southwestern, a junior college. She commuted by riding to college in the mornings with a neighbor who worked in Americus and returned home on a Greyhound bus. A friend, Allene Timmerman Haugabook, remembered that many Plains students attended Georgia Southwestern. She reported, "Never was getting to and from Americus an easy task." Allene even had a recurring dream of being in Americus and having no way to get home. In her dreams, she walked home in the dark.[36]

Rosalynn continued to visit with Ruth Carter, still a high school student. She remembers, "That was the year I fell in love with Jimmy's picture. . . . I couldn't keep my eyes off the photograph of her idolized, older brother. . . . I thought he was the most handsome young man I had ever seen." That fall, she and Ruth worked to get the two together. During Christmas, "Jimmy teased me about falling in love with his uniform, and I'll have to admit he took my breath away in his dress blues."[37] They then got to know each other by mail. Photos of handsome Midshipman Carter helped make sure that Rosalynn Smith did not forget him.

IN 1943, THE SON OF A GEORGIA PEANUT FARMER HEADED TO ANNAPOLIS. His years at the Naval Academy forever shaped his life, just as the military academies have affected generations of students. When he graduated from the Naval Academy, Jimmy Carter had two women pinning his uniform: his fiancé, Rosalynn Smith, and his mother, Miss Lillian. Graduates more commonly got pinned by one woman. Rosalynn turned down the first proposal that he made during the Christmas holidays of 1945. She accepted his second proposal, which came a few months later.

The Carters married on July 7, 1946, in a small ceremony at Plains United Methodist Church with family and friends. Jimmy picked Rosalynn up and drove her to church. They walked down the aisle together as they became Mr. and Mrs. Jimmy Carter. They began married life by heading to Norfolk, Virginia, where he started his Naval career. Between 1947 and 1952 they had three sons, John William "Jack," Donnel Jeffrey "Jeff," and James Earl III "Chip."

CARTER OBSERVES THE WORK OF SAILORS in the main control room of the USS K-1 between June and October 1952. Jimmy first worked on a ship in the navy. After Norfolk, the Carters moved to Hawaii, Connecticut, New York, and California with the service.[38] As a sailor, Carter knew of and respected Admiral Hyman G. Rickover. Carter decided to go into submarines and wanted to be in the nuclear program. He remembered, "Obviously this was a position that was hotly sought by almost every young naval officer who was in the submarines. I mean, it was the ultimate position in the navy. And I had my first encounter with Rickover . . . a stern, brilliant, dedicated, innovative, nonconformist officer—in my opinion, the best engineer who ever lived on earth. He was instrumental in evolving the peaceful use of nuclear power. . . . Rickover had a great impact on me and my life."[39] In 1975, Carter wrote his first book, *Why Not the Best?* The title came from the admiral who challenged his men to always do the very best they could.

In that book Carter talked about his first meeting with Rickover. He had applied for the nuclear submarine program and sat with Rickover in a large room for over two hours. Carter had to choose subjects he wanted to discuss. "In each instance, he [Rickover] soon proved that I knew relatively little about the subject I had chosen." Next, Rickover asked about how Carter stood in his Naval Academy class. Carter proudly responded "'Sir, I stood fifty-ninth in a class of 820!' . . . 'Did you do your best?' . . . I finally gulped and said, 'No sir. I didn't *always* do my best.'"[40]

BOTH JIMMY AND ROSALYNN expected he would make the navy a career but life for the Carters took a different direction. In 1952 his father, Earl Carter, won election to the Georgia House of Representatives by closely defeating the incumbent.[41] He took office in January 1953 but soon afterward became ill. A diagnosis of pancreatic cancer meant that he only had a few more months to live. He died in July 1953.

Jimmy, Rosalynn, and their sons came back home to see Earl when he got sick. Jimmy had been mostly gone from home for twelve years. Returning to Plains for an extended visit gave him time to get to know his dad as an adult. Jimmy also saw how much people in Sumter County loved his father. The death of Earl caused Jimmy to reflect on his own life. "My job was the best and most promising in the navy, and the work was challenging and worthwhile. The salary was good, and the retirement benefits were liberal. . . . I had only one life to live, and I wanted to live it as a civilian, with a potentially fuller opportunity for varied public service."[42] The family business in Plains needed a leader and Jimmy soon began to question how much he wanted to stay in the navy. The pull of family, Plains, and the land itself proved to be stronger than the lure of the navy and the seas. Jimmy soon decided that his family should move back to Plains.

Carter remembers, "When I first came home my ambition in life was to have a very complete involvement in the community life my father had. . . . I spent a couple of weeks with my daddy just before he died and I saw the impact that he had on Plains and the friends that he had accumulated, the responsibilities that he bore to improve other people's lives, and I thought to myself that, even if I got to be the chief of naval operations someday, that my life may not be as significant as my father's was in this little town."[43] He also said, "I could see that my father's life, in all its multi-faceted aspects, was more exciting, more challenging, more interesting, and had a greater promise than the one I had in the navy."[44]

Hugh Carter has stated that Earl had a net worth of over a quarter million dollars when he died, while others have implied that the family business faced serious financial troubles in 1953 due to many loans and gifts.[45] In those days, women seldom ran businesses and Lillian had no desire to run a peanut warehouse. Gloria and Ruth had gotten married and had no interest in the business. Sixteen-year-old Billy, a rebellious teenager, had not yet finished high school.

JIMMY, ROSALYNN, AND THEIR SONS moved home and he took over the Carter family business in 1953. Due to a postwar housing shortage in Plains, they moved into a new public housing project less than three blocks from Plains High School, becoming the first tenants of unit 9.[46] The trip from New York back to Georgia had to have been a long drive. Rosalynn wanted Jimmy to stay in the navy—she liked being away from Plains and getting to know other parts of the world—but Jimmy insisted they move back. The Carters quickly adapted to life in Sumter County. They moved a few months later when a house became available in town. Carter recalls of those days that "we wanted to have a successful business and be rich someday . . . so we worked hard, Rosalynn and I as partners. I was head of the Lions Club and I was a Sunday school teacher." Rosalynn added, "The business was very small and we were buying seed peanuts and reselling them. We decided to grow our own seed." They also cleaned peanuts they bought from farmers.[47]

Carter followed the lead that his father had set and focused on seeds for peanuts and later other crops as well. Carter's Warehouse grew and prospered as it added services. Jimmy Carter worked with seedsmen from all over Georgia to improve the quality of seeds available to farmers. He later became president of the Georgia Crop Improvement Association, which worked to make high-quality seeds available for a wide variety of different crops.[48]

In the mid-1950s, the Sumter County grand jury asked Carter to fill an open seat on the school board. The *Brown v. Board of Education* decision by the U.S. Supreme Court sent shock waves across the South. This landmark 1954 ruling declared that "separate educational facilities are inherently unequal" and violated the equal protection clause of the

Fourteenth Amendment.[49] After Carter joined the school board, he asked that board members tour all the schools in Sumter County. "There were three fairly nice schools for white kids, including the one here at Plains . . . and there were twenty-six different places where black kids went to grammar school, mostly in the basement of homes or in the back end of churches. . . . It was a shocking realization, I think, even to members of the school board, how unequal educational facilities were when we were claiming to be separate but equal."[50] Board members also realized that white children rode buses to school while black children had no transportation, and that black children received worn-out text books discarded by white students.

Carter later said, "We made a real effort to correct those deprivations of blacks. . . . There was not any equality about it at all. This really preyed on my mind. It was a very serious reflection, I felt, on our country and on our region and on our county."[51] During this time, members of a local organization, the White Citizens' Council, visited Carter at the warehouse and demanded that he join them and pay dues. Carter refused to join even when the Council threatened to boycott the business. Jimmy and Rosalynn decided to stand firm and their business managed to survive the crisis. Carter stated, "It wasn't just our family that was affected. It was a lot of families who were struggling with what to do and how to be fair and right, and of course the South made the transition, I think, very well."[52]

CARTER JOINED THE PLAINS LIONS CLUB in 1953, soon after he moved back home. He served as president of the club from 1957 to 1958. During this time, Carter and other members decided that Plains needed a community swimming pool. They raised some money and then relied on donated labor to complete the project. An Americus friend in the cement business, John Pope, remembered that Carter found farmers from the area who brought in "their tractors and small dirt pans. They dug this large hole—35 by 75 feet—and furnished their own tractors. . . . The project took a lot of hand labor."[53] Women in the community also played an important role by operating the pool. They took turns keeping the pool open and running the small concession stand. Everyone showed "a willingness on the part of the adults to see that the children had a nice place to swim and that it cost nothing to keep the pool open."[54]

DURING THE 1968–69 YEAR, Carter served as a district governor for the Lions Club, an international service organization. He joined other district governors of Georgia for the photograph. They are, from left: Carter, Wallace Greeson, Vivian Yawn, Olin Newby, Carl Donaldson, and Harvey Jones. Once he started running for political office, his connections to the civic club meant that he would frequently speak to other Lions Clubs during campaigns. He has also maintained a lifelong interest in improving eyesight and preventing blindness, major goals of the organization.

LIFE FOR JIMMY AND ROSALYNN CARTER focused around their children, their extended family, work, and politics. Here the family plays a game around the table at their home, probably in 1966. The next year, Rosalynn gave birth to daughter Amy on October 19, 1967.

Carter family members, including the children and especially Rosalynn, helped with the family business and political activities. The Carter sons assisted around the farm and the peanut warehouse beginning at young ages. They continued to help their father when he began campaigning for office.

Carter taught his sons about two of his favorite pastimes, hunting and fishing. Jeff Carter realized early on that he and his father experienced hunting differently. "I sort of enjoyed going bird hunting, but my daddy was a great shot. I mean, we would go hunting, and I would take a box of shells, and if I killed two birds, I had a great day. Dad would take a box of shells, and if he missed one, he had had a lousy day. Because he was that good. And I just assumed that when you got to be older and had done it as long, that everybody was that way. I later found out that he was really an excellent shot."[55]

CHAPTER 2

Georgia Politics

JIMMY CARTER BEGAN his political career the same way so many citizens across this democracy do: he served on local and regional boards and then moved on to serve state government. He first focused his energies on Sumter County and then on regional planning and economic development commissions. Carter had returned to Plains after serving in the navy and within a few years he had the family peanut business and farms operating successfully. His involvement in local civic affairs soon led him to seek elected office. The 1960s saw Carter gain narrow political wins and suffer devastating losses while he ran issue-oriented campaigns. Nothing about his early political career indicates a predestined greatness at other levels of government, but both he and Rosalynn learned much from these early wins and losses. Along the way, they attracted a loyal contingent of followers and allies who provided important support in their endeavors during and after Carter's years in political office.

Jimmy Carter actively participated in Plains society after his return to south Georgia in 1953. After being appointed to the Sumter County School Board in November 1955, he tried to do what he considered to be the right thing even if that meant taking controversial positions. In the process, he met many county residents.[1] In 1962 he decided that the time had come for a new challenge. On the morning of his birthday, October 1, he put on his Sunday clothes. Rosalynn found out that he had decided to run for higher office when she asked him if there was a funeral to attend. He told her he was going to qualify for the Georgia Senate seat representing Sumter County.

Carter later reflected on that day with a bit of chagrin. "I hadn't discussed it with her in advance, which to me now is inconceivable. I still can't believe I did it then."[2] Certainly in 1962, with different dynamics between spouses, husbands

often made major decisions without talking to their wives. Rosalynn, however, reported in her memoir that she was thrilled with the idea. Jimmy had occasionally mentioned running for office and the time had come.[3]

Election laws in Georgia had changed earlier that year thanks to a ruling from the U.S. Supreme Court in *Baker v. Carr* that eliminated the county unit system. Carter said that he "ran for the Senate with a sole purpose of improving or protecting the education system in the state. When I got to the Senate, my only request was to be put on the Education Committee." He was soon named as secretary for the Education Committee.[4]

During a symposium in 2007, Carter explained his decision further. "The reason that I ran for politics in the first place was that I was the chairman of the Board of Education in Sumter County, Georgia, when the threat was made to the Georgia public schools to close them down. We had a very good former governor in Georgia, that his campaign promise was to raise one finger, and he would say 'No, not one.'

And his premise was that if a single black child went into a Georgia school, that the schools would be shut down. So I decided to run for the Georgia Senate."[5] The fact that Jimmy, Rosalynn, and others wanted Georgia Southwestern College to become a four-year institution provided another motivation for him to seek the senate seat.

CHANGES IN STATE LAW had greatly shortened the time between qualifying and elections in Georgia. Carter had only two weeks to shake hands with as many people as possible and ask for their votes. In the primary election on October 16, 1962, Carter won his home county of Sumter plus Chattahoochee County, but he lost to Homer Moore in Quitman County, which had been controlled by political boss Joe Hurst for years. John Pope had been at a Quitman polling station and assured Carter that he had witnessed voting fraud.

After a desperate search for a sympathetic ear, Carter connected with attorney Charles Kirbo and journalist John Pennington, both from Atlanta. Quitman County had several voter irregularities: 163 more votes were cast than the official number of people who voted; 117 of the votes cast occurred in alphabetical order, down to the third letter of the alphabet; and several of the votes came from people who had died before the election. After debating the issue and realizing that the odds of winning were long, the Carters decided to take the case to court. He testified in hearings about the voter fraud and the judge ended up overturning the vote. Carter then won the general election in November by 831 votes. His state political career began on January 14, 1963, when he

was sworn into the Georgia Senate at the capitol building in Atlanta.[6] He has said that the episode caused him to lack confidence in the electoral system and the political party structure.[7] He wrote a book, *Turning Point: A Candidate, a State, and a Nation Come of Age*, about this election.

Once in the senate, Carter realized he had much to learn about bills being proposed. He vowed to read every bill being voted on by the senate. He ended up generally being the first senator in the office each morning and usually left last. Given the number of bills and amount of verbiage in some of them, he regretted saying he would read all of them. During his state senate terms he chaired the university committee and served on the corporations committee.[8]

VOTE FOR
JIMMY CARTER
CANDIDATE FOR
State Senator
PRIMARY OCTOBER 16th, 1962

Your Vote and Support Will Be Appreciated

AFTER SERVING TWO TERMS in the Georgia Senate, Jimmy decided that he would seek a different political office in 1966. He might have easily won the congressional seat being vacated by Howard H. "Bo" Callaway, a west Georgia native who was running to become the first Republican governor of Georgia in modern times. Carter soon decided to instead run for governor, the same office that Callaway sought. He dismissed Bo as a rich kid who got by on his family name. The Callaway family had operated textile mills in Georgia since the mid-1890s. Bo attended the United States Military Academy at West Point and would later serve as secretary of the army under President Gerald Ford. As a member of the Georgia Board of Regents, Callaway had opposed making Georgia Southwestern a four-year college and instead wanted the newly established Columbus College to be made four years.[9]

Carter had only family and friends to help him garner support and little name recognition beyond southwest Georgia. Carter used his motorcycle to reach out to people and he tried to get around the state to meet as many

Georgians as he could. Talking with voters in Gainesville, from left to right are Jack Bailey, Carter, Jo Caldwell, and John Allison. His opponents in the primary included former governors Ellis Arnall and Ernest Vandiver, plus arch segregationist Lester Maddox. Carter pushed for better government and allied himself with neither the segregationist side nor the moderates, declaring himself to be neither conservative nor liberal. He came in third in the Democratic primary, losing to the eventual governor, Lester Maddox, who had never won an election before and didn't technically win this one. Four years earlier, Maddox had stood in front of his Atlanta restaurant, the Pickrick, with a pickaxe to make sure that no African Americans tried to enter. In the general election, Callaway received a plurality of votes. Former governor Ellis Arnall, who had lost the Democratic runoff election, had entered the race as an independent write-in candidate and this led to no candidate receiving at least 50 percent of the vote. By law, the Georgia legislature decided the issue and selected Lester Maddox to be governor. Thirty-four more years passed before Georgia elected a Republican as governor.

For Jimmy Carter, the third-place primary finish came as a shock that sent him into depression. The fact that the voters of the Peach State had elected a man who stood with a pickaxe to keep his restaurant whites only embarrassed him deeply. In *Faith: A Journey for All*, Carter remembered that, "heartbroken and discouraged, I felt my life was a failure and I was disillusioned about my religious faith." He told his sister Ruth, an evangelist, "It's not my goal just to grow peanuts, sell fertilizer, gin cotton, and build up a bank account. I have nowhere to go! God has rejected me through the people's vote."[10] With guidance from his sister, he rededicated himself to Christ and went on mission trips to Pennsylvania and

Massachusetts. These mission trips helped refresh him and give him renewed energy. He has also said that he gained a greater appreciation of people during those journeys and has felt "ever since that when I meet each individual person they are important to me."[11] This feeling may have made him a more effective campaigner in the 1970s, since journalists called him a brilliant in-person campaigner.[12]

AS PART OF HIS GEORGIA GUBERNATORIAL CAMPAIGNS in 1966 and again in 1970, Carter spoke at various places around the state, including Pinkie Masters Lounge in Savannah. With Rosalynn, his mother Miss Lillian, a son, and Pinkie Masters in attendance, candidate Carter spoke at a "get out the vote" event. Carter, a regular church attendee and Sunday school teacher, visited Masters Lounge during his 1966 and 1970 campaigns for governor. On St. Patrick's Day, 1978, he stood on the bar and paid homage to his friend, the original owner, who had died the previous year. Carter had long been friends with Luis Christopher Masterpolis, a.k.a. Pinkie Masters, the owner of the Drayton Street bar located across the street from the DeSoto Hilton.

Masters frequently supported underdog candidates, including Carter.[13] By the late 1960s and 1970s the bar had become a hub for politics in downtown Savannah as many politicians and newsmen often talked there late into the night.

The dive bar, known for its cheap beer, has had its ups and downs since the 1970s, but in 2017 Jimmy Carter sent a letter to its current owner, Matt Garappolo, saying, "I will always remember the times I had in your establishment. When I ran for governor, Pinkie himself was one of my most important supporters. And when I was back in Savannah as President of the United States, I will never forget standing on the bar to say thank you." A bronze plaque marks the spot where Carter stood on the bar.[14]

JIMMY CARTER PLANNED CAREFULLY for his next bid to become governor of Georgia. He officially announced his intentions on April 3, 1970, in the old Supreme Court room of the Georgia capitol with three-year-old daughter Amy in his arms. As the first candidate to announce for the position, he had a better organization supporting him and a more thoughtful plan than he had had four years earlier. He referenced his 1966 defeat when he told supporters at the capitol, "Show me a good loser and I'll show you a loser. I don't intend to lose again."[15]

From the start, Carl Sanders, governor from 1963 to 1967, appeared to be his main opponent. An Augusta native and Atlanta attorney, Sanders has been identified as Georgia's first New South governor thanks to his progressive leadership and the variety of reforms he made during those turbulent years.[16] Historian Gary Fink wrote, "In the first race Carter had positioned himself as a moderate progressive alternative to the more liberal Arnall and the staunchly conservative Maddox. During his second campaign Carter subtly appealed to class antagonisms, running as the representative of the ordinary people. It was a successful campaign strategy in which Carter projected himself as a traditional southern conservative."[17]

Carter criticized Sanders for failing to invite Alabama segregationist and 1968 third-party presidential candidate George Wallace to address the Georgia General Assembly. He referred to the former governor as "Cufflinks Carl" and depicted him as a rich man with wealthy friends. Just before the primary on September 9, 1970, leaflets appeared in mailboxes picturing Sanders, part owner of the Atlanta Hawks basketball team, celebrating a victory with their star Lou Hudson, an African American.

Several days before the runoff, controversy arose over the size of the Carter farms and the laborers and sharecroppers who worked there. Investigative teams from the Sanders campaign and the Atlanta newspapers went to Plains to tour tenant houses on the Carter farm. An *Atlanta Constitution* article identified the tour leader as "Bill Carter," younger brother of the candidate. He led teams from the Atlanta newspapers and Sanders campaign headquarters. Showing the sarcasm and humor that he would become well known for later in the decade, Bill asked the group, "You want to see the tenants we keep penned up or do you want to see the ones we let out to pick peanuts?" At least some of the houses had cold water but no bathrooms while others needed more windows. Some of the tenants had not worked the land in recent years and paid no rent.[18] A few days later Carter responded in a brief statement: "I'm a Christian, I love God. I do not love [black activist] Hosea Williams, I do not hate old folks, I'm not a land baron, I do not have slaves on my farm in Plains and I did not inherit 2000 acres."[19]

IN MAY 1970, candidate Jimmy Carter visited with students at Georgia Southern College in Statesboro. During the 1970 campaign, Carter visited most of the towns and counties in Georgia. He, Rosalynn, and their family members shook many hands across the state during this campaign and appeared on radio and television whenever they could. During this campaign, Rosalynn transitioned from being a shy businesswoman, wife, and mother to a seasoned campaigner who knew the issues and wanted others to know about her candidate. She gave her first speeches ever during this campaign. After stumbling through a talk that she had not expected to give, she wrote a few sentences, practiced her delivery, and gradually became a more polished public speaker.[20] As her sister-in-law and childhood friend Ruth Carter Stapleton said, "She was a formidable campaign partner. . . . Jimmy, with her considerable aid, spoke in every city, town, and hamlet of Georgia. He alone gave more than 1800 speeches. He and Rosalynn shook hands with some 600,000 people."[21]

JIMMY CARTER AND CARL SANDERS shook hands during the 1970 campaign. Sanders later described the campaign: "Jimmy Carter, much to my chagrin, took the opportunity that he was going to play the racial card. He took the position that he was a supporter of George Wallace, which I was not. . . . He put himself in the position as a south Georgia farmer who supported the white race and not the black race and that's how the campaign was run. It was a mean, dirty, campaign. But it was politics."[22] Zell Miller joined the Georgia Senate the same year as Carter. He wrote about the 1970 election, "Georgia's political campaigns have always been rough. . . . It was much rougher in 1970. It worked. Carter won."[23]

Sanders went on to say that Carter accomplished little during his governorship, due in large part to having Lester Maddox as his lieutenant governor. According to Sanders, "They never got along and every day they'd have a fight over what kind of legislation they were going to try to entertain . . . and that went on for four years."[24] Hugh Carter, a first cousin who lived in Plains and served in the Georgia Senate, agreed with the description of their relationship. "Maddox and Jimmy, they just did not get along. Their personalities were just opposite." Hugh Carter thought his cousin accomplished much as the leader of the state in areas of government reorganization, health care, prison reform, and education.[25]

ROSALYNN AND JIMMY CARTER celebrated three different election nights in 1970. In the Democratic primary on September 9, Jimmy Carter and Carl Sanders succeeded in reaching the runoff since no candidate won the majority of votes. Then, on September 23, Carter became the Democratic nominee for governor. He and Rosalynn shared their excitement about the results with the crowd and the photographer. Then, he won the general election on November 3, 1970. An editorial in the *Valdosta Daily Times* noted that "Georgia's voters have demonstrated . . . they want something new in the way of a governor. They have essentially said they want no ties with the past."[26] For the position of lieutenant governor, the voters chose a known candidate and elected Lester Maddox: the incumbent governor, who could not seek reelection to that position, became the second-in-command.

As she got to know the people in the state, Rosalynn gradually became more concerned about mental health issues. One morning during the 1970 campaign she stood outside a cotton mill shaking hands with employees who had worked the night shift. As one lady with cotton lint in her hair left the plant, Rosalynn asked if she was headed home to sleep. The woman said she would get a little rest but she had a child with developmental problems. "The child's expenses were more than her husband's income, so she had to work nights to make ends meet." By chance, Rosalynn realized Jimmy would be in the same town that afternoon. She generally never saw her husband during the week but she attended his talk and then stood in the back of the line to shake his hand. He reached for her hand before realizing that the hand belonged to his wife. She promptly asked him about his plan to deal with mental health policy. He replied, "We are going to have the best mental health system in the country and I am going to put you in charge of it." As governor and as president, he followed through on this campaign promise by establishing mental health commissions, though with Rosalynn serving as a member of the boards, not as chair.[27] Her concern about mental health became a lifelong cause and concern for Rosalynn.

ON JANUARY 12, 1971, when Jimmy Carter became governor of Georgia, he gave a brief, eleven-minute inaugural speech. He started by saying, "It is a long way from Plains to Atlanta. . . . I realize that the test of a man is not how well he campaigned, but how effectively he meets the challenges and responsibilities of the office." Then he stunned many in the state by declaring, "At the end of a long campaign, I believe I know our people as well as anyone. Based on this knowledge of Georgians North and South, Rural and Urban, liberal and conservative, I say to you quite frankly that the time for racial discrimination is over. . . . We who are strong or in positions of leadership must realize that the responsibility for making correct decisions in the future is ours."[28] Carter referenced these comments when talking to Stuart Eizenstat, his chief domestic policy advisor from 1977 to 1981, noting, "That statement got me on the front cover of *Time* magazine." Eizenstat went on to say, "While the statement gave the new governor of Georgia national prominence, it was a politically courageous and deeply unpopular sentiment among white voters in his own Deep South state."[29] A sketch of Carter appeared on the cover of *Time* on May 31, 1971, with the caption "Dixie Whistles a Different Tune."

Young Amy, along with other family members, joined her parents for the swearing-in ceremony. Later, Jimmy and Rosalynn danced at the inaugural ball. Rosalynn wore a gold embroidered sleeveless coat over a gold-trimmed blue chiffon gown while Jimmy donned a tuxedo with white tie for the formal event.[30] She chose to wear this dress again in 1977, creating controversy in the process when the national media, along with many citizens, wanted the president and First Lady to show more glamour at a presidential inaugural.

JIMMY CARTER SWORE IN HIS STAFF soon after he gave his inaugural address. The group included core members who had worked with him before and would stay with Carter as he moved onto the national stage. Jody Powell stands just behind Carter; Charles Kirbo and Hamilton Jordan are on the far right. Other aides who served the governor and later the Carter presidency included Stuart Eizenstat, an Atlanta native, and Frank Moore from Gainesville.

Hamilton Jordan first joined the Carter team during the 1966 campaign. He and Nancy Konigsmark, his girlfriend and later his first wife, lived in Albany and volunteered in the Carter campaign office. Konigsmark worked for the Carters until shortly before her 2012 death. Jody Powell, from nearby Vienna, came onboard during the 1970 gubernatorial campaign. Carter recalls, "I remember the first time Jody Powell ever came to the door. He was one of the few volunteers that I had that was mature enough to drive an automobile that I would trust."[31] Powell had been at the Air Force Academy and was a Ph.D. student at Emory in 1970. Two years later, Jordan and Powell helped Carter develop a plan to become president. In Washington, the group became known as the Georgia Mafia. Eizenstat later commented on the loyalty these people felt toward the man from Plains. "For the rest of Jimmy Carter's Georgia team, he had been the sole focus of their political lives; as deeply committed to him as I became, I was a relative latecomer. When I was finally admitted to Carter's inner circle on the strength of my policy papers in his run for governor . . . I was under no illusion that my relationship with him could ever be as deep as the others'. Like Carter himself, they were not only from the South but *of* it, going back generations."[32]

JIMMY AND ROSALYNN CARTER TALK TO GEORGE WALLACE at the Southern Governors' Conference in 1970. The group met in the Phoenix Ballroom at the Regency Hyatt House in Atlanta. The ballroom's name referenced the image of Atlanta as a phoenix rising from the ashes of the Civil War to become a world city. At the formal dinner, the background image gives an appearance of flames shooting out of the head of the Alabama politician.

Jimmy Carter had a complicated relationship with Governor Wallace, an ardent segregationist and three-time candidate for president. Carter alternated between denouncing and courting him. During the 1970 gubernatorial election, Carter seemed to seek out the segregationist vote, especially when he met with Roy V. Harris, president of the Citizens' Councils of America, a white supremacist network. He criticized opponent Carl Sanders for never having Wallace address the Georgia General Assembly. At his inaugural he declared that the time for racial segregation was over, but two years later he invited Wallace to address the Georgia legislature.

POLITICAL ASPIRANTS spend much of their time shaking hands, asking for votes, giving speeches, and kissing babies. The magazine *Mother Jones* once published a tongue-in-check article on the topic of candidates kissing babies. "The first politician to lay lips on an unsuspecting infant is unknown, though President Andrew Jackson is credited with the first use of a supporter's baby as a political prop." The piece credits an 1888 story as recounting that the president from Tennessee had held the baby during an 1833 tour of eastern states, and then held the baby up for his secretary of war to kiss. The *Mother Jones* article concludes by quoting the London *Daily Mail*'s website, which proclaimed in 2012 that "the baby-hugging photo opportunity is an age-old test for any politician and can sometimes define an entire campaign."[33] On May 4, 1972, the office had been won and no one expected the baby to be kissed, but Governor and Mrs. Carter spent time with this little one at the Yerkes National Primate Research Center at Emory University. The Yerkes Center conducts biomedical and behavioral studies on primates with a goal of improving the health and well-being of both primates and humans.

GEORGE WALLACE spoke to the Georgia legislature on February 24, 1972. As a candidate for the Democratic nomination for president, Wallace addressed the issue of busing students to achieve racial balance and discussed the possibility of an amendment to the U.S. Constitution to prohibit such actions. During his appearance at the capitol, Wallace received enthusiastic support for his candidacy from Lester Maddox, while Carter introduced Wallace as a "personal friend of mine" whose voice "is being heard throughout the country." In another speech that day to the Georgia Press Association, Wallace called busing "silly and foolish . . . senseless, asinine, and atrocious."[34]

Arthur Bremer shot Wallace ten weeks later in Maryland and left the candidate permanently paralyzed from the waist down. Memos written in 1972 by Hamilton Jordan expressed concern that a Wallace candidacy could be a major threat to Carter in 1976.[35] Carter, Wallace, and Maddox all ran for president in 1976. From early in the campaign, Carter and Wallace battled for votes in various state primaries, with Carter finally defeating Wallace in the crucial Florida primary. Wallace endorsed Carter in September. Maddox ran as the nominee of the American Independent Party, the same party that had nominated Wallace in 1968. Maddox received less than 1 percent of the vote.

Tom Johnson, editor of the *Montgomery Independent*, summed up the competition between Wallace and Carter in an article in the *New York Times*. "Mr. Wallace showed . . . that a Southerner could do it. In the most conspicuous way, he expunged the stigma that had clung to the Deep South since the Civil War—the notion that access to national politics was automatically foreclosed to a Southern candidate. . . .

A much larger irony is that had there been no Wallace in all those years past, there might well have been no Carter running for the Democratic Presidential nomination in 1976."[36]

In spring, 1978 Wallace announced that he had decided not to run for the U.S. Senate. On May 17, President Carter wrote the Alabamian a letter, saying, "I would like to take this opportunity to express again my sincere appreciation for what you have meant to me. Your friendship, support at a critical time, sound advice, and a gentle sensitivity about some of the important political issues have all been very important. I value this friendship."[37]

THE YEAR 1972 proved to be a transformative one for Governor Jimmy Carter. He got involved in the presidential election and nominated Henry "Scoop" Jackson for president at the 1972 Democratic National Convention. He considered George McGovern to be excessively liberal, though there were discussions in the Carter camp about his being the vice presidential candidate once McGovern became the party nominee.[38] Here Carter welcomes Terry McGovern, daughter of the candidate.

In 1974, Carter agreed to serve as the Democratic National Committee's campaign chairman for that year's congressional and gubernatorial elections. He learned the inner workings of the party and met with Democratic leaders from around the country. As his friend Bert Lance noted, "His appointment was a real windfall. He learned the rules of the Democratic party inside out. He structured an election campaign for the party within those rules. . . . He learned the process, and then he became a victor of the process he had just chaired."[39] Leaders he met included North Carolina lieutenant governor James Hunt and Congressman Roy Taylor from the western part of the Tar Heel State in 1973. Jimmy Carter got to know many national and state leaders of the Democratic party by inviting them to stay in the Governor's Mansion whenever they happened to be in Atlanta.

IN HIS YOUTH, Jimmy Carter spent most of his free time fishing, hunting, and playing in the outdoors and has continued to enjoy such activities as an adult. In 1972, he canoed on the Chattooga River in the north Georgia mountains, the setting for much of the scenery in the movie *Deliverance*, which came out that year. After seeing the success of the movie, Carter created the Georgia Film Commission in 1973. It was only in 2008 that the state legislature approved substantial tax credits for movie projects, but in the 1970s a "can do" attitude of providing what movie companies needed helped lure them to the state.[40] Early movies included *Smokey and the Bandit* (I and II), *Sharky's Machine*, and the critically acclaimed *Driving Miss Daisy*.

A major fight during his governorship involved the Flint River, which flows from East Point south to join the Chattahoochee River at Lake Seminole near the Georgia-Florida line. Carter battled the U.S. Army Corps of Engineers,

Congressman Jack Flint, local chambers of commerce, and other groups to prevent construction of Sprewell Bluff Dam on the Flint River. The major long-term advantage of the dam would have been recreational, while short-term economic benefits would arise from the creation of over two hundred jobs. Carter opposed the plan because the dam would disrupt the longest stretch of free-flowing water in Georgia. Carter later wrote about the river, "Lakes and dams are everywhere. But to experience something that is undisturbed and has its natural beauty? You hope and pray that it will be there a thousand years in the future, still just as beautiful and undisturbed."[41] Others have echoed this appreciation for the Flint River. In 1976, the Georgia Department of Natural Resources named the Flint the most scenic stream of the fifty-three it studied that year.[42] In 1974, Carter wrote that "with the exception of reorganization itself, I spent more time preserving our natural resources than on any other one issue."[43]

IN THE EARLY 1970S, Jimmy and Rosalynn walked a trail at Callaway Gardens in Pine Mountain with Virginia Callaway and Gardens president and chief executive officer Hal Northrop. Virginia and her husband Cason Callaway founded Callaway Gardens in 1952 when they decided to share their gardens, lakes, and other natural areas with the public on a regular basis. Virginia and Cason, who died in 1961, were the parents of Bo Callaway. Both Callaway and Carter had strong-willed and independent mothers. By the early 1970s, Virginia Callaway and others actively opposed plans to route what became Interstate 185 over Pine Mountain. Bo Callaway supported that route but Virginia wanted lands in and around Callaway Gardens to be preserved. Ultimately, Jimmy Carter and the Georgia Department of Transportation, led by Bert Lance, opted for conservation and chose a route west of the gardens.[44]

JIMMY CARTER AND OTHER MEN TALK WITH EVANGELIST BILLY GRAHAM, an ordained Southern Baptist minister who preached before millions and counseled every president between Truman and Obama plus many other political leaders. Governor Jimmy Carter served as honorary chairman of Graham's 1973 crusade at the Atlanta–Fulton County Stadium. Carter attended most evenings and sat on the podium. Graham admired Carter and appreciated his Christian stance. Graham wrote, "Jimmy Carter did not present himself as perfect or pious. . . . Neither did he compromise his understanding of the Gospel by verbal dodging or double-talk. He took a political risk by being so forthright about his faith; in the end, though, I believe his candor worked in his favor."[45]

As a Southern Baptist, Carter had long respected Billy Graham. In 1966, he headed up a Billy Graham crusade in Americus. Graham, who required that his crusades be integrated, sent a crusade film. Carter had trouble finding a room to have a mixed-race planning session and then had to persuade a local theater owner to allow them to show the film in the theater. Carter led an invocation after each showing of the film. He reported, "Everyone was startled because [there were] black and white people walking down the aisles, together, in front of the theater, to place their faith in Christ. Together."[46]

Carter, who has talked more about his religious beliefs than most other political leaders of the late twentieth century, decided against having Graham visit him at the White House. "Although President Nixon and some of my other predecessors had invited Billy Graham to speak to groups and to pray in the White House, I decided that this was not appropriate."[47] Graham reported that they never discussed the matter but they agreed on this point: "Visibility on my part could easily have been misunderstood by the public, leading to the suspicion that I was somehow taking advantage of our shared faith to influence political decisions."[48] Others have speculated that Carter and Graham never became friends, in part because Graham spent time with President Nixon and expressed public support for President Ford.[49]

GOVERNORS TRAVEL THEIR REGION AND SOMETIMES THE NATION AND THE WORLD

promoting their states and supporting economic development. Governor Carter joined Ed Cole, president of the Georgia Municipal Association, and Mayor Gerald Thompson (right) in 1973 at the groundbreaking ceremony for the Delco-Remy Battery Plant in Fitzgerald. On such occasions, Carter met and got to know political and business leaders of the state.

Reorganization of state government proved to be the centerpiece of the Carter administration. Carter disagreed with most things that Lester Maddox had done as governor, so he considered government reorganization a necessity. Carter estimated that he spent one-fourth of his time on the reform efforts.[50] Special study teams made many recommendations, including some controversial ones. The governor urged the teams to make their recommendations on the basis of merit without consideration of politics or possible cost savings. He told them, "I want you to submit the perfect system. . . . I don't want to lower our sights simply because something is politically expedient."[51] Thus, the Georgia Bureau of Investigation gained the authority to investigate in a locality without letting the police chief or sheriff know. Sometimes recommendations caused turf wars, such as when all social and medical services ended up moving under the Department of Human Resources. At the national level he continued to espouse this philosophy of working for what he considered to be the right thing while generally dismissing political implications.

IN THE EARLY 1970S, an energetic group of people tried a variety of different ways to "Save the Fox." Beauchamp Carr gave Governor Jimmy Carter a Save the Fox T-shirt. The state of Georgia did not contribute to the fund but the group ultimately succeeded in saving the historic theater.

During the Carter governorship, community leaders established the Georgia Trust for Historic Preservation in 1973. Bulldozers and new development threatened historic sites that dated back to the founding of the state. "We established and funded the Georgia Heritage Trust, designed to inventory and assess more than two thousand such sites. We acquired many of them while I was governor."[52]

Carter also did much for the archives and records management program of the state of Georgia. At the urging of State Archivist Carroll Hart, Carter sent a letter to department heads in February 1971 telling them to implement a records management program immediately. He declared that effective management of agency records would be considered during program evaluations. The following year, the Georgia General Assembly passed the Georgia Records Act. Retention schedules having the force of law were developed and implemented, and the state began to save thousands by not buying more filing cabinets. The Georgia Historical Records Advisory Council presented President Carter with a lifetime achievement award in October 2019. The award recognizes that "had it not been for Governor Carter's enthusiastic support, such accomplishments would not have come about as rapidly or not at all."[53]

A PROUD MOMENT for the Carter governorship came when a special legislative committee hung a portrait of Martin Luther King Jr. in the Georgia capitol. The unveiling occurred on February 17, 1974. Members of the national press covered the event and King family members attended while the Ku Klux Klan protested outside. The painting shown here hangs in the Georgia capitol and replaced the original picture which was smaller than other paintings hanging there.

The committee had recommended that three African Americans be honored with portraits at the state building. Later in 1974, committee members plus a few others gathered to see the installation of images honoring Lucy C. Laney, a black educator, and Henry McNeal Turner, a minister and back-to-Africa advocate. The second unveiling attracted little attention from either the press or protest groups.

Martin Luther King Sr. ("Daddy King") later endorsed Carter in his presidential bid and provided much-needed support in the black community. In December 1978, President Carter and Coretta Scott King toured the Lorraine Motel in Memphis where her husband, Martin Luther King Jr., lost his life on April 4, 1968.

JIMMY CARTER HAS LOVED BASEBALL since his youth. The Braves started playing in Atlanta in 1966. On April 8, 1974, Governor Carter watched the Atlanta Braves play the Los Angeles Dodgers at Atlanta–Fulton County stadium. Henry Louis "Hank" Aaron entered the major league record books that day when he hit home run number 715 and passed the record set by Babe Ruth in 1935. With much of the world media focused on Atlanta, Carter got to be both a Braves fan and a spokesman for his state.

African Americans first joined the major leagues in 1947 when Jackie Robinson, a native of Cairo, Georgia, played for the then Brooklyn Dodgers. (Carter's mother, Miss Lillian, promptly became a huge Dodgers fan after they brought Robinson onto the team.) Aaron retired in October 1976 with 755 home runs and held onto the record for thirty-three years. He received much hate mail and multiple death threats after he surpassed Ruth. Aaron held management positions with the Atlanta Braves for many years.

Jimmy Carter stands with Aaron and his wife, Billye. Before the game, Carter joined actor Sammy Davis Jr., Richard Kattel, head of Citizens and Southern Bank, and Atlanta mayor Maynard Jackson. On the fortieth anniversary of the breaking of the home-run record, Carter recalled that "having integrated sports in the Deep South, Aaron already was a hero to me as I sat in the stands that day. As the first black superstar playing on the first big league baseball team in the Deep South, he had been both demeaned and idolized in Atlanta. . . . He became the first black man for whom white fans in the South cheered." Carter remembered cheering wildly as he sat in the front row that historic day.[54]

JIMMY CARTER PAUSED during a contemplative moment in the 1970s. He gave a couple of major addresses to students during this time period. Governor Carter addressed a group at Emory University at the Barkley Forum on May 18, 1975. The forum, the debate organization for Emory, named Carter as its speaker of the year for 1975. The previous year, he gave a major speech at Law Day at the University of Georgia, an occasion to recognize the accomplishments of students and featured guest speakers. Senator Edward Kennedy delivered the keynote address and spent the night at the Governor's Mansion as the guest of the Carters. Already seriously considering a run for the presidency, Carter agreed to speak at Law Day since the law school graduating class included his son Jack.[55] Carter addressed the Law School Association at their luncheon and gave a widely acclaimed talk, which he changed at the last minute after he heard Kennedy give virtually the same speech he had intended to present.

Carter spoke mostly about the importance of including "hope and compassion" in the Georgia penal system. He lamented the fact that so many of the incarcerated are poor people with few resources. He said, "My heart feels and cries out that something ought to be analyzed, not just about the structure of government, judicial qualification councils, and judicial appointment committees and eliminating the unsworn statement—those things are important. But they don't reach the crux of the point, that now we assign punishment to fit the criminal and not the crime." Carter also mentioned the old county unit system. "To think about going back to a county unit system, which deliberately cheated for generations certain voters . . . of this state is almost inconceivable. To revert back or to forego the one man, one vote principle, we would consider to be a horrible violation of the basic principles of justice and equality and fairness and equity."[56]

This concern about poor prisoners had been shared by progressives for much of the twentieth century. Peter Bourne, who served President Carter as special advisor for health affairs, declared this to be "a defining speech in Carter's career embodying his deepest beliefs and values and his rationale for being involved with politics."[57] Journalist Hunter Thompson, who drank Wild Turkey in his iced tea glass during the luncheon, helped propel Carter to national attention with an article he wrote for *Rolling Stone*.[58] "I have heard hundreds of speeches by all sorts of candidates and politicians, but I have never heard a sustained piece of political oratory that impressed me any more than the speech Jimmy Carter made."[59]

JIMMY CARTER LEAVES PLAINS BAPTIST CHURCH IN SEPTEMBER 1976.

Jimmy Carter belonged to this church for many years. Churches and ministers have played important roles in his life. In August 1962, Allen Comish, a well-known Baptist minister from Columbus, conducted a revival meeting at Plains Baptist. He had dinner one evening with Miss Lillian, Rosalynn, and Jimmy. Carter remembers that they discussed his decision to run for state senate. Comish asked, "'If you want to be of service to other people, why don't you go into the ministry or some honorable social service work?' Somewhat annoyed, I asked him, 'How would you like to be the pastor of a church with eighty thousand members?'"[60] In recalling that event, Rev. Comish did not remember questioning Carter's interest in politics, since members of his family and his congregations served in the legislature and held other political offices. Instead, he remembered advising Carter, "You won't find a political life easy. You'll lose friends. You'll be subjected to personal attacks. You'll be pressured by special interests. You'll have to compromise a little and get a coalition to get your bills passed."[61] Carter has long realized that a commitment to church and public service do not easily meld together, but he has always worked to find a way to serve both church and the public.

The Carters faced controversy at the church. In 1965, someone made a motion that the deacons, the church governing body, accepted and presented to the members, stating that "Negroes or any other civil rights agitators" could not attend worship services at the church. Jimmy recalls, "Rosalynn and I and my mother were the main ones around Plains . . . who were distressed about these things enough to try to do something about it openly. One of the early tests came when . . . our church decided not to let blacks come in to worship. . . . We had about 250 people in the church. There were six that voted to integrate the church, or to accept black worshippers. Rosalynn and I, my mother, Chip and Jeffrey, my two sons. Jack was off somewhere. . . . About fifty voted against it and almost two hundred didn't vote, which I thought was very significant."[62]

In 1976 and 1977, the question of integration of Plains Baptist Church again surfaced. The fact that Jimmy Carter, a national political leader, had been a member of the church most of his life attracted others to join or try to join the church,

including Rev. Clennon King of Albany. Rather than welcome him into the congregation, the church did not hold services on the Sunday in late October when he proposed attending. The controversy continued for several months. On November 14, 1976, the board of deacons asked for the resignation of Rev. Bruce Edwards, who supported integration. People and families argued as the church split. Edwards resigned in late April 1977 and within weeks many congregants started meeting at a new church, Bottsford Baptist. Members soon adopted the name Maranatha Baptist Church. The national press covered the split of the church.[63] The spotlight shone on both Maranatha and Plains Baptist whenever Jimmy Carter came home. His first Sunday back, he and Rosalynn attended Sunday school at Plains Baptist and then listened to the minister at Maranatha.[64] They joined the new church in 1981.

JODY POWELL, LEFT, AND HAMILTON JORDAN
helped Jimmy Carter get elected governor and president.
Carter and Jordan first met during the 1966 gubernatorial
campaign and Powell during the 1970 campaign. They both
remained loyal Carter friends for the rest of their lives. In
November 1972, at age twenty-seven, Jordan drafted a memo
outlining the steps needed for Carter to become president.
The memo turned out to be a remarkably accurate assess-
ment of how a south Georgia businessman and peanut farmer
could transition from the governor of Georgia to becoming
nationally known and winning the Democratic presidential
nomination. The Carter team followed most of the steps suggested in the 1972 memo, including the need for Carter to
develop greater expertise in foreign affairs, write a book, and
win the support of the media world in which members of the
"eastern liberal news establishment" dominated. The memo
advised Carter to carefully select in which states to launch
primary campaigns, but due to changes in the Democratic
Party rules, Carter and Jordan ended up deciding that he
should enter all of the state primaries.[65]

CHAPTER 3

The Presidency

SOON AFTER HE BECAME GOVERNOR OF GEORGIA, Jimmy Carter began to think about the ultimate political prize in the United States, the office of president. As Carter got to know other national political leaders, he realized that he had as much to offer the country as they did. He also appreciated the fact that a man of high moral character who did not lie to the public could help a nation reeling from Watergate and Vietnam. This belief grew even stronger with the resignation of Richard Nixon in 1974. Once in office, he surrounded himself with Georgians, several of whom had served with him while governor, but he also worked with people like Vice President Walter Mondale who brought in needed expertise and helped give national balance to his group of advisors. As president, Carter tended to focus on issues and positions that he considered to be the most important for the nation, even when those issues lacked widespread political support and appeal. His presidency accomplished much, but, in the end, a struggling economy with high inflation and the fact that Iranian students held fifty-two American hostages for 444 days meant that Jimmy Carter would only serve one term as commander in chief.

JIMMY CARTER has said, "I began to think about a national office shortly after I became governor, fairly early in 1971. . . . After the Democratic Convention in 1972, I decided to go for the presidency. And so we had a few very secret meetings in the Governor's Mansion, just six or seven people there, and slowly but surely the plans evolved. . . . So by the time the term of office was over as governor in January of '75, I had my thoughts fairly well clarified and my goals for the nation were certainly . . . in outline form and I began to campaign." He had gotten to know Democratic candidates for president during the 1972 campaign and as campaign chairman of the Democratic National Committee in 1974. He felt that his time as governor, state senator, and even local school board member had given him knowledge about domestic programs and the workings of government, and that his time in the navy had given him familiarity with defense issues and had broadened his perspective in general. He added, "I didn't feel inferior to these famous Democratic candidates in 1972."[1]

Carter officially announced his candidacy for the highest office of the land on December 12, 1974. He addressed a group of journalists and political leaders at the National Press Club in Washington, D.C. In his speech, he spoke about his

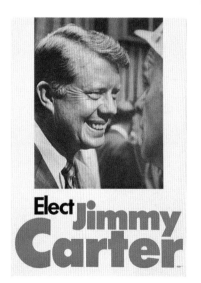

belief in the "greatness of our country" and declared, "We Americans are a great and diverse people. . . . We have dared to dream great dreams for our nation. We have taken quite literally the promises of decency, equality, and freedom—of an honest and responsible government." Then he went on to note that "there must be no lowering of these standards, no acceptance of mediocrity in any aspect of our private or public lives."[2] He said in his first autobiography, *Why Not the Best?*, "I have always looked on the presidency of the United States with reverence and awe, and I still do. But recently I have begun to realize that the president is just a human being."[3]

PLAINS, GEORGIA, and members of the Carter family first appeared on the national radar during the 1976 election. The town stood at the heart of the Carter campaign. Early in the presidential race, members of the local community decided that the depot should be the campaign headquarters. The depot had served passengers on the Seaboard Air Line Railroad from 1888 until 1951, when the company discontinued passenger service in Plains. Carter's Warehouse held the lease on the depot and stored materials there. Billy Carter approved using the depot for the campaign and sent a crew to help with cleaning.[4] A close friend and supporter of Jimmy Carter, John Pope remembered having to steam clean the entire dirty building before it could be used.[5]

The Carter campaign leased the depot and opened its headquarters on April 18, 1975.[6] The depot soon became a required stop when tourists visited Plains. As many as ten thousand people a day came to town. Hugh Carter recalled, "Whenever Jimmy came to Plains, he had to have a place to make his speeches, to make his appearances, and the platform of that depot as well as the inside of the depot was the place that he did this, the place that he made those appearances . . . and it got to be kind of a symbol of the center of all the activity around his campaign."[7]

Maxine Reese, a campaign coordinator, reported that the town had a large gathering outside the depot after the first primary in New Hampshire. Carter told her, "Maxine, I appreciate y'all staying up this late at night. . . . You can't do this every time." But the people of Plains gathered in front of the depot after every primary. She added, "I feel like the people of Plains gave a good deal and helped tremendously in his campaign because we were always here, we were always visible."[8] Miss Lillian quickly became one of the most popular people in south Georgia. As friend Betty Pope said, "Miss Lillian . . . she stood up for what she felt. . . . She was very popular . . . with the people that came because they looked up to her so much. . . . Miss Lillian would entertain them. She had a ball."[9] She would often greet people at the depot. "She came down nearly every day and she would sit for hours in her rocking chair in the back room talking to people and signing autographs."[10]

Men and women from Georgia, who traveled to eighteen different states the during primary season, made a big difference in the 1976 presidential election. They would spend a week or two weeks at a time trying to get the local voters to support Carter. The idea for the group originated with the "Hi Neighbor" contingent of mostly Sumter County residents who had campaigned for Carter in 1970. In 1976, Hamilton Jordan wanted supporters to be on the ground in New Hampshire for the first state Democratic primary. Peanut Brigade members generally traveled to other states at their own expense and put in long days knocking on doors and telling people why they should vote for Carter. They generally traveled together from the South but then divided up and covered the state to share their message.[11] John and Betty Pope remembered that people from the Granite State wanted to hear the Georgians, with their southern accents, talk. The Popes also recalled temperatures leading up to the February primary being as low as twenty degrees below zero. Betty said, "We had layers and layers of clothing on. If we would stop and eat, say, clam chowder, and get warmed up, then we'd be refueled and ready to go again. But the staying up late at night and writing those notes made it just unbelievably worthwhile. That was actually one of the keys."[12] This personal contact helped overcome the "Jimmy who?" questions that people voiced often in the early months of 1976 campaign.

Florida proved to be a critical primary. The contest took place on March 9 after Carter had placed fourth in Massachusetts. Jordan and Powell worried about how George Wallace would fare in Florida, particularly in the Panhandle in west Florida. Members of the Peanut Brigade went down and Carter won the state. Rudy Hayes, a newspaperman from Americus, was in Orlando on election night. He later recalled, "That evening in Orlando, I think, was one of the most memorable evenings I had during the entire campaign. . . . it was just a tremendous joy and happiness because this was a real landmark."[13]

Changes in national election rules helped the Carter campaign. Public financing for presidential elections had been established as part of the national reaction to Watergate. Candidates had to raise at least five thousand dollars in amounts of $250 or less in at least twenty states. The federal government matched funds raised by candidates. Another new rule meant that state primary results dictated the selection of more of the delegates to the Democratic National Convention than had occurred in past elections. This meant that dark-horse candidates could compete with nationally known candidates. These rule changes led Carter to enter every primary and have a slate of Carter delegates in every congressional district.[14]

BILLY CARTER AND SOME FRIENDS GATHERED AT BILLY'S GAS STATION. The public loved him. As Mrs. Pope said, "Billy was one of their favorites, I think, because he was colorful and you could just about always find him laughing jollily over at the gas station."[15] Cousin Hugh Carter said, "People think that Billy has always had the gas station that he made famous. That also isn't true." He bought the station a few years before the presidential campaign started. "Billy had the good sense to know it was a good moneymaking proposition and Billy improved on gasoline sales vastly by promoting himself as the picturesque fellow with a beer can always in hand."[16]

Billy Carter entered the Plains political arena in the 1970s. He served on the Plains City Council for two years and then ran for mayor in 1974. Leonard Blanton learned that Billy was running that year and at the last minute decided that he, too, would run for mayor. Blanton defeated Carter by four votes in a town with 225 registered voters. The two men ran against each other again in 1976. Mayor Blanton won the December 6, 1976, election with ninety-six votes versus seventy-one for Billy. Carter told the *New York Times* that "it was the antidrinking vote that beat me."[17] Blanton knew Billy well through the years. He has said, "I didn't know he drank until I saw him sober one time."[18] President-elect Carter played no role in the 1976 election but did show up at the gas station late on election night and declared, "He would have made a great mayor." He also mentioned that maybe there were too many Carters in politics for all family members to win elections.[19]

ON JULY 4, JIMMY CARTER STOPPED AT HISTORIC WESTVILLE, located about thirty miles west of Plains, to visit and ask for votes. He and Rosalynn rode in a carriage at the living history museum, which recreates life in the 1850s. During the 1976 presidential race, the Carter campaign used several different tactics that worked greatly to his advantage. The Iowa caucuses were a major focus. Carter went there 110 times between December 1974 and primary day, with some trips lasting a week or longer.[20] The 1970 campaign for governor of Georgia provided the model for the 1976 Carter presidential campaign. As Numan V. Bartley wrote, "Carter and his advisers sought to reenact on a larger scale their gubernatorial victory of 1970. In that campaign Carter had started from a base in southwest Georgia and expanded from it to the rest of the state. In his presidential effort Carter endeavored to extend his Georgia base to encompass first the rest of the South and then the rest of the nation through campaign techniques similar to those that were successful in 1970."[21]

Through it all, Carter did not forget his home state. Several times during the year he came back to Georgia to regroup and see his family. On May 4, 1976, Carter overwhelmingly won the Georgia Democratic primary. Voters from both rural and urban counties voted for him and he won counties with white and with black majorities. Conservative candidate Ronald Reagan beat eventual nominee Gerald Ford in the Republican primary in the Peach State that day.[22]

DEMOCRATIC PRESIDENTIAL NOMINEE JIMMY CARTER appeared at the 1976 Democratic National Convention with his choice for vice president, Senator Walter "Fritz" Mondale of Minnesota, and members of their families. Mondale had been a candidate for president but withdrew his name from consideration. In his autobiography, *The Good Fight*, he says, "That turned out to be a tough period. . . . After more than a year of constant travel, constant fund-raising, and constant speeches, I had pulled about even with 'None of the Above' in national opinion surveys, and I dropped that bid."[23]

In late May, he knew that Jimmy Carter had compiled a list of possible candidates for vice president that included him. "I wasn't too excited because I didn't know Carter well and I was happy in the Senate."[24] Fellow Minnesota senator and former vice president Hubert Humphrey urged him to consider accepting the job. On July 8, 1976, Walter and Joan Mondale flew first to Atlanta and then to Plains for a meeting. Mondale grew up in the small town of Elmore, Minnesota, with a population of about seven hundred. He remembers that after they arrived in Plains, Carter asked him what he thought of the town. "I said it was pretty big." The two men both had religious backgrounds: Mondale had a Methodist minister for a father and a half-brother who was a Unitarian minister. Jimmy and Fritz talked for several hours and walked around Plains and the Carter farm. They talked at length about civil rights as Mondale made sure that he and Carter agreed on that important point. Mondale then spent the time trying to determine how he would fit into the administration if he became vice president. "I was not interested in being a vice president who stands by until the president dies." He shared with Carter that "for me, my dignity, my sense of respect, are very important. . . . If I get in there and people start pushing me around and there is nothing I can do about it, that is going to be horrific for me. I hope we can have a relationship where none of that occurs." Carter responded, "I guarantee that is the way I want to do it."[25]

The day went well and Carter agreed with Mondale that the vice president should have a significant role in the administration—to be in the know and be more than just the designated person to attend ceremonial events. On July 15 during the Democratic National Convention, Mondale received a call from Carter, who said, "Good morning, Fritz. Would you like to run with me?" He agreed and both his life and the role of the vice president changed forever.[26] Mondale recalls, "We got along very well. We understood each other. He never did anything underhanded to me. I don't think any other vice president has been treated the way he treated me."[27] The liberal Democrat appreciated several things about Carter, including the fact that the man from the Deep South fully supported civil rights.

Richard Moe, chief of staff for Mondale, recalled the close personal connection between his boss and Carter. "After the election . . . they really spent large amounts of time together. Mondale would take a shuttle to Plains a couple days a week. . . . It's not really an easy place to get to . . . But the flip side of this, this was a very positive sign, because it was the first time in American history a president-elect was involving his vice president in cabinet selection and policy development."[28] The practice of the vice president being a real part of the White House team has continued ever since, though specifics differ with each administration.

THE ENTIRE CARTER FAMILY, including Rosalynn, Amy, Lillian, sons, and their wives gathered at the Democratic National Convention in 1976. The convention took place in New York City at Madison Square Garden, July 12–15. During the rest of the campaign, family members spread out across the country. As Chip Carter said, "At one point in the presidential campaign we had eleven different family members in eleven different states at the same time."[29]

Barbara Jordan, the first African American woman elected to the U.S. House of Representatives from the Deep South, gave the keynote speech on the first day. During her speech, which has been recognized as one of the hundred most significant American political speeches of the twentieth century, she noted that the mere fact that she was giving the speech was significant. "I feel . . . that my presence here is one additional bit of evidence that the American Dream need not

forever be deferred. . . . We are a people in a quandary about the present. We are a people in search of our future. . . . We are attempting on a larger scale to fulfill the promise of America."[30] Martin Luther King Sr. delivered the invocation at the convention and strongly supported his fellow Georgian.

Carter proudly stood for election as a man from the South. Lyndon Johnson, president from 1963 to 1969, did not try to gain office as a southerner and the South did not embrace him. Indeed, Johnson received a cool welcome when he spoke in Augusta just before the 1964 election with loud hecklers in the audience.[31] As Carter would later say, "Johnson was [the] incumbent president. . . . He did not want to be stigmatized, in his mind, as a southerner—he was a southwesterner. And the major issue then was Johnson's commitment to civil rights. . . . That became a major issue in the southeast."[32]

JIMMY CARTER SPOKE AT THE LITTLE WHITE HOUSE in Warm Springs, Georgia, on Labor Day, September 6, 1976, as he kicked off the final run down to the presidential election. Franklin Delano Roosevelt had the house built while still governor of New York and continued to use it as a retreat while he served as president from 1933 to 1945. Georgians voted solidly for Roosevelt in each of his four presidential elections. During his Labor Day speech, Carter commented, "I owe special interests nothing. I owe the people everything."

Carter gathered his brain trust at Miss Lillian's Pond House at the start of Labor Day weekend in 1976. Attendees included Walter Mondale and his aide, Richard Moe, plus Carter staff members Hamilton Jordan, Jody Powell, Gerald Rafshoon, Pat Caddell, Charles Kirbo, Robert Lipshutz, Tim Kraft, Stuart Eizenstat, Rick Hutcheson, and Greg Schneiders. Jordan later admitted that those meetings made one point clear: advisors had not given adequate thought to how they should present policies and plans to the public. Carter and his staff had developed basic themes but effectively explaining them to the public continued to be a challenge in the last weeks of the campaign.[33]

After leaving Warm Springs, the candidate headed to the Darlington 500, a stock car race held in South Carolina. Carter, a longtime fan of stock car racing, arrived after Bob Dole, the Republican vice presidential candidate from Kansas. Dole told the large crowd that Republicans would be making the South a battleground. The crowd had its favorites. The *New York Times* reported, "And with the Confederate flag flapping in a favorable breeze beside Old Glory, the Georgia Democrat, after exchanging greetings with Senator Dole, was brought to the speakers' stand with a call to 'welcome the next President of the United States, Jimmy Carter.'"[34] As the race was about to start, Carter rode in the lead car while Dole rode in the pace car. That November, a majority of South Carolina voters selected Jimmy Carter for president, though in the next ten presidential elections majorities would go to the Republican candidate.

CRITICS COMPLAINED about many different aspects of Carter, his staff, and his personal activities, with the fault-finding starting as soon as Carter announced that he would run for president. Candidate Jimmy Carter got his luggage out of the car to load on his campaign plane, Peanut One, in September 1976. He continued to carry his own bags while serving as president. Stuart Eizenstat has stated that the people of the United States like a little pomp and circumstance with our presidency. He wrote, "We . . . begged him to abandon his campaign habit of carrying his own luggage. . . . The country did not want him to jettison the symbols of the office that help raise any president of the United States from being just another jumped-up politician to a figure who represents the majesty of our country."[35] Carter consented and let others do these tasks.

Bert Lance thought that Carter got criticized just for being himself. He wrote about the opposition from people in Washington, D.C., "He was an outsider and that was plenty bad enough. . . . Even worse was that he was a *southern* outsider. . . . Jimmy was ridiculed . . . for the way he talked. . . . The Washington crowd mocked him for taking his own carry-on luggage. . . . They snickered about his sweaters."[36] People respected Carter for being a normal person but they wanted the leader of the country to exude power.

JIMMY AND ROSALYNN CARTER FLASH BIG SMILES while a sleepy Amy signals that election day has been a long day. The fall 1976 run for president by Jimmy Carter had its ups and downs, as often happens with campaigns. Controversy erupted in late September after Carter declared in a *Playboy* interview that he had "committed adultery in my heart many times. This is something God recognizes I will do—and I have done it—and God forgives me for it."[37] People expressed shock that a born-again Christian granted an interview with *Playboy* though others thought he merely shared too much information.

The three debates with Gerald Ford brought mixed results. Many considered Ford to be the winner of the first debate while Carter won the second. Most commentators rated the third and final debate as a draw.[38] By late October, Carter had lost his early lead and the race became too close to call. Members of the Peanut Brigade headed to Iowa, Texas, Oklahoma, and elsewhere. "Their person-to-person campaign style and down-home charm were certain to make a favorable impression and gain votes for the Democratic nominee."[39] Despite a statement Carter made in Philadelphia about "ethnic purity" on April 3, 1976, while discussing public housing, blacks in both the South and the North supported Carter.[40] Carter said that he thought communities should be able to preserve the ethnic purity of their neighborhoods, a statement many thought indicated his support of segregated housing. He soon issued an apology for using that phrase.

Rosalynn Carter has written that "election days are no fun. My stomach stays in knots, the tension almost unbearable. The worst time is from the hour the polls close until the returns start coming in."[41] She remembered waiting in

a suite at the Omni Hotel in Atlanta on election night. "On November 2, 1976, we paced and laughed nervously and talked too loud and prayed silently. Jimmy was there, as was all our family. . . . It was chaotic, as all election nights are, but this evening was particularly tense. . . . This was *the* night. The night in which all our work, all our hopes and dreams, would either be realized or shattered."[42] About 2:00 a.m., Jody Powell went to speak to over three thousand restless Carter supporters in the World Congress Center in Atlanta. He urged patience. "We have waited more than a hundred years for this moment. We can wait a few minutes more."[43] Finally, after 3:00 a.m., Governor Cliff Finch of Mississippi called Carter to tell him he had won the state. Rosalynn heard her husband gleefully saying to the governor, "'We won. We won Mississippi! . . . That puts us over the top!' The room erupted in cheers, tears, and embraces."[44]

MISS LILLIAN CELEBRATES IN PLAINS with friends and neighbors. The T-shirts came from Maxine Reese, campaign coordinator. She ordered 144 shirts in Carter green and white. Earlier in the evening, they took Miss Lillian into a room at the depot and had her put a shirt on. Cold weather pervaded that evening, so the locals had coats on over their shirts. They let the national news teams know they would take off their coats when they found out that Jimmy won. "It hit every newspaper in the country. We were still doing our little thing here in Plains. But immediately when he said that he had enough votes that he was going to win, we pulled our coats off. . . . And it was just—it's hard to describe the feeling at a time like that, and the camaraderie of everybody. . . . We were working for a local boy who wanted to be president of the United States."[45]

Carter and his supporters soon flew back to Plains. They arrived about 5:00 a.m. Some people had been there all night, others had come and gone. Betty Pope recalled, "There were young people, old people, Plains people, people from all over the nation had come in. And it was an unbelievable experience. The emotions were extremely high."[46]

Miss Lillian enjoyed being in the thick of things on election night. Walter Mondale remembers her: "I thought she was great. She was her own independent spirit. She was a good mother to the president. She always wanted to play a role to help in some way."[47]

JIMMY CARTER BECAME THE THIRTY-NINTH
PRESIDENT of the United States on January 20, 1977.
Carter took the oath of office on the East Portico of the U.S.
Capitol. In his swearing-in ceremony, he used two Bibles, a
family Bible and one used by George Washington when he
became president in 1789. He became the first man elected
president from the Deep South since the 1840s, when James
K. Polk won the seat in 1844 and Zachary Taylor triumphed

in 1848. As one observer noted, "The day of his inauguration,
Carter immediately accomplished one impressive long-range
achievement without lifting a finger. His Presidency reinte-
grated the South with the nation. . . . He is the ideal figure to
release the South from the burden of its past, bringing it back
into the mainstream, while preserving its special nature."[48]

On the parade, the Carters walked from the Capitol to
the White House, the first time a president ever walked the

pavement of Pennsylvania Avenue after his inauguration.[49] James Reston noted in the *New York Times* that "he walked Pennsylvania Avenue, defying the advice of the Secret Service. He didn't talk about the South. . . . He made a point in his speech about the family as the heart of any society, but mainly he walked the avenue hand in hand with his wife, with his children and grandchildren at his back, and acted as if nation and world were all one big neighborhood."[50]

A train transported supporters from Georgia to Washington, D.C., for the inauguration. The "Peanut Special" recalled another train, the "Presidential Express," which transported supporters in 1933 from Warm Springs to Washington to attend the first inaugural of Georgia's adopted son, Franklin Delano Roosevelt.

Later in the day, the Carters attended inaugural balls. Mrs. Carter decided to wear the gown she had worn in Georgia in 1971 for the gubernatorial inaugural. She received much criticism for wearing the same dress twice. Journalist Sally Quinn mused, "They are not our king and queen. . . . They refuse to ride in a limousine. . . . She wears her 6-year-old evening dress from his gubernatorial inaugural ball for 'sentimental reasons.'"[51] Many members of the press did not appreciate the fact that Mrs. Carter took the nostalgic option by wearing a dress she had worn on a special night in Atlanta in 1971. (The dress is now part of the First Ladies exhibit at the Smithsonian's National Museum of American History.)

PRESIDENT CARTER ENJOYED A FEW MINUTES OF RELAXATION with daughter Amy and grandson Jason at a tree house on the White House grounds on March 10, 1977. Family has always been a central focus for Jimmy and Rosalynn Carter. During the White House years, they tried to spend what little free time they had with each other and with family. Amy Carter turned ten years old during her first year at the White House. Her nephew Jason, the son of Jack Carter and Judy Langford, was eight years younger than Amy.

Members of the Carter family helped when running election campaigns and the peanut business and they continued to be close to Carter during the presidency. Jeff Carter, the youngest son, received a graduate degree from George Washington University and he and his wife, Annette, lived in the White House while he attended school. Chip Carter, his wife, Caron, and their son James Earl Carter IV also lived at the White House for a period. A cousin, Hugh Carter Jr., worked on the staff in the White House. Family members and friends visited often during the White House years.

JIMMY AND ROSALYNN CARTER MET WITH ADMIRAL HYMAN G. RICKOVER on May 28, 1977, on the USS *Los Angeles*. Carter first met Rickover during his Navy days. Carter has described him as a "stern, brilliant, dedicated, innovative, nonconformist officer—in my opinion, the best engineer who has ever lived on earth." He acknowledged that Rickover had faults. "Rickover could have done more had he been more sensitive to other peoples' weaknesses, had he been willing to accommodate the vicissitudes of Navy life. But he couldn't abide solidly anything that departed from his own ideas or his own standards." He added, "When I was President, Rickover came to see me often. He was very deferential to me as commander in chief. . . . He gave me gratuitous advice often. I protected him as best I could because I saw his value." Carter also extended his active duty status. In 1982, during the Reagan administration, Secretary of the Navy John Lehman forced Rickover to retire at age eighty-two.[52]

JIMMY CARTER STAYED IN TOUCH with family and life in Georgia while he served as president. He and Rosalynn placed their financial interests in a blind trust but he continued to watch things like how peanut plants looked in the field and how much rainfall south Georgia had received. Here President Carter and his brother Billy examine plants. In addition to caring about the agriculture, the Carters also quickly came to appreciate the solitude and seclusion they had while on their farm and at other isolated places in the South. Rosalynn said, "We did learn that we could slip away on occasion and do a few things privately. We . . . walked in the fields on our farms at home, and vacationed on an island off the coast of Georgia out of view of the television cameras and reporters."[53]

Jimmy Carter, the farmer who became president, brought agriculture into the forefront of world politics. Carter has commented that his father disagreed with Franklin D. Roosevelt, whose Depression-era projects dictated to farmers what they could do on their land and with their products. He stated, "My father was a strong supporter of Roosevelt in 1932 but he turned against Roosevelt quite bitterly after the government made farmers kill their hogs and plow up their cotton after it was planted. Daddy thought that was an excessive interference in the freedom of American farmers."[54]

During much of the 1970s, the Soviet Union suffered from poor agricultural output and bought tons of wheat, corn, and soybeans from American farmers. In December 1979, the Soviet Union invaded Afghanistan, a country on its southern border. The Soviets invaded because of the rise of militant Islamic political forces. Carter viewed this as an expansion of the Soviet Empire and as a serious threat in an unstable region of the world. He told a group of congressmen soon

afterward that the attack constituted "the greatest threat to peace since the Second World War." Carter ordered an embargo and cancelled grain sales to the Soviet Union. U.S. farmers bore the brunt of this decision and Senator Ted Kennedy and others opposed it. In the end, farmers sold their grain to other countries but the embargo became a symbol of the farm crisis of the 1980s.[55] Ronald Reagan ended the embargo in April 1981. The Soviet invasion in 1979 also led the United States and other countries to boycott the 1980 Summer Olympics, which were held in Moscow.

THE FRIENDSHIP BETWEEN JIMMY CARTER AND BERT LANCE dates back to 1966. They met when the regional planning and development commission gathered at Berry College in Rome. Lance, the president of First National Bank of Calhoun, had much in common with Carter. He and Carter, the first chair of the state planning commission, cared deeply about economic development in the area and especially in small towns. Soon Lance started campaigning for Carter during the 1966 gubernatorial race. After Carter won the office in 1970, he asked Lance to head the state highway department, which had been the focus of much controversy, partly due to the power held by its director of twenty-three years, Jim Gillis. Later, the north Georgian led the governor's reorganization efforts and together they got things done. As Lance noted, "Folks around Atlanta and the rest of the state began saying that Carter and I had a peer relationship. . . . Word had it that I was the one person who could speak candidly to the governor and still keep his respect and support. . . . I never stopped being completely honest with him on any subject where I thought he needed to hear the truth from somebody who had nothing in mind except the best interests of the people and of Jimmy Carter himself."[56]

Lance lost a bid to become governor of Georgia in 1974 and then served as an advisor to Carter during the 1976 presidential election. He also became president of the National Bank of Georgia, based in Atlanta. In 1977, President Carter named him the director of the Office of Management and

Budget. Within months, controversy surrounded Lance. Allegations of mismanagement and corruption at the Calhoun bank finally forced his resignation on September 24, 1977.

The scandal damaged the Carter administration, which had run on a truth stance. Lance thought his departure hurt the administration in other ways. He said, "When I left Washington . . . he didn't have that kind of personal give-and-take with anyone in any job anywhere in his administration. It was a glaring deficiency that undercut his effectiveness every day."[57] In 1980, a jury acquitted Lance of all charges. He went on to be involved with the Democratic party and periodically appeared in Plains for special events during the post-presidency. Jody Powell reflected on the episode, "It would have been better for the president if we had brought that to an end sooner. It threw us off stride. It made it harder for us to talk about other things, and sort of played into questions about whether we could lead and run the country."[58] Walter Mondale agreed: "Jimmy Carter really respected him. It was a loss to the administration. Poor Carter was shaken by it but the stories were too bad to keep him in the administration."[59] Stuart Eizenstat added, "His administration was never again tainted by scandal, and he became steeled to the rough political realities of Washington."[60]

JIMMY AND ROSALYNN CARTER have had a close marriage and one that has evolved since the 1950s and 1960s, when he made most of the major decisions and she took care of their young sons. She has been his business and campaign partner for many years. Once Carter assumed the presidency, she assumed control of family finances, events involving Amy, and social activities. According to Stuart Eizenstat, in the early days of his term "Rosalynn would meet Jimmy at the end of the day on the elevator to the private living quarters with a list of things she needed his help to decide. She remembered that he dreaded seeing her with those lists, so he suggested they meet every Wednesday for lunch."[61] They generally ate inside the White House but enjoyed the patio outside whenever weather permitted, and she always arrived with a list of things to review.

Mrs. Carter represented the United States by traveling to foreign countries and served as the president's eyes and ears, gathering information as she went. Some members of the press criticized her activities, especially when she started attending cabinet meetings. This happened after she asked Jimmy about the accuracy of press reports about the sessions. The president recommended she come to the cabinet meetings and decide for herself. She never participated in meetings but sat to the side and occasionally took notes.[62] She addressed the issue of the widespread criticism of her activities as a member of the first family during a 2007 conference at the University of Georgia. "I was just doing what I've been doing all my married life with Jimmy Carter, being a partner in everything he did. And so I soon decided that I was going to be criticized no matter what I did, so I may as well go ahead and do the things I wanted to do. I tried to

ignore the criticism, it was hard at times, but I think I accomplished it. I never did stop doing the things I wanted to do."[63] Mondale and others in the administration supported her. He said, "Her attendance at those cabinet meetings worked out very well." In general, he thought that she "enhanced the role of women. She was always productive, always helpful . . . always well-informed."[64]

HAVING A PRESIDENT of the United States who is an alumnus attending a sporting event means that the person might get as much attention as the actual game. A president who had attended both schools in a contest definitely drew attention to Annapolis, Maryland, on November 12, 1977. Carter recalls, "I know when I was governor, every year when Georgia Tech and the Naval Academy played football in Atlanta . . . the Naval Academy superintendent and the commandant and others would come down . . . and one of the main topics of their conversations then from '71 through '74 was criticizing Rickover."[65] A strong wind and cool temperatures on that day in 1977 made for a tough day to watch football. Navy got the victory.

In 1984, Carter commented on his strong attachment to Tech. He declared, "As is generally recognized, there is a special air and loyalty about Georgia Tech. I've never really understood exactly why. But there is a spirit there that I don't think is equaled in—I know is not equaled in any other college I've been to. Now even, my visceral reaction to events at Tech exceeds that of my reaction to the Naval Academy." He added that "I'm very proud of my honorary degree. I've been very reticent about not accepting many degrees. That is one of my greatest honors."[66] He received that honorary degree in 1979.

JIMMY CARTER PLANTS A RED MAPLE at the White House on November 17, 1977. Joining the Carters for the occasion were Ray Shirley, chief of the Georgia State Forestry Commission, Henry E. Williams, chairman of the board of the commission, and John R. McGuire, chief of the Forest Service, U.S. Department of Agriculture.[67] Jimmy and Rosalynn Carter left their mark on the grounds of the White House by planting two trees. As the oldest continually maintained landscape in the United States, the White House lawns provide a focal point for many events each year. John Adams requested that a garden be planted before his arrival in 1800. His son John Quincy Adams, the sixth president, established flowerbeds on the grounds during his time at the White House. Most presidents since the 1870s have chosen to plant at least one commemorative tree on the grounds, so the landscaping continually grows and changes. Carter planted a cedar of Lebanon tree on April 28, 1978, presented by the American Lebanese League, and this red maple, which represented Georgia.[68]

ON JANUARY 15, 1978, Jimmy Carter met with the two most recent and only surviving presidents of the United States. Gerald Ford and Richard Nixon came to Washington for the funeral of Hubert Humphrey. Humphrey served as the thirty-eighth vice president from 1965 to 1969. He represented Minnesota in the Senate and ran for president in 1968 as the Democratic Party nominee, losing that election to Richard Nixon. In the last months of his life he talked to many old friends and acquaintances, including Nixon, the victor in the 1968 national election. A newspaper headline at the time of his death noted, "Nixon leaves exile to honor HHH." This was the first time Nixon had visited the Capitol since he resigned in disgrace on August 8, 1974, after the Watergate hearings. The body of Hubert Humphrey lay in state in the Capitol rotunda, a practice which honors the most eminent citizens of the United States. Both his political protégé, Vice President Walter Mondale, and President Carter eulogized the man known as "the happy warrior."[69]

PRESIDENT AND MRS. CARTER entertained many world leaders during their time in the White House. Some occasions had a southern flair, with musicians and barbeques on the White House lawn. Legendary Texas musician Willie Nelson and his band visited on April 25, 1978. Shown are, left to right, Connie Koepke, wife of Nelson, Frank Moore of the Carter administration, unidentified, and country musician and wife of Waylon Jennings, Jessi Colter, who is standing next to Nelson and Carter. Nelson also performed on September 13, 1980. At one point, Rosalynn Carter joined him onstage to do a duet of "Up against the Wall, Redneck Mother."[70] The Carters invited drivers and their crews from the Atlanta Speedway and other supporters from Georgia for that concert.

The press and Washingtonian society disparaged the Carters' style of entertaining. In both Georgia and Washington, D.C., the Carters seldom served hard liquor and instead offered wine and beer. They felt that this saved taxpayers money, and they did not drink much themselves. The Carters practiced their belief in fiscal conservatism throughout their lives. Rosalynn received an unwanted nickname, "Rosé Rosalynn." She protested, "They make me sound like a real prude. I'm not a prude!"[71] The Carters participated relatively little in the Washington, D.C., social scene. They generally preferred to stay home with family or host events at the White House rather than attend events elsewhere in the city. Rosalynn once told a reporter, "When Jimmy was governor, we weren't involved in Atlanta society. We were busy. And when we had an evening at home we wanted to be at home, like any other couple that works."[72] She has noted, "If there is one thing Jimmy dislikes more than anything I can think of, it is a cocktail party or reception or dinner every night."[73] Despite avoiding most Washington social events, the Carters reached out to members of Congress and others, including hosting a square dance for Congress on July 20, 1977, on the South Lawn at the White House.

THE FACT THAT HIS PARENTS RAISED A SOUTHERN GENTLEMAN periodically showed itself during the Carter administration. In 1978, the president poured water for William Tapley "Tap" Bennett Jr. while they attended an event. Bennett, a career diplomat and native of Griffin, Georgia, served as the U.S. permanent representative on the North Atlantic Council of NATO, the North Atlantic Treaty Organization, from 1977 to 1983. Sheryl Vogt, director of the Russell Library at the University of Georgia, remembers, "As the longest serving career foreign service officer, Ambassador Bennett was well versed in protocol. Much to Bennett's chagrin, the President began pouring his water before he could serve the President. When Ambassador Bennett told me of the incident years later, he still expressed his embarrassment."[74]

Though he had limited experience in the international arena prior to becoming president, Jimmy Carter had some of his greatest achievements in foreign affairs. In 2011, he told the *Guardian*, "We kept our country at peace. We never went to war. We never dropped a bomb. We never fired a bullet. But still we achieved our international goals. We brought peace to other people, including Egypt and Israel. We normalized relations with China, which had been non-existent for 30-something years. We brought peace between [the] US and most of the countries in Latin America because of the Panama Canal Treaty. We formed a working relationship with the Soviet Union." Regarding not going to war, he added, "In the last 50 years now, more than that, that's almost a unique achievement."[75]

ROSALYNN CARTER SIGNED A RESOLUTION in support of the Equal Rights Amendment (ERA) on October 20, 1978. President Carter signed a congressional bill the same day extending the deadline for ratification of the ERA for two years. Many supporters of the women's movement thought the 1970s would be the decade that the Equal Rights Amendment passed. Alice Paul and others first introduced the concept of equal rights for women under the law in 1921. A leader in the women's suffrage movement, Paul astutely argued that getting the right to vote in 1920 with the passage of the Nineteenth Amendment did not guarantee women equal rights. The U.S. House and Senate approved the ERA in 1971 by huge bipartisan majorities. Presidents Nixon and Ford supported the amendment, though the president plays no official role in the passage of a constitutional amendment. Indiana became the thirty-fifth state to ratify the amendment in 1977. Three-fourths, or thirty-eight states, are needed to support an amendment for it to pass.

In 1979, Rev. Jerry Falwell organized the Moral Majority, which portrayed the amendment as an attack on the family. This new evangelical movement linked Christian beliefs with traditional values and brought religion into the Republican Party and American political life. The ERA had not previously been a partisan or religious issue. Phyllis Schlafly organized conservative Republican women and argued that the ERA and other new laws would give women, including house-wives, less protection. Opposition to abortions also became entangled with the ERA vote. Rosalynn and Jimmy Carter personally opposed abortion but they did not want to see *Roe v. Wade* overturned. The 1973 Supreme Court decision first recognized the constitutional right to have an abortion. The Carters also did not advocate for laws or a constitutional

amendment banning abortion, positions which some religious and political groups opposed.[76]

Mrs. Carter has stated, "One of my biggest disappoint-ments in the four years is that we failed to get the Equal Rights Amendment passed. We made call after call after call. We knew every single legislator in the state legislatures in the country who had not supported it."[77] Jimmy Carter reflected in *A Full Life*: "Surprising to me, it was people with whom I felt most friendly and whom I attempted to help who caused the most trouble. . . . I had more women in my cabinet and at other high levels than any predecessor, and appointed more female federal judges than all previous presidents combined. . . . Despite our best efforts, leaders of women's organizations were the most demanding and unappreciative. . . . I believe the issue was my disagreement about abortion rights."[78]

PRESIDENT JIMMY CARTER CHATS WITH ARKANSAS GOVERNOR-ELECT BILL CLINTON on December 1, 1978. Clinton became the youngest governor in the United States when he took office a few weeks later at age thirty-two.[79] He became the forty-second president of the U.S. in 1993 and served until 2001. Clinton ran the 1976 Carter campaign in Arkansas, but the two have had a lukewarm relationship at times. The two Democrats from the South had few things in common. Carter family roots in Georgia went back for generations, while Clinton had few roots in his home state. Earl and Lillian Carter and their four children had a close-knit family in the small farming town of Plains. Clinton grew up with his mother and grandmother after his father died in an accident before his birth. Carter had an engineering background and served in the U.S. Navy for eleven years, while Clinton attended Yale and Oxford and worked as an attorney.

Differences in their personalities abounded. As Douglas Brinkley said in *The Unfinished Presidency*, "Carter married his high school sweetheart at age twenty-two and never had an extramarital affair. Clinton, by most accounts, did not place marital fidelity high as a life priority. . . . Where lying was anathema to Carter, for Clinton it was synonymous with being a good politician; while Carter scorned compromise to his political detriment, to Clinton deal making was what politics was all about."[80] Steven Hochman, director of research at the Carter Center and faculty assistant to President Carter, has noted, "Certainly, there are many differences, but both came to stand for civil rights and had strong connections and support in the African-American community. Both have a global perspective and see themselves as global citizens. They are committed to environmental issues. They came together as Baptists to try to bring other Baptists together. While both appreciate elite culture, they also appreciate the traditional culture of Southerners. They were influenced by populism and understand and appeal to ordinary people."[81]

Several months after this meeting in 1978, relations between Carter and Clinton began to sour. Cuban president Fidel Castro opened the port of Mariel to anyone wanting to leave the island and Carter responded by offering asylum to those who wanted to come to the United States. Thousands fled Cuba on the Mariel boatlift between April and October 1980, so the president set up tent cities to deal with these immigrants. Over eighteen thousand went to Fort Chaffee, Arkansas. This proved to be a contentious point in the 1980 Arkansas gubernatorial election and Clinton lost his bid for reelection as governor. Clinton later said that Carter "screwed me," though he won his bid for that office in 1982.[82]

PRESIDENT AND MRS. CARTER SING with Martin Luther King Sr., civil rights activists Andrew Young and Coretta Scott King, and others during a visit to Ebenezer Baptist Church in Atlanta on January 14, 1979. They gathered to observe the birthday of Martin Luther King Jr. and to see Carter receive the Martin Luther King Jr. Nonviolent Peace Prize. The King holiday had first been proposed in Congress just days after his assassination on April 4, 1968. The King Center sponsored the first observance of the birthday in 1969. The bill establishing a King holiday languished until President Carter vowed in 1979 to support the day. Finally, in November 1983, President Ronald Reagan signed the King holiday bill into law. The first official holiday observance came in January 1986. Jesse Helms and John P. East, senators from North Carolina and Mississippi, led the opposition to the bill in the Senate. Helms urged senators to not elevate King to "the same level as the father of our country and above the many other Americans whose achievements approach that of Washington's" by establishing a federal holiday to observe his birthday.[83] When Carter addressed the group in Atlanta that day in 1979, he noted, "My administration and I personally stand with you. We are committed to civil rights. We are committed to equal opportunity. We are committed to equal justice under the law."[84]

Carter had a long relationship with Andrew Young. Young served as executive director of the Southern Christian Leadership Conference and a congressman from the Fifth District of Georgia from 1973 to 1977. President Carter appointed the former aide to Martin Luther King Jr. as ambassador to the United Nations in January 1977. Young served as the first African American in that post and took several controversial positions while serving as ambassador. Finally, in 1979, he resigned due to an unauthorized meeting with the U.N. representative of the Palestine Liberation Organization. Rumors declared that he had been fired. Young told *Time*, "It is very difficult to do the things that I think are in the interest of the country and maintain the standards of protocol and diplomacy. . . . I really don't feel a bit sorry for anything that I have done."[85] In 1981, Atlanta voters selected Young as mayor of Atlanta. Young and Carter have maintained a close friendship despite this episode.

CARTER TALKS WITH REV. JOSEPH E. LOWERY, a civil rights activist and the third president of the Southern Christian Leadership Conference, and others at Ebenezer Baptist Church. The SCLC criticized economic policies of the Carter administration. They thought that proposed austerity measures placed the heaviest burden on poor people, especially poor blacks who faced unemployment rates of 12 to 15 percent.[86]

ON MARCH 26, 1979, the Carter family took a few minutes before a state dinner honoring the signing of the peace treaty between Israel and Egypt to have a family portrait taken. During the dinner, President Carter exchanged toasts with Israeli prime minister Menachem Begin and Egyptian president Anwar Sadat. All four of the Carter children attended the momentous occasion, as did Miss Lillian and Allie Smith, mothers of Jimmy and Rosalynn, plus spouses and Carter grandchildren.

Negotiations leading to the Camp David Accords and the subsequent peace treaty took place the previous September when Begin and Sadat came to the Maryland retreat at the invitation of President Carter. They spent thirteen days in private negotiations. No public statements were allowed during the process. Sadat and Begin shared the 1978 Nobel Peace Prize for the work. Stuart Eizenstat sums up the peace activities of September and the treaty signing in March: "No president has dedicated himself so exclusively to one project, or taken such a risk to his prestige."[87] Carter wrote in *Faith*, "There were a number of times as president when I prayed that I would be able to succeed in reaching one of my political goals. . . . One of my most vivid memories of this kind was toward the end of my negotiations with President Sadat and Prime Minister Begin at Camp David."[88] Eizenstat added, "Everyone agreed that it was Jimmy Carter who unlocked the compromise to achieve an improbable agreement, not once but twice. . . . Carter's success was without precedent in American diplomatic history: no president of the United States was so closely engaged in drafting and negotiating agreements."[89]

JIMMY CARTER RECEIVED AN HONORARY DOCTOR OF LAWS DEGREE from Emory University on August 30, 1979. Officials presented the degree during the groundbreaking ceremony for the William R. Cannon Chapel and Religious Center at the Candler School of Theology. Cannon, a bishop of the Methodist Church, served as dean of the Candler School from 1953 to 1968. He and Carter had been longtime friends and Bishop Cannon gave the prayer during the presidential inauguration of 1977. Behind Carter on the left is Henry Bowden, former chairman of the Emory Board of Trustees, and to the right of Carter is James T. Laney, who became president of Emory in March 17, 1977.

Laney commented about Carter and his religion, saying, "His religion is so natural to the South and so enigmatic to the rest of the nation."[90] Many southerners understood how his religion was just part of Jimmy Carter and his being, though others found his Christianity more mysterious.

Griffin Bell also attended the ceremonies at Emory that day. The Americus, Georgia, native served as the attorney general of the United States from 1977 until 1979. Bell had strong principles and an independent streak. Though a Democrat, he did not always stand by the party. He stuck with decisions which he felt were rooted in U.S. laws even when those beliefs clashed with the desires of the president.[91]

PRESIDENT JIMMY CARTER AND OTHERS

examined energy sources for the future during an Energy Research Symposium at Georgia Tech on September 2, 1979. Carter sits with Dr. Ruth Davis, U.S. energy secretary, and former president of Coca-Cola Charles Duncan on his right, and Georgia Tech president Dr. Joseph M. Pettit and Stuart Eizenstat on his left. Ten of the leading energy research experts in the nation attended the symposium, which was organized at the request of the White House.[92] Eizenstat has noted that "over four full years Jimmy Carter struggled more than any other president with energy, accomplished far more, and suffered politically for it."[93]

Carter later said, "I wanted to honor Tech as Tech was honoring me, by picking a subject of major importance to present there."[94] In February of that year, Carter gave an address at Tech about foreign policy, including expressing concerns about the need for an agreement on the limitation of strategic arms with the Soviet Union and the importance of an independent Iran. He also greeted students before his alma mater presented him with their first Honorary Doctor of Engineering degree and the Alumni Distinguished Service Award.

Jimmy Carter devoted much time and effort to the national energy crisis. During his governorship he criticized President Nixon for not having an energy policy. After having been president less than ninety days, Carter said in a televised speech that the energy crisis of the 1970s was the "moral equivalent of war," and he placed more emphasis on conservation than on developing new resources. Four months later, he signed the Department of Energy Organization Act of 1977. He pushed his National Energy Plan through Congress the following year, though he never received a lot of support for the plan from the Senate and the general public. In 1979, he signed the Energy Security Act, a third energy package, into law. In the course of four years, historic changes occurred in America's energy policy. Americans began to realize that the United States had a limited supply of oil and gas and that relying on imported oil posed a national security risk.[95]

JIMMY CARTER SWINGS AT A PITCH on July 7, 1980. Some of the most famous ballgames played in the country between 1977 and 1981 occurred in Plains, Georgia, when the president and the Secret Service took on Billy Carter and members of the press. The national media covered these softball games. ABC correspondent Sam Donaldson wrote in *Hold On, Mr. President!* about playing in these games and following Carter as he jogged in his hometown. "On Sundays, we all went to the Plains Baptist Church. . . . Then, in the afternoon, we would play softball. . . . I wasn't very good, and Carter would often strike me out. . . . In between such recreational events . . . we worked hard chasing Carter up and down Georgia roads, dogging him."[96]

Billy Carter remembered how huge crowds of people attended the games and photographers documented events. "In the middle of one game, my service station blew up. I ran like hell to get over there. . . . Some photographer started blocking my way, and I just hauled off and hit him." Billy was worried that his oldest son might have been injured but media coverage that day focused instead on Billy hitting the cameraman. "It made me look like a fool. The media could be your friend one minute and turn on you the next."[97] Donaldson noted that the press left the game to cover the fire at the gas station and then returned to finish the game after the fire ended.

ROSALYNN SMITH CARTER BEGAN SUPPORTING MENTAL HEALTH ISSUES during the 1970 Georgia gubernatorial campaign and she has continued to care deeply about such issues ever since. The president established a commission in 1977 to review mental health care in the United States that looked beyond fragmented individual programs. As First Lady, Mrs. Carter took her position seriously and she and her staff worked hard on projects. She expressed frustration that "the press was more interested in what I was going to wear than in the projects I intended to take on. . . . They wanted to know why I was only serving wine at state dinners rather than how I expected to improve care for people with mental illnesses."[98]

The commission made recommendations to the president that soon translated into legislation. Rosalynn's assistant Kathy Cade said, "It was extraordinary that one could go from a commission . . . to implementation in three and a half years and Rosalynn accomplished all of this because of her interest and persistence in mental health. It is not very appealing on the Hill."[99] Carter signed the Mental Health Systems Act into law on October 7, 1980, and recognized the thirty million people in the nation with mental health problems. This law provided grants to community mental health centers that coordinated health care, mental health care, and social support services. The Reagan administration later repealed most of this act. Rosalynn Carter has written about this bill and its passage, "We were jubilant! Sadly, our elation

was short-lived. Within a few weeks, Ronald Reagan was elected president. . . . Thus, the many facets of the Mental Health Systems Act were effectively nullified by the Omnibus Budget Reconciliation Act of 1981. It was a bitter loss, but I have always been pleased about the commission and its recommendations, for they served as a guide for many states that have adopted more humane, up-to-date policies."[100] Mrs. Carter worked diligently to focus national attention and discussion on mental health issues.

JIMMY CARTER FACED MANY DIFFICULTIES
that made his 1980 reelection campaign harder. Relations
between Billy Carter, Libya, and its dictator Muammar
Gaddafi between 1978 and 1980 did not help the image of
his brother Jimmy. William Carter, the oldest son of Billy
and Sybil, said, "The beginning of the Libya deal was hardly
something to sit up and take notice of. The old man was
approached in July 1978 by a state senator from Georgia and
a couple of other people. They . . . asked him if he would go
to Libya as part of a 'goodwill trip.'"[101] Peter Bourne, who
held several positions under the Carter administration, wrote
that "Billy Carter was the only member of the family really
damaged by Jimmy's ascendancy to the presidency. . . .
His already serious drinking problem became significantly
worse."[102] Then the Libyan connection started and Billy
accepted a loan of over two hundred thousand dollars from
the Libyan government. Billy appeared before a Senate
committee in 1980, "coming across as a plausible and sympathetic figure. . . . Nevertheless, at a time when he was beset
by a plethora of other problems, this episode only served to
further weaken Carter's standing with the public."[103] The suggested impropriety of the episode hurt both Billy and Jimmy
Carter.

Walter Mondale recalls Billy and his role as the brother
of the president. He recognized that Billy was a very

independent person. "I don't think he intended to be a problem but he gave the country a chance to ridicule the Carters,
not something the president deserved at all, but he loved
his brother and protected him. . . . I remember asking the
president one day whether he thought his brother was out to
destroy him. Of course, he didn't, but it took a whack out of
our public image."[104]

THE FINAL YEAR OF THE CARTER PRESIDENCY
is remembered by many as the year of the Iranian hostage crisis. Iranian college students, who were Islamic militants and sought to oust Western influence from the country, took sixty-six American citizens hostage on November 4, 1979, and later released fourteen of them. For the next 444 days, Americans saw reminders every time they watched the news. The hostage takers supported the Iranian Revolution and took over the U.S. Embassy in Tehran. Jimmy Carter denounced the event. Much of life for the Carters began to revolve around the hostages. Rosalynn wrote that, very quickly, "the hostages seemed like family to us as Jimmy schemed and plotted to bring them home. And every time we saw them on television, I counted quickly to see how many there were. . . . I could always tell . . . that Jimmy was filled with anger and revulsion as he watched the terrorists."[105] Carter did not campaign as much as he would have normally and the election seemed up for grabs, but Carter won the Democratic nomination. Edward Kennedy, who had also sought the nomination, would not shake his hand on the stage during the Democratic convention.

Jimmy Carter wrote in *Keeping Faith: Memoirs of a President*, "Before leaving for my last thirty-six-hour campaign swing around the country, I believed I had pulled almost even with Reagan over the weekend."[106] Then the Carters received word from their pollster Pat Caddell that defeat was inevitable. Walter Mondale remembers that year and the campaign: "We kept going hard up to the election. . . . It was tough going. . . . We were delivered a very hard hand. We already had serious inflation. We never did get control of that. . . . We're not babies, we've been through tough times, but we didn't get one break."[107]

The year 1980 had other difficulties as well. A deep recession hit the U.S. economy. Oil prices continued to be high. The Peanut Brigade lacked its novelty and effectiveness in reaching out to voters. Betty Pope said later, "The 1980 campaign did not work the same way at all. . . . It was old hat. . . . The Peanut Brigade did not have the youth and the newness of it all. . . . It just didn't go over as well."[108]

The Carters went to Plains to vote on election day. Hugh Carter remembered seeing Jimmy after he voted. "I looked at him. I could tell he was very—you know, I could tell that he was depressed about . . . something."[109] On election night, the networks began calling the election for Ronald Reagan by 7:30 p.m. eastern time. Carter conceded about 9:30 p.m. "My decision to concede so early was later criticized because the polls had not closed on the West Coast. . . . I did not want to appear a bad loser, waiting until late at night to confirm what everyone already knew."[110]

CARTER STAYED BUSY DURING THE LAME DUCK SESSION working diligently to free the hostages. At times during those two and a half months, Carter got little sleep and Rosalynn had to remind him to eat. Finally, on January 20, 1981, inauguration day for Ronald Reagan as the fortieth president of the United States, they knew that freedom for the hostages would come soon. After the swearing in of the new president, a Secret Service agent came through the crowd and told Rosalynn that the first aircraft had taken off from Iran with a second plane leaving a few minutes later. She wrote, "It was time to leave Washington and we filled Air Force One with the people who had been with us from the beginning. . . . The next morning Jimmy would fly to Wiesbaden."[111]

Mondale spoke about the hostages and that long period of turmoil. "While we put the hostage crisis behind us, it was miserable all the way. . . . Even on the day we transferred power to Reagan, they held the hostages until one minute after that."[112] On the trip to Plains, Carter spoke about the timing of the release of the hostages to Hamilton Jordan: "Hamilton, I was personally disappointed, but the most important thing is that they are out and safe."[113] Jimmy Carter wrote in *Keeping Faith*, "It is impossible for me to put into words how much the hostages had come to mean to me, or how moved I was that morning to know they were coming home. . . . I was overwhelmed with happiness—but because of the hostages' freedom, not mine."[114]

Carter later expressed that his major regret about his years in the White House was the fact that he failed to share with the general public "the clear sense of direction I tried

to impart to the country, and my administration's significant accomplishments—as they were achieved." He felt that many of their accomplishments got lost behind headlines about crises and emergencies, while the press focused on problems. They overlooked the first comprehensive energy policy for the country, his environmental policy, deregulation of major sections of the economy, reorganization of government and civil service, ratification of the Panama Canal treaties, the Camp David Peace Accords, and more.[115]

CHAPTER 4

Post-presidency Begins

ON JANUARY 20, 1981, minutes after the swearing in of Ronald Reagan as president, Jimmy and Rosalynn Carter returned home to Plains. They had made a decision to leave life in big cities and return to their rural roots. Neighbors and friends threw a party to welcome them home and then gave the couple time to settle back into their 1960 ranch-style home, work on their memoirs, and figure out what they would do with the rest of their lives. They set about writing and establishing new routines in a world far from the glitz and glamour of Washington, D.C. Carter found creative solace in woodworking, a hobby he first learned decades earlier as a boy on the farm and in school. The public honored the Carters with parades, and world leaders stopped in Plains for visits. Just as the community had done when the Carters came back from the navy in 1953 and after Jimmy lost his first bid for governor in 1966, the people of Sumter County and the South helped the couple adjust to their new life and thrive in their post-presidency.

ROSALYNN AND JIMMY CARTER BOARDED AIR FORCE ONE to fly South and begin the next chapter of their lives. By this point, they had accepted the fact that Jimmy Carter had lost the November election and become the first Democrat to lose the presidency after one term since Grover Cleveland in 1888. They waved goodbye to cabinet members and others who gathered to watch the Carters leave Washington, D.C. The fate of the Iranian hostages had been a major distraction since the election loss, just as it had for the past year. Rosalynn wrote, "I didn't feel very sentimental during the [Reagan] inauguration. . . . I had long since accepted Jimmy's defeat—though with continuing regrets. . . . It was done, over, accomplished. . . . Now we were going back to where it had all begun. We were going home to Plains."[1]

She wrote further about going home. "When Jimmy lost the election in 1980, there was no question about where we would go: We would go home. I was hesitant, not at all sure that I could be happy here after the dazzle of the White House and the years of stimulating political battles. . . . We slowly rediscovered the satisfaction of a life we had left long before."[2] In the next few years, they started writing, decided where the presidential library would be and established an adjacent action center, got involved in Habitat for Humanity, and generally plotted the course of their lives for the next few decades.

GEORGIA LIEUTENANT GOVERNOR ZELL MILLER
and his wife, Shirley, joined the crowd in Plains to welcome the Carters home. Miller served as second-in-command of the state from 1975 until 1991. Georgians then elected him governor of Georgia for two terms, an office he held until 1999. Miller had known Carter since they were both in the state senate in the early 1960s. Other political leaders in the crowd at Plains that day included former head of the Office of Management and Budget Bert Lance, future governor of Georgia Joe Frank Harris, and Norman Underwood, a Democratic leader in Georgia who also ran for governor in 1984.

Maxine Reese, a Carter campaign coordinator in Plains, described the night that the Carters came home. "We had this big party planned for when he came back home, probably the only defeated president in the history of this country that had a big party planned for when he got back home. . . . We were sad that he lost but we were happy that he was coming home. And our party was billed as the world's largest covered-dish supper. I never saw so much food in my life and the street was full of people." She said they had had good weather for every Carter event. Plains did not have a building big enough for everyone, so everything happened outside. "We never had it to rain on us. But when Jimmy came home to stay, it rained. And the whole street was full of umbrellas, it was just a sea of umbrellas." People brought food from several states.[3] Not everyone disliked seeing the rain. A farmer from the area noted that they desperately needed the precipitation. "The Lord was sure with us today. He sent us rain so we can get our seed in."[4]

Lewis Grizzard, a humorist and columnist for the *Atlanta Constitution*, also wrote about the night. He described

Carter: "He looked awful . . . he looked tired, he looked drained." The crowd knew that Carter had been working diligently for release of the hostages over the last few days. Grizzard considered comments made by "Jimmy Earl" (as he called him) to be fitting for the occasion. Carter urged everyone to support Reagan. He talked about the hostages and how he would soon be in Germany to meet them. Grizzard added, "I got the distinct feeling that why that crowd showed up in that awful weather Tuesday was to soften a hometown boy's abrupt fall from the most powerful office in the world." He added that while Ronald and Nancy Reagan danced at inaugural balls in Washington, D.C., "the last thing [Carter] did before the public eye was stand tall on the platform in front of the cheering crowd and take his wife in his arms and dance with her. The tune was 'Dixie.'"[5]

IN 1981, THE CARTERS RETURNED TO THE ONLY HOME THEY HAVE EVER OWNED, the house they had built at 209 Woodlawn Avenue twenty years earlier. The modest ranch-style house served as home base for the Carter family throughout his time in the Georgia Senate and the offices of governor and president. Hugh Gaston, an Albany architect, designed this home and several others in Plains, including the Pond House the Carters built for Miss Lillian in 1968. Many meetings with political allies, including ones with vice presidential candidate Walter Mondale in 1975 and 1976, took place at the Carter home and the Pond House.

A major renovation of the home took place in 1974 when the Carters enclosed the screened-in back porch with windows, converted the garage into an office, and added a new garage. Another renovation happened in 1981 when Carter converted the new garage into a woodworking shop, which housed tools given him as a farewell gift from the White House by staff members. By then the Secret Service provided transportation for the Carters and they no longer needed to park their vehicles at home. Gaston oversaw these renovations.[6]

As Jimmy Carter said in *Faith*, "Back home, we resumed our role as active members of our local church, repaired our house and grounds, put a floor in the attic to store possessions . . . became reacquainted with our farms and woodlands, and settled our urgent business affairs."[7] Carter is one of the few presidents in recent history to move back into the home he lived in before he became president.

JIMMY CARTER HAS ALWAYS BEEN PHYSICALLY ACTIVE.
He and Rosalynn rode on a bicycle built for two in Plains during Christmas holidays in 1980. They knew that leaving the White House meant they had more time to relax and enjoy life, though they also had concerns. As he said in *Faith*, "We decided to return to our home in Plains, but we still had no idea what to do. Our farms and warehouse business had been in a blind trust, and we learned from our trustee that we had suffered heavy financial losses while we were away. . . . It seemed that we might have to sell all our farmland to pay what we owed."[8] Within three months, the Carters sold their peanut warehouse to a large agricultural corporation.

Though Rosalynn had not wanted to return to Plains in 1952 when her father-in-law died, she received significant support from the people of the area in 1981. She has stated, "I think it makes a lot of difference when you're off traveling around the world and you're off in politics like we have been . . . to know that you've got a home and I think it just gives you a stability to know that there are people there who care about you."[9]

Jimmy Carter worried about money and business when they returned to Plains, but he never wanted to be rich, and he did not want to "capitalize financially on being in the White House." Gerald Ford and other former presidents received large sums to speak to groups and serve on boards. Carter has said, "I don't see anything wrong with it; I don't blame other people for doing it. It just never had been my ambition to be rich." He decided to make income by writing books. He also receives the same annual pension all former presidents receive. (Carter received $210,700 in 2018, pay equal to the salary of federal executive department heads.)[10]

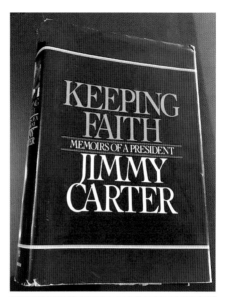

WHEN JIMMY AND ROSALYNN CARTER RETURNED TO PLAINS, they knew they both wanted and needed to write their memoirs. They both had stories to tell, and proceeds from the book contracts would help their finances. They began writing with word processors they got after they left Washington, D.C., putting the typing skills they had learned years earlier at Plains High to good use.[11] President Carter had learned shorthand and typing in high school and used them through college. Mrs. Carter had used her typing skills when Jimmy ran for governor to keep up with the names of people they met. Her book *First Lady from Plains* ended up outselling his volume.[12]

A few years later, the Carters coauthored a book and found the process less than pleasant. Jimmy described the process: "The joint project soon turned out to be a disaster, however, and came as near as any other experience to destroying the harmony of our marriage." They wrote about their life together, and he drafted about half the project and she wrote the rest. They soon realized that their memories of the events or reaction to events of about 3 percent of their lives differed dramatically. Also, he wrote fast and edited later, while she labored to get every sentence just so. "We soon found that we could communicate about our book only by writing ugly notes back and forth on our computer. . . . Understandably, we also agreed never to write another book together."[13] Thus, *Everything to Gain: Making the Most of the Rest of Your Life* became a one-time-only collaboration, though the Carters often comment on drafts and even edit each other's speeches, editorials, and books.

JIMMY CARTER HAS BEEN WORKING WITH WOOD since his youth. He learned the basics of making furniture on the farm and from Future Farmers of America starting in junior high school. He first built items to use on the farm. "I was making simple structures for chickens and hogs and storage bins, as well as furniture for around the house. And then my daddy was a fairly competent carpenter and blacksmith. . . . You didn't hire people to come in and do work for you; you did it yourself."[14] Successful farming, especially during the Depression years when Carter grew up, requires self-sufficiency. Later, in the navy, Carter had access to a well-stocked hobby room in Hawaii manned by warrant officers who were expert cabinetmakers. Through the years, Carter has also attended woodworking workshops and met with talented craftsmen around the world to discuss the hobby.

He has made extensive use of the tools given to him as a parting gift by former staff members. Carter recalls, "When I learned that they were planning to purchase a Jeep, I sent word that this was not something I wanted, with a hint that furniture making was what I would like to resume. My friends then gave the same funds to Sears, Roebuck and Co. . . . This has turned out to be one of the best gifts of my life."[15] He spends part of most of his days in Plains creating furniture. For several years, a typical day included time spent on his latest furniture project as a change of pace from writing speeches, books, or emails and correspondence. Over time, he has focused more of his spare time on painting, a favorite hobby after leaving the presidency.

In addition to the satisfaction that Carter receives when he completes a project, woodworking offers a way for him to relax. His woodworking shop is next to his house. "So when I get tired of indoors, I can just take twenty steps out here and I'm pounding on boards or using a saw." Rosalynn talked about the value of his workshop, especially during his first years back in Georgia. Carter would be in the house and would "work till he got frustrated with things he's writing about; he would come out here and beat on something."[16]

A FEW MONTHS AFTER THE PRESIDENCY ENDED, Jimmy and Rosalynn Carter bought twenty acres in a gated community on Turniptown Creek near Ellijay with John and Betty Pope. They built a small cabin plus another small structure nearby for the Secret Service. The north Georgia area offers ample opportunities for Carter to go fly-fishing, one of his favorite activities. Carter designed and built much of the furniture used in the cabin at his shop in Plains. He used some "ancient long-leaf pine, virgin timber board" from the house where Rosalynn was born. The house was being torn down and he got wide boards to use for furniture and paneling.[17]

THE CARTERS SPENT MUCH of their first year back in Georgia focused on getting resettled in Plains, writing, and making sure Amy found a school where she could flourish. They made a major public appearance on July 4, 1981, to celebrate the birth of America. Jimmy, Rosalynn, and Amy served as grand marshals for the WSB Salute to America Parade in Atlanta. Col. Charles Scott of Stone Mountain joined the Carters as celebrity guests. Scott had been one of the fifty-two Americans held hostage by Iranians. He served in the U.S. Army for thirty-one years and had been chief of the Defense Liaison Office in the American Embassy in Tehran.

Amy had been sad to leave Washington, D.C., in January. At the last minute, two of her friends decided to fly to Plains on board Air Force One with the family. The friends hated seeing the "first daughter" go back to Georgia.[18] Amy had been criticized while in Washington, D.C., for always reading. Jimmy Carter grew up in a family where they read around the dinner table each night. He has commented that Amy reads more than anyone he has ever known. Rosalynn notes that Jimmy became governor three years after the birth of Amy. "She got to where she didn't want to go with us because all she did was go listen to political speeches . . . so we started letting her take a book. . . . She learned to be just alone in her own little world no matter where she was."[19] Amy attended public school in Plains, just as she had in Washington, D.C., but opted to attend Woodward Academy, a private school in Atlanta, for her senior year before heading to college.

MANY PEOPLE CAME TO VISIT the Carters in Plains after the presidency ended. Anwar Sadat, president of Egypt, visited in 1981, as did his fellow Nobel Peace Prize winner, Prime Minister Menachem Begin of Israel. The two won the Nobel in 1978 following the Camp David Accords. Carter has said, "They came by as a matter of courtesy and we had a party in our house and invited a lot of Plains people. And as you can imagine, now, scattered all around this part of Sumter County, there are very proud owners of photographs with them and President Sadat or Prime Minister Begin."[20]

Sadat and his wife, Jihan, traveled to Plains from Washington, D.C., in August 1981. They had visited with President Ronald Reagan and former presidents Gerald Ford and Richard Nixon earlier that week. Following an enthusiastic welcome by the band majorettes from Westover High School in Albany, Carter and a crowd of approximately twenty-five hundred greeted the Egyptian leader. Carter noted that the "high hopes" brought about by the Camp David Accords no longer existed. Carter criticized Palestinian leaders for using violence and terrorism against Israel and wanted full autonomy for Palestinian refugees. Sadat referred to Carter as his "deep friend" and noted that the president had "risked everything" as he negotiated peace in the Middle East.[21] Begin visited Carter in Plains on September 15, 1981.

On October 6, Sadat lost his life when fundamentalist army officers assassinated their leader of eleven years. The Secret Service recommended that President Reagan and Vice President George H. W. Bush not attend the funeral due to safety concerns. Instead, former presidents Carter, Ford, and Nixon led a large U.S. contingent that included Rosalynn Carter and elected officials to Cairo, Egypt, for the service.

AFTER JIMMY CARTER LEFT OFFICE, he and
Rosalynn did several things to help future generations of
historians, archivists, and interested people. They wrote
their memoirs, planned for the Carter Presidential Archives
and Library, and gave oral history interviews. On November
29, 1982, he and a panel of nine scholars, assembled by the
Miller Center, gathered in Plains. The historians questioned
him and also interviewed other Carter staff members. A
nonpartisan affiliate of the University of Virginia, the Miller
Center has documented the presidency, public policy, and
political history since 1975. Professor James Young stands
on the left of Carter. A member of the Miller Center staff,
Young put the Jimmy Carter Presidential Oral History project together. Others in the group included college faculty
like Richard Neustadt of Harvard and Erwin Hargrove of
Vanderbilt. The center interviewed about fifty people
who had worked with the Carter presidency in twenty-
one sessions, with most of the interviews taking place in
Charlottesville. In the back row, second from left, is Steven
H. Hochman, the only Carter staff member present. Carter
has given many interviews through the years.

JIMMY AND ROSALYNN CARTER have attended some Georgia and Democratic Party events in the decades since he left public service. They attended the Georgia gubernatorial inauguration on January 11, 1983. Joe Frank Harris, in the center looking toward the Carters, became the chief elected officer of the state that day. Harris had represented Cartersville in the Georgia House of Representatives and entered the race for governor in 1982 as a long shot candidate in a crowded field. He had strong support from Speaker of the House Tom Murphy, standing behind the podium. Harris won the Democratic primary runoff by defeating Bo Ginn, a U.S. representative, and then solidly defeated Robert H. Bell of the Republican Party in the general election. Harris served as governor from 1983 until 1991.

THE FORMER PRESIDENT PROVIDED THE KEYNOTE ADDRESS of the Carl Vinson Memorial Lecture at Mercer University on April 28, 1983. Robert L. Steed, seated on the left, paid tribute to John Adams Sibley, who funded the lecture series. In the center is Lamar Rich Plunkett, chairman of the Board of Trustees at Mercer University. The lecture had to be moved to the Macon City Auditorium because of the large crowd who wanted to hear Carter speak. He gave a talk entitled "Negotiation: The Alternative to Hostility." Mercer University Press published the presentations plus tributes to Carter. He gave guidelines for establishing more stable peace in the world and for using negotiation in resolving disputes, whether they occur on the world stage or locally. According to him, the goal for negotiating on the local level is to "reduce the growing burden of unnecessary litigation that is overloading" the justice system.[22] Carter mentioned that he had discussed the issue with Chief Justice Warren Burger of the Supreme Court. Burger thought that despite the rising acceptance of mediation, courts in the United States had made little progress in settling disputes outside of courtrooms. Carter then focused on an area where he had found success during his presidency: negotiations between countries. He also outlined ground rules needed to initiate negotiations.[23]

FAMILY HEALTH ISSUES surely caused Jimmy Carter to ponder his own mortality in the decade after his presidency ended. Miss Lillian, the mother of the president, plus his brother and both sisters all died during those years. All of them had pancreatic cancer, except his mother, who also had breast and bone cancer. His sister, Ruth Carter Stapleton, died on September 26, 1983, while sister Gloria Carter Spann died on March 5, 1990. His father had died at the age of fifty-eight, also of pancreatic cancer. Also, in 1985 the Carters learned that Hamilton Jordan, his former chief of staff, had been diagnosed with cancer.[24] Jimmy and Billy chat at Georgia Tech on February 20, 1979, after Jimmy received an honorary doctor of engineering degree. Carter hugs his mother during the 1976 election.

The subject of many investigations after Jimmy Carter became president, Billy told Senate investigators that he realized he brought many problems on himself, but "I refused to conform to an image that a lot of people thought a President's brother should adopt, I considered myself to be a private individual who had not been elected to public office and resented the attention of different Government agencies that I began to hear from almost as soon as Jimmy was sworn in."[25] Billy was cleared of any wrongdoing in that Libyan case but did have to sell land in Plains in 1981 to cover taxes before the Internal Revenue Service foreclosed on his home and property.[26]

Miss Lillian played a major role in life in Plains, especially in the 1970s when Jimmy served as president. Her brother-in-law, Alton Carter, described her: "She's a real politician. That's where Jimmy's political instinct comes from. It wasn't from any of the Carters." Her father, Jim Jack Gordy, developed a reputation as a political leader in southwest Georgia whose support could greatly help a candidate.[27]

JIMMY CARTER VISITED WITH TOMMY IRVIN,
the commissioner of agriculture for Georgia from 1969
until 2011. Governor Lester Maddox appointed the north
Georgian to the job. Irvin holds the title as the longest-
serving statewide official in Georgia.[28] Jimmy Carter later
said, "Tommy Irvin was the most effective commissioner of
agriculture in Georgia in my lifetime. He was a friend, supporter, and adviser for many decades. His towering presence
filled a room with good humor and sound judgment."[29]

Agriculture has been an important part of life for Jimmy
Carter. He worked on the family farm in his youth and again
in the 1950s and 1960s, but in 1981, after having served as
president, he did not return to that work. Carter has not been
an active farmer since returning from Washington, but he has
had renters who plant and harvest the fields. He also manages
timberlands with the aid of a trained forester.

Jimmy Carter became a member of the Georgia
Agricultural Hall of Fame on November 9, 2018. He told the
group, "This has been the highlight of my life in agriculture,
my induction tonight." The Hall of Fame was established
in 1972 and is housed at the University of Georgia. The
College of Agricultural and Environmental Sciences Alumni
Association maintains the Hall of Fame. Tommy Irvin is one
of the former inductees. In inducting Carter, Van McCall,
president of the alumni association, noted, "When you think
of notable Georgia farmers, you can't help but think about
President Carter." McCall also noted that during the days
before Carter became governor, "He wasn't just a farmer;
he was a community and agribusiness leader in southwest
Georgia and really worked to develop agriculture in that
region."[30]

JIMMY CARTER, MAX CLELAND, and two other men got together in the mid-1980s. Jimmy Carter closed the first book he authored in the post-presidency by writing about Max Cleland. He noted that his fellow Georgian had been his first official visitor in the Oval Office on January 20, 1977. The administrator of Veterans Affairs also stopped by for a visit on January 20, 1981, and became the last official Carter presidential visitor. Cleland gave him a plaque with a Thomas Jefferson quote: "I have the consolation to reflect that during the period of my administration not a drop of blood of a single citizen was shed by the sword of war."[31] Cleland later served as Georgia secretary of state and as a U.S. senator.

Hamilton Jordan had invited the Vietnam War veteran to come to the White House at 5:00 p.m. on the day of the 1977 swearing in. Just getting through the streets of Washington, D.C., with the inaugural parade happening took a major effort. When he got to the White House in the limousine he had rented for the day, the guards did not know Max Cleland. Finally, he reached the Oval Office about twenty minutes late. Cleland was overwhelmed to be in that location on such a historic day. He told an interviewer, "Talk about the shadow of the presidency or the shadow of the Oval Office? Jimmy Carter was the ultimate good old boy. . . . I couldn't hardly say my name. . . . So I was his first official appointment. And on the way out, I said, 'Mr. President, this is only my second time in the Oval Office.' He said, 'It's only my second time, too!'"[32]

CHAPTER 5

The Carter Center and Emory University

AFTER BECOMING the former president, Jimmy Carter had one last official duty: he had to build and establish a presidential library. Carter soon decided to join the faculty of Emory as a "university distinguished professor." This would be the start of over four decades of lecturing, hosting town hall meetings, and being involved with the school. A late-night dream or vision soon after his return to the South led Carter to start a new action center next to his library where he could work with governments and people around the world to mediate and help societies avoid conflict. Much of the work and activity of the Carter post-presidency would revolve around the Carter Center, the Jimmy Carter Presidential Library and Museum, and nearby Emory University.

Ironically, the proposed site for the Carter Center, just east of downtown Atlanta, generated much controversy because of a road. The state of Georgia owned the suggested site and Georgia Department of Transportation officials wanted a new highway to be constructed from downtown Atlanta to the center. Carter supported those efforts but opponents feared that the route would eventually be expanded and disturb historic neighborhoods. Eventually, compromises helped assure the building of the library on that site. After hard work by Carter and others on design and fundraising, the goal of the Carter Center playing a role in promoting human rights and fighting disease became a reality.

THE CARTER CENTER was photographed in 2004, almost two decades after opening. Much thought and debate went into the establishment of the Carter Center and the Jimmy Carter Presidential Library and Museum. At age fifty-six, Jimmy Carter left the White House as the youngest former president since William Howard Taft exited the office in 1913. Also fifty-six, Taft went on to serve as chief justice of the U.S. Supreme Court. Carter, in good health and always energetic, expected to have at least a couple more decades of productive life. Late one night about a year after he left office, he suddenly woke up and startled Rosalynn. He'd had a thought or a vision about what they could do in addition to building a presidential library. "We can start an adjacent institution," he told her, "something like Camp David, where people can come who are involved in a war. I can offer to serve as a mediator, in Atlanta or perhaps in their countries. We might also study and teach how to resolve or prevent conflict."[1] Thus, a vision in the middle of the night helped define the focus of much of the future for Jimmy and Rosalynn Carter.

Questions about location and logistics still had to be settled. The president had offers for faculty positions and land for his library from several universities, including the University of Georgia, Georgia Tech, Morehouse College, and Vanderbilt. Others hoped the museum would be in a different city than the library. Several cities and towns across Georgia hoped to land the museum, including Plains and Americus.[2]

The *Atlanta Constitution* credited Atlanta architect John Portman with first suggesting that the state create a "Great Park" as a possible site for a Carter Presidential Library in 1979, though decisions would not be made until after the 1980 election at the earliest. According to legend, Union General William Tecumseh Sherman watched Atlanta burn during the Civil War from the site where the Carter Center would be built.[3] The site had been owned by the state for several years. Plans for a proposed Interstate 485 to go through the area had been rejected by a federal judge in 1975 following a bitter battle between neighborhoods and Tom Moreland, the powerful Georgia transportation commissioner. Portman had been appointed by Georgia governor George Busbee to develop a plan for the area. Interestingly, the name "Great Park" has not been associated with the Carter Center or the library and museum since the completion of construction.

JIMMY CARTER HAS HAD A LONG RELATION-
SHIP WITH EMORY UNIVERSITY. The president
received an honorary doctorate in August 1979. Emory president James Laney contacted him early in 1981 while the
Carters were pondering their future. As Laney said, "It was
hard to bring up the issue of the post-presidency when Carter
was running for office."[4] Following brief negotiations, Laney
officially named Carter as the university distinguished professor in 1982. Carter publicly announced in April 1982 that he
also planned to establish an institute. The former president
said many years later that becoming associated with Emory
gave him a "tremendous boost in spirits and commitment and
ambition."[5] With his assistant Dr. Steven Hochman, a historian from the University of Virginia, he soon had a temporary
office for the Carter Center on the top floor of the Woodruff
Library at Emory.

Laney knew that Emory "should make a play for him. At
that time there was only talk of a library. When he lost, I got
in touch with him and said we will appoint you to the faculty
and you can lecture anytime, anywhere you want to." As the
only president ever to come from Georgia, Laney wanted
Carter to stay in the state, plus the two men had similar
backgrounds, much as Carter and Mondale had had in 1976.
Laney said, "I'm a Southerner and we both are religious. . . .
I'm a minister and a so-called scholar. . . . We had a lot in
common. We got to be friends. We hit it off."[6] Carter recalls,
"People often ask why I came to Emory University. I invari-
ably answer, 'Jim Laney.' . . . In 1981, when Rosalynn and I
were trying to decide what we should do with the rest of our
lives . . . we chose Emory because Jim Laney convinced us
that he had a moral and ethical vision for the university that
we could share and help to advance."[7]

The Carter appointment brought national attention to
Emory. A 1987 issue of *Newsweek on Campus* focused on the
hiring of "superstar" faculty. Regarding the value of Jimmy
Carter to Emory, the article stated, "While his occasional
classes are popular, Carter's chief value to the university is
his ability to draw admissions and attention."[8] Another article
mentioned that before Carter, national references to Emory
always described the school as "Emory University in Atlanta."
After his arrival, the identifier became just "Emory."[9]

Despite these benefits of Carter coming to Emory, decisions at the time also generated controversy. The proposed road connecting the Carter Library and Carter Center with downtown Atlanta upset many Emory faculty and staff members plus the general public. The Great Park controversy erupted in 1981 with protests and picket signs. Jim Laney remembers, "That kind of roiled on campus. . . . It was a terrible spot for me to be in. There were signs all around Druid Hills [the surrounding neighborhood] to 'Stop the Road. Stop Jimmy Carter.'"[10] According to the *Atlanta Constitution*, "Carter has said repeatedly that if the library couldn't be built on the Great Park land with the provision of adequate access, he would be forced to have it built elsewhere."[11] Eventually all sides reached a compromise with smaller roads leading to Carter Center.

CARTER BECAME PART OF LIFE AT EMORY UNIVERSITY ALMOST IMMEDIATELY. He held a book signing at Woodruff Library for his presidential memoir, *Keeping Faith*. He signed copies of the book for faculty and staff and spoke briefly to the group. Special Collections shared the top floor of Woodruff Library with Carter during the early 1980s. Carter's former chief of staff, Hamilton Jordan, also had an office on the top floor of the library for about a year. He wrote his book, *Crisis: The Last Year of the Carter Presidency*, during the 1981–82 academic year and taught political science. Jordan had contacted Laney in the fall of 1980 and expressed his plans to leave Washington, D.C., regardless of the election outcome.[12]

An early and ongoing concern was how the Carter Center would function as part of Emory University. The Carters and others visited several universities and institutes to study things that worked well and look for possible conflicts that might limit activities. Warren Christopher, deputy secretary of state during the Carter Administration, served as chairman of the Stanford University trustees. He knew that relations between relatively liberal Stanford and the more conservative Hoover Institution had sometimes been rocky. Christopher and a group of advisers recommended a framework for an agreement reached between the Carter Center and Emory in 1994 which governs operations. The Carter Center has permanent independence from Emory, with half of its board of trustees being selected by and approved by Emory trustees. The other half of the center's trustees are selected by the Carter Center and approved by the university. The Carter Center raises its own funds and employs its own staff, though in compliance with the university's personnel policies. Through it all, Emory and the Carter Center have worked to make sure the connection between the two organizations remains strong. Dr. Laney says they worked to ensure that "the Carter Center would be part of Emory. Carter used to say in speeches, the Carter Center is just like the medical school. It is part of Emory."[13]

Emory committees have struggled with the question of how the center will continue its work, once Jimmy and Rosalynn Carter are no longer present. Carter penned a humorous poem about this, which contains the lines,

> Some shy professors, forced to write
> about a time that's bound to come
>
> . . . .
>
> not by saying
> I have passed on
> joined my Maker
> or gone to the promised land
> but stating the lamented fact
> in the best of terms
> that I, now dead, have
> reduced my level of participation.[14]

Here he is signing books for Dr. Linda Matthews, director of Special Collections, and Theodore Johnson, director of Emory Libraries.

IN HIS FIRST YEARS WITH EMORY, Carter reached out to every department. A report from February 2000 declared that "within Emory, President Carter is one of the few symbols of excellence that can be shared by the entire community. From the beginning, President Carter served the entire university, teaching in every school and college. During the first decade of his service, when he was devoting two full days to Emory activities, he also met frequently with faculty, staff, and extracurricular student groups."[15] Carter had town hall meetings where he answered a wide variety of questions from the audience. This started a new tradition at Emory where all the first-year students received tickets, with remaining spots being taken by upper-class students, faculty, and staff. Carter attended receptions where he met with students, faculty, and staff on campus. He had monthly meetings with the university president. For three and a half years, Carter had an office in Special Collections, on the top floor of Woodruff Library. Here, he greets members of the library staff during a welcome coffee. Located in what had once been part of the exhibit area of the library, the Carter office had a panoramic view of downtown Atlanta. Carter and other staff members moved into the Carter Center, located three and a half miles away, in fall 1986.

IN 1981, Carter knew he had to fund a presidential library and archives. Once he decided to add the center and link them to Emory University, he knew he had to raise funds for both entities.[16] He sought out support from large corporate donors and also looked to people who had assisted him in the past. The Peanut Brigade had been very important in the 1976 presidential election. Georgians spent hundreds of hours in key election states ringing door bells, shaking hands, and asking people to vote for their former governor. The brigade members came through one last time as they helped with fundraising for the Carter Center and Library, holding a reunion and a fundraiser in March 1986. The invitation stated that "the Peanut Brigaders spirit and uniqueness cannot be forgotten." Over four hundred people attended that night, including Max Cleland, a Georgia native and Vietnam veteran who served as administrator of Veterans Affairs during the Carter administration. Party attendees also got to see the partially finished structures. Many of those people who had campaigned for Carter in 1976 made donations to the Carter Center. Their donations helped create a Peanut Brigade gallery in the Carter Library, which recognized their contributions to the winning 1976 campaign.[17]

THE OPENING OF THE CARTER CENTER offered a time to recognize and thank donors with a black-tie event held before the official opening and to show the facilities to the press. Billy Carter joined his brother at the event. Fundraising had been a necessary but tough part of developing the Carter Center and building the Carter Presidential Library and Archives. Jim Laney reports that the incumbent who had lost his bid for reelection had a tough time raising funds just a few years later. Laney joined Carter on fundraising trips to New York, San Francisco, Tokyo, and elsewhere. Laney said, "It was hard. Also, getting donations from one person might mean no donations from someone else."[18] The center borrowed several million dollars in the early 1980s to complete the buildings and get the project started, but they repaid the debts and have maintained a balanced budget. They have also developed an endowment of over $500 million to ensure the future activities of the center.

In his post-presidency, Carter never wanted to serve on the boards of major companies for personal gain but he willingly called on companies and foundations in the United States and elsewhere in order to secure support for the Carter Center. Foundations that have contributed include the Ford Foundation, the Rockefeller Foundation, the William and Flora Hewlett Foundation, the MacArthur Foundation, the Robert W. Woodruff Foundation, and others. In recent years, the center has worked closely with the Bill and Melinda Gates Foundation to jointly fight diseases around the world. The Carter Center has also sent out mailings and seeks donations as small as five dollars. Over time, many of those donations grew to larger amounts. Carter devoted much time to the process. He wrote in 2007, "I spend a day each month calling these unknown partners personally, to thank as many

as possible and to invite them to visit our Center to learn more about us." He has also visited corporate headquarters and foundation boards.[19]

The center also works with other groups when their goals gel around a particular project. Lions Clubs International has focused its charitable efforts on eyesight for decades. The international organization has joined one of its former club presidents and district governors as they fight river blindness (onchocerciasis) and trachoma. The Conrad N. Hilton Foundation, which also has an interest in eyesight issues, has been another partner in that fight.

DEMOCRATIC POLITICAL CANDIDATES also turned out for the opening gala event. Many of these people had been friends with Carter for years. Atlanta city councilman John Lewis, a civil rights hero who worked with Martin Luther King Jr., and Wyche Fowler Jr. talk at the library opening. That November, Georgia voters elected Fowler to the U.S. Senate while Atlanta voters chose Lewis to represent them in the U.S. House of Representatives. A few weeks after the official opening, Jimmy Carter personally convened the first major meeting at the center, "Democracy in the Americas." Twelve current or former heads of state participated.

Human rights have been the focus of the Carter Center since its opening. As author Douglas Brinkley noted, "More than any other previous American political figure—save perhaps Eleanor Roosevelt—Jimmy Carter promoted, protected, and championed human rights at home and abroad."[20] Author Louise Slavicek wrote, "The Carter Center is a testament not only to Carter's profound commitment to live his Christian beliefs by helping others, but also to the former president's perseverance and resiliency."[21] Jim Laney shared a story of a chance meeting at Emory. In 1983 or 1984, he and Carter were walking across campus when Karl Deutsch, the Stanfield Professor of International Peace at Harvard University who later became associated with the Carter Center, came up to them. "He said, 'Mr. President, a thousand years from now, there will be very few names of American presidents that will be recalled, but yours will be one of them because you introduced human rights into the political lexicon.' Carter had tears in his eyes—a lovely moment and an endorsement of the first order. The validations began to come."[22]

PRESIDENT RONALD REAGAN spoke at the dedication of the Carter Center on October 1, 1986, a very warm and beautiful day in Atlanta. He and his wife Nancy joined Jimmy and Rosalynn Carter and over five thousand dignitaries, donors, and other guests. Speakers included Bishop William R. Cannon; Atlanta mayor Andrew Young; Roberto Goizueta, CEO of Coca-Cola; Governor Joe Frank Harris; President Reagan; Dr. James Laney; Greek Orthodox Archbishop Iakovos; Frank G. Burke, acting archivist of the United States; and keynote speaker Warren Christopher, who served as deputy secretary of state for Carter and later as secretary of state under President Clinton. President Carter also spoke.

Reagan addressed the group and thanked his predecessor for his contributions to the nation and recognized his intellect, passion, and commitment. The Carters raised funds for the center and grounds, consisting of two man-made lakes, a traditional Japanese garden, and four interconnected circular buildings on a hill overlooking downtown Atlanta.

The library and archives house more than twenty-seven million pages of materials about the Carter presidency. The Carter Center and Carter Museum opened immediately, while the library opened three months later. Scholars and the general public could go into the space which had been gifted to the National Archives and Records Administration and study the documents and photographs generated during the Carter administration. They could study the role that Carter and his administration had played in developing policies and promoting programs and how plans developed over time. Carter has written, "My instructions have always been to expedite the availability of the classified documents." Carter also noted that the Carter Center and library have worked together as they "shared responsibility for the exterior grounds and parking areas, as well as an agreement that no substantive changes can be made in the museum exhibits without my approval."[23]

Housed with the Carter Presidential Library and next door to the Carter Center, the Carter Museum contains an exact replica of the Oval Office plus gifts the Carters have received. A permanent exhibit spotlights significant events occurring during Jimmy Carter's life and political career. The library and museum also host a variety of authors, speakers, and events each year and host school groups.

Established in 1982, the Carter Center functioned as a public policy center. Per the *Carter Center News* of Summer 1987, "President Carter envisions the Carter Center of Emory University as a place where individuals of differing perspectives can come together to address carefully selected issues of public policy, especially issues with international implications. The Center . . . continues to pursue this mission through nonpartisan study and research by resident and visiting fellows, public forums, and special publications."[24] Over time, the scope of work would expand to include human rights, nuclear arms control, global health, and the environment.

The Carter Center developed seven guiding principles. They would not compete with effective work being done by others, such as agencies of the United States or the United Nations. They would be nonpartisan. The center would be an action agency and would seek to cooperate with others. They would not let the prospect of failure keep them from undertaking worthy projects. Carter personally agreed not to intrude on sensitive areas without obtaining "at least tacit permission" from the White House. They would at times use the generic name "Global 2000" instead of the name of the center. Finally, Carter and others would prepare detailed reports after foreign visits and would share them with family, staff, and key supporters of the center.[25]

ACTIVITIES AT THE CARTER CENTER REFLECT THE CONCERNS AND INTERESTS OF BOTH JIMMY AND ROSALYNN CARTER. Mrs. Carter, who has worked to improve the quality of life of people who are suffering from mental illness since the 1970 Georgia gubernatorial campaign, spoke at a mental health symposium on November 8, 2006. Gains made during the Carter presidency regarding the care of those with mental illnesses proved to be short lived. President Reagan quickly cut much of the funding for the Mental Health Systems Act. A 2002 study by the President's New Freedom Commission on Mental Health shared news that many of the issues surrounding the care of the mentally ill in 1978 continued to be problems into the twenty-first century.

Those involved with the Carter Center have worked through the years to fight the stigma of having mental illness. One goal has been to bring mental illness out into the open and make insurance and financial resources available to sufferers. Mrs. Carter has cowritten three books on the subject.[26] The center has hosted symposiums on mental illness with national and international speakers since 1985. Participants at each symposium develop action items to pursue in their community and with partners, including government agencies and nonprofits. The center works in Georgia to develop community-based solutions to mental health care in the state.

The center also has a Mental Health Program which established the Rosalynn Carter Fellowships for Mental Health Journalism and encourages participants to do in-depth studies and share their findings. Fellows have produced more than fifteen hundred articles, books, documentaries, and other works on topics related to mental health.[27] Their work focuses on Georgia and the South as well as global issues.

As Mrs. Carter notes in *Within Our Reach*, "I know that they are making important contributions in lifting some of the stigma."[28] Additionally, Emory University established a Rosalynn Carter Chair in Mental Health at its Rollins School of Public Health. This is the first such endowed chair at a school of public health. Periodic "Conversations at the Carter Center" focus on mental health topics. Those events include speakers like Kathy Cronkite (daughter of Walter) and actor Rod Steiger talking about their experiences with mental illness while recordings of the events continue to draw viewers to the discussions.

DESMOND TUTU CHATS WITH JIMMY CARTER at Emory University in May 1988. Tutu gave the commencement address that spring and received an honorary doctor of divinity degree. Tutu and Emory had a long, close relationship and Tutu worked closely with the Carter Center. In 1986, he was the speaker in Texas at the awards ceremony for the Carter-Menil Human Rights Prize, which promotes the protection of human rights throughout the world. He served as a council member of the center's International Negotiation Network. On February 17, 1998, Carter and Tutu conducted a forum in Cannon Chapel at the Candler School of Theology, "A Conversation about Peacemaking with President Jimmy Carter and Archbishop Desmond Tutu."

A native and lifelong resident of South Africa, Tutu is a cleric in the Anglican Church of Southern Africa. He is archbishop emeritus of Cape Town and has spent his life working in the anti-apartheid movement and seeking greater human rights for all. One day, Dr. James Laney took Tutu to speak at an Atlanta public high school. As Laney said, "All the school officials were very excited but students were bored. In about two minutes, Tutu had them in the palm of his hand. It was just a marvel. They were riveted."[29] Tutu and Carter have met a variety of times.

Tutu also spent several months at Emory in 1992. Tutu spoke at international conferences on Christianity and religious human rights in 1991 and 1994. In 1995, Tutu joined with President Carter, President Julius Nyerere of Tanzania, and President Amadou Touré of Mali to facilitate the summit meeting arranged by the Carter Center in Cairo, Egypt, on the Great Lakes crisis. He served on the faculty during the fall semester of 1998 and taught two courses. While he worked on a book during the 1999–2000 academic year, he also taught courses at the Candler School of Theology as the William R. Cannon Visiting Distinguished Professor of Theology. Dr. Kevin LaGree, Dean of the Candler School, declared, "Archbishop Tutu's very public commitment to human rights and his singular ministry to the people of South Africa has made a profound impact on Candler as he shares his unique insights in the classroom. We have been deeply moved by his witness and enriched by his presence with us in the Emory community."[30]

JOINING JIMMY CARTER IN MARCH 1989 for the New Hemispheric Agenda consultation at the Carter Center were former president Gerald Ford (right) and James A. Baker III, secretary of state for President George H. W. Bush and secretary of the treasury for President Reagan. They brought together leaders from various countries in the western hemisphere. The Council of Freely Elected Heads of Government organized the two-day consultation as part of an effort to support democracy in the region. The Carter Center works deliberately to take a nonpartisan approach when dealing with government leaders. Gerald Ford cochaired many conferences at the Carter Center until his death in 2006. The two presidents and one-time rivals formed an intensely personal friendship and enjoyed working together.

Through the years, Carter has collaborated with other former presidents and has also kept the sitting president informed of his international activities. Over a hundred reporters covered this consultation. Carter once flew to Washington, D.C., following a trip to Panama to give President George H. W. Bush a report on recent elections in that country. Peter Applebome of the *New York Times* mused about Carter, "He is in some ways the last person one might expect to be sitting at the right arm of a Republican President and reporting on world affairs."[31]

President Ford also participated in a consultation with the Freely Elected Heads of Government at the Carter Center in 1997. He and Carter held a Q&A session with the press. They discussed relations in Latin America, the Caribbean, and elsewhere in the Western Hemisphere. They promoted democracy and economic cooperation in the area. Vice President Al Gore, a Democrat, and Speaker of the House Newt Gingrich, a Republican, along with the presidents of Mexico and Bolivia joined more than 130 other attendees at the program. Conversations focused on a moratorium on arms purchases and the illegal drug trade.

JIMMY CARTER, LEFT, AND FORMER U.N. AMBASSADOR ANDREW YOUNG, center right, pause as they walk near the Carter Center. Young served as mayor of Atlanta from 1983 until 1990. Through the years, Young participated in numerous events at the Carter Center. He and Carter served as two of the keynote speakers for the dedication of the Cecil B. Day Chapel and the opening of the Ivan Allen III Pavilion on October 21, 1993. Young told the audience that "this place is about breaking down walls. This place is about making peace. This place is about human rights and justice. We dedicate it, but more than dedication, we commit it to the continuation of breaking down barriers between races, clans, creeds, rich and poor, and to the waging of peace."[32]

Ivan Allen III, son of Ivan Allen Jr., the mayor of Atlanta from 1962 to 1970, served on the Carter Center's Board of Advisors and chaired the Board of Councilors. He was the principal volunteer coordinator of Carter Center fundraising efforts before his unexpected death in 1992 and worked tirelessly for the center. Carter has said that "Ivan was unique . . . in his eagerness, without attracting credit or attention to himself, to do things that stimulate the idealism and the moral character and the humanitarian nature of Atlanta and also of Georgia."[33] Cecil B. Day established Days Inn of America. His widow, Deen Day Smith, was a founder of the Carter Center. Major early contributors to the Carter Center comprised the "founders" and their names are on the wall in the lobby of the Jimmy Carter Presidential Library and Museum.

In his remarks, Carter noted, "What has strengthened us is the blending of deep friendships with the hopes and ambition of the future of this center." The chapel allowed the center to accommodate worship services and larger conferences.

IN 1992, CARTER GOT MIKHAIL GORBACHEV TO COME TO ATLANTA to visit the Carter Center and speak at commencement at Emory. The Emory University timeline reports for 1992 that "Mikhail Gorbachev, former president of the former USSR and a Nobel Peace Prize winner, draws such intense interest as Emory's Commencement speaker that the Quadrangle must be fenced for the first time."[34] Emory officials conferred an honorary law degree on Gorbachev at graduation on May 11, 1992.

The Russian leader spent two weeks in the United States trying to raise money for the Gorbachev Foundation, a Moscow policy institute he was establishing. He gave the commencement address to over twenty-six hundred graduates at Emory and assured them that "from your ranks will emerge the formulators of policy in the 21st century. I feel that you will be leaders of a new type, thinking on a broad scale and without prejudices, leaders who are not thinking just about the next elections but about mankind's long-term goals and common interests."[35] He and Jimmy Carter spent time discussing nonprofit policy centers and what a former president could achieve by establishing a policy center and nongovernmental organization. He met with the heads of major corporations in Atlanta.

IN THE 1990s, the Carters, the Carter Center, and Emory University all spent considerable energies on the Atlanta Project (TAP). From 1991 to 1999, they raised funds and poured resources into examining how the lives of the poor and disadvantaged in the city of Atlanta might be improved. The roots of the project go back to discussions between Carter and James Laney at one of their monthly meetings. Carter mentioned problems in Africa. Laney then asked him if he had ever considered taking care of problems at home. They were soon looking at issues in Atlanta, including "health, education, economics, and residential housing." Laney mentioned focusing on a defined Atlanta neighborhood and involving all the schools at Emory. An excited Carter went on a planned overseas trip and then held a press conference when he returned. The project had grown tremendously in the intervening days.[36]

Mark O'Connell, president of the United Way of Metropolitan Atlanta, remembers the day he and other local leaders heard about the plan from Carter. After a presentation by the former president, the leaders started discussing what they liked and did not like about the plan. Carter listened but then told them, "I didn't get you here to get a sense of whether or not I should do it. I'm here to tell you I'm going to do it and to ask for your support."[37] The Atlanta Project quickly grew to encompass an area extending through most of the southern part of the city with over half a million people in three counties. They divided the area into twenty cluster communities. TAP studied the needs of the poor in Atlanta to determine how groups of volunteers from local communities, universities, and businesses might play a legitimate role in assisting the poor and underserved of the city. Carter sought donations from influential citizens and raised

over $32 million for the project.[38] He pledged the support and energy of the Carter Center toward tackling these problems. He got business and professional leaders to serve on TAP committees. Problems identified included lack of easily accessible grocery stores and banks, and health problems like few children being immunized against diseases. Carter had been governor and president of these people but did not fully appreciate the size of these issues until the TAP studies were undertaken.

Atlanta civic leader Dan Sweat assumed the role as TAP coordinator. Local community members became vocal and persistent in their demands about what they wanted to see happen. Jimmy Carter had to periodically mediate between neighborhood groups.[39] TAP used a variety of means to accomplish its goals, including holding a concert by Michael Jackson to encourage immunizations. Jackson agreed to give free tickets to each local family that provided health department certificates showing that all its children had been immunized.[40]

THE ATLANTA PROJECT received intense press coverage and both local and national delegations of civic leaders and nonprofit staff came to learn more about what was being done in Atlanta. They formed a new organization, the America Project, which had a full-time staff. Carter devoted much of his time working on this project and gave many speeches about fighting urban poverty.

During the TAP years, Atlanta hosted the 1996 Olympics. In keeping with its 1960s slogan, "The city too busy to hate," Atlanta has long been big on boosterism and loves to point out the shining lights of the town. Historian Douglas Brinkley noted that "its chronic shortcomings aside, at least TAP was forcing Atlantans to grapple with their economic

and racial divisions. . . . TAP forced residents to recognize that real urban problems could not be glossed over. . . . Carter also had gained respect for raising social concerns that are too often ignored."[41] At the end of the initial five years, they raised funds to extend the project three additional years. The service area was reduced and the cluster community idea ended, thus eliminating artificial boundaries established by the project.

Atlanta Journal-Constitution reporter Jill Vejnoska wrote in 2002, "The Atlanta Project was perhaps Carter's most ambitious domestic project and one of his few undertakings that turned out not to be a resounding success." TAP had successes, including streamlining the public assistance process and conducting a high-profile, door-to-door immunization campaign to reach 16,650 preschoolers. Offering his view for the article, Douglas Brinkley added, "If there's a downside to Jimmy Carter's approach, it's his belief that everything can be solved through volunteerism, dedication, and hard work. If only that were so."[42]

As Jimmy Carter says in *Beyond the White House*, "It is difficult to quantify the results of The Atlanta Project, but we accomplished our original goals. . . . There is little doubt that some of the high expectations that evolved among the poor families were not realized. . . . Of all the projects of The Carter Center, this has been one of the most difficult, challenging, exciting, and gratifying."[43] In 1999, the project ended with unused funds being transferred to Georgia State University for it to continue the project by involving students, faculty, and community residents.

FOR JIMMY CARTER, his birthday on October 1 sometimes means quiet family time but other times the day provides a date for public observances, such as the date of the dedication of the Carter Center and Carter Library in 1986. In 2009, after the museum had been closed for several months for renovations, the site reopened with a preview of recent renovations and an eighty-fifth birthday celebration for the former president. The exhibit area had been stripped down to concrete floors and rebuilt. The $10 million five-month project included a large section devoted to the various activities of his post-presidency.[44] The museum has always spotlighted the Oval Office but the updated display includes "A Day in the Life of the President," which focuses on December 11, 1978. The exhibit makes use of video screens, declassified documents, and Carter's personal calendar. The Carters and library staff raised funds for the renovations. The exhibit takes visitors from Carter's birth in south Georgia, to his time in the navy, to his political life, and ends with a large section about the Carter Center and his work in fighting disease and promoting human rights.

IN 1999, Rosalynn Carter visited Miami's Abriendo Puertas (Opening Doors), a human services agency initially founded in 1992 by the Annie E. Casey Foundation under its Mental Health Initiative for Urban Children. Abriendo Puertas is a community-based agency in the Little Havana neighborhood. The Casey Foundation's Mental Health Initiative lasted until 1999, and Abriendo Puertas now offers a variety of programs to community members. Through the years, the various divisions of the Carter Center have partnered with Emory University and a number of agencies.

Benjamin Druss, Rosalynn Carter Chair of Mental Health at Emory, has noted that the Carter Center plays a role in research, training, and real-world service by working with Emory faculty and students. "I am not aware of any university in the country that has within it an organization specifically and actively dedicated to improving lives globally, nationally, and locally."[45]

JIMMY CARTER PARTICIPATED IN AN ONLINE VIDEO DISCUSSION of global health at the Carter Center on September 10, 2013, hosted by Google+. *New York Times* op-ed columnist Nicholas Kristof in New York and Dr. Donald Hopkins, the world's leading authority on public health and head of the health programs at the Carter Center, also participated in the discussion. Carter views global health as an important part of human rights campaigns. The three men discussed efforts to eradicate diseases around the world, including a major effort by Carter and the Carter Center to eradicate Guinea-worm disease. They also discussed the importance of fundraising and having journalists write stories about the issues to raise awareness.

While working for the Centers for Disease Control, Hopkins had engaged in the smallpox eradication campaign, the first successful effort to completely do away with a human disease. Hopkins led efforts at the Carter Center to support efforts to eliminate Guinea-worm disease, which, if successful, would make it the second human disease to be eradicated. (He remains engaged in this effort, although he has relinquished the day-to-day administration of the program.) The global health community currently targets only Guinea-worm and polio as diseases that can be eradicated completely from the earth. The Carter Center also seeks to eliminate river blindness, trachoma, schistosomiasis, lymphatic filariasis, and malaria from particular geographical areas. Carter points out that while much work remains to be done in freeing the globe of these and other diseases, great progress has been made in a relatively short amount of time.

THE AMERICAN BAR ASSOCIATION held a National Symposium on the Modern Death Penalty in America on November 12, 2013, at the Carter Center. James Silkenat, president of the American Bar Association, left, Steve Bright, president of the Southern Center for Human Rights, and symposium emcee Virginia Sloan, chair of the Steering Committee of the ABA's Death Penalty Due Process Review Project, joined President Carter for the discussion. Capital punishment is a state matter in the United States. In 2013, Carter called for the United States to abolish the death penalty, noting evidence of an "extreme bias" in the way that the punishment affects the poor, minorities, and those with diminished mental capacities more than others. He added, "The United States is the only country in NATO or North America that still executes its citizens."[46] In his book *A Call to Action*, he pondered whether the death penalty violates the provision of the U.S. Constitution which prohibits cruel and unusual punishment. He concluded that section of the book by noting that "90% of all executions are carried out in China, India, Saudi Arabia, and the United States."[47]

Carter noted that his thinking on the subject has evolved since he served as governor. He signed legislation in 1973 that revised Georgia's capital punishment laws to be in compliance with U.S. Supreme Court rulings against cruel and unusual punishment. The previous year, the Court had ruled in *Furman v. Georgia* that capital punishment was inconsistently and arbitrarily applied, and often against minorities. Georgia officially resumed capital punishment in 1973 but the next execution did not occur until 1983.[48] Carter believes that life imprisonment and other sentences imposed by judges serve society better than capital punishment.

THE PRESIDENT TALKS WITH CARTER CENTER INTERNS in fall 2002, during an excursion to the Jimmy Carter Boyhood Farm, part of the Jimmy Carter National Historic Site. Groups of interns have made visits to Plains for many years. The Carter Center internship program began in 1984 and has involved several thousand students.

Internships and graduate assistantships focus on peace, health, and operations programs at the center. Interns come from Emory University and other schools around the world. Undergraduate, graduate, and professional students can apply for internships, though one has to be at least a college junior to apply. The Carter Center also has graduate assistantships. Thirty percent or less of internship time revolves around paperwork.

Heejun Yoo said, "In the Democracy Program, I really feel like I am involved in changing society, and that's why I appreciate this experience." Jacqueline Mullin urged new interns to "just throw yourself in and immerse yourself and learn all that you can and realize this can be a stepping stone for anything you want in your life."[49] Internships and graduate assistantships help the Carter Center extend its mission and reach around the world.

JIMMY CARTER SPOKE IN SEPTEMBER, 2016, at the thirty-seventh annual Carter Town Hall at Emory. Holding town hall meetings for freshmen attending Emory University and Oxford College has been a major way that Jimmy Carter has reached out to the Emory community. He has held town hall sessions since 1982. At the first one, he agreed to answer all questions with no holding back. He continues to do that. As expected, students ask about a wide variety of topics, including the Affordable Care Act, campaign finance reform, and lighter matters such as whether he prefers crunchy or smooth peanut butter (he likes crunchy). On September 13, 2012, he told the more than two thousand students who gathered that "my immersion in all of the facets of Emory life has been the best thing about it and the best thing of all has been getting to know the student leaders every year for this occasion . . . and also to have questions from you, not only in the town hall meeting . . . but in your classes during the year."[50]

In June 2019, Emory University announced that Jimmy Carter, at age ninety-four, had been granted tenure. In announcing this new status, Emory noted that Carter would be the first tenured faculty member at Emory to hold a Nobel Peace Prize and the first to have been a U.S. president. Emory president Claire E. Sterk stated that "across nearly four decades, he has given Emory the full measure of what it means to be a public intellectual and an engaged faculty member. He has viewed teaching as a revered calling—the same humble approach he has brought to every undertaking, large and small, across a lifetime."[51]

Dr. James Laney reports that in the 1980s he and Carter kidded about the fact that the president did not have tenure. Laney says he jokingly told Carter that "he had to write enough books." The two saw each other at the Carter Center in July 2019 and discussed the new honor. According to Laney, Carter said, "I wrote thirty-two books and I think that satisfies everybody." Laney added, "Tenure wasn't discussed on campus. He never raised it. . . . Early on, I don't think the faculty would have been happy with it. . . . It wasn't really necessary."[52]

Sterk initiated the process after hearing President Carter joke about not having tenure at a town hall meeting. An Emory faculty committee considered tenure for him, just as they do with all candidates. Steven Hochman of the Carter Center put together a lengthy report documenting the academic career of the former president. The faculty committee voted to confer tenure. Granting tenure in 2019 was another way for Emory to honor Jimmy Carter and the school happily shared the story with the national press. President Carter considered this a thoughtful gesture.[53]

CHAPTER 6

Habitat for Humanity

JIMMY AND ROSALYNN CARTER BECAME AWARE OF THE MISSION OF HABITAT FOR HUMANITY International soon after its founding in 1976, and got to know its founding leaders six years later. Carter first participated with Habitat by welcoming board members to Sumter County during their October 1982 meeting. The Carters soon donated money to the group and helped with builds in Americus and New York City in 1984. Since then, the Carters have spent one week a year at sites in the United States or elsewhere in the world constructing homes for people needing a place to live. The Carters don't lead projects, but work with hammers and other tools alongside other volunteers and the future homeowners. They have attracted thousands of volunteers to Habitat and many donations. At the same time, the respect that people have for Jimmy and Rosalynn Carter has grown tremendously due to their involvement.

MILLARD AND LINDA FULLER founded Habitat for Humanity in 1976 in Americus, Georgia. Jimmy and Rosalynn Carter became involved in Habitat for Humanity a year after he left the White House. They have tackled many different tasks when working on Habitat houses. Jimmy watches Rosalynn attach house numbers in Charlotte in 1987. The Carters led 235 volunteers as they built fourteen homes.

The Carters plaster the prefabricated steel mesh and Styrofoam walls with a concrete mixture in Tijuana, Mexico, in 1990. Over a thousand volunteers gathered in Mexico and nearby San Diego, California, to construct new homes. The Carters stayed in tents in Tijuana, just like the other volunteers.

The Carters learned about Habitat for Humanity International during his presidency. The president saw and was impressed by Habitat homes built in southwest Georgia. The Fullers, who formed Habitat while working with Clarence Jordan of Koinonia Farm, had a goal of ending poverty housing and providing affordable, quality homes around the world. The Carters had lived in public housing when they returned to Plains in 1953 and sympathized with people worried about having a place to live.

Initially, "we were willing to consider putting in a few hours to help with a project."[1] They met with Millard and Linda Fuller in 1982 and soon decided to get more involved. Jimmy and Rosalynn Carter have picked up hammers and other building tools around the South and the world. They have attracted many volunteers, much attention, and significant donations to Habitat projects. They have also supported the organization by serving on the board and helping raise funds through their own contacts. The Carters have become the most famous spokespersons in the world for Habitat.

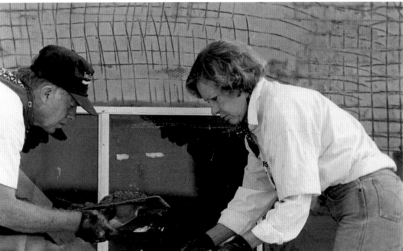

IN JANUARY 1985, Carter showed Millard Fuller the land and cabin that the Carters and Popes own in Ellijay, in the mountains of north Georgia. More than two years earlier, leaders of Habitat for Humanity had invited Carter to greet board members at their October meeting in Americus. David Rowe, president of the board of Habitat, sent Carter a letter even though he knew the former president had a busy schedule. Rowe soon received a call saying that Carter would speak to the group on October 16, 1982, at First Presbyterian Church in Americus. Carter addressed the group for about ten minutes and mentioned Koinonia Farm and "the profound impact of

Clarence Jordan on this country. . . . And to have known this quiet man . . . with human fallibility, yes, but with the inspiration of Christ. I think I will be a better Christian because of Clarence Jordan, Koinonia, and Habitat. And I hope to grow the rest of my life, along with you."[2] Carter then departed so he could prepare his Sunday school lesson for the next day.

Millard Fuller, the son of a textile mill worker in Valley, Alabama, and his wife, Linda, went to live on Koinonia Farm in the late 1960s. A self-made millionaire by his late twenties, Fuller gave up his businesses when his wife threatened divorce. She felt his attention to work and making money took him away from their marriage and children. He sold his share of his business to his partner and the Fullers gave away a million dollars to worthy causes.[3] Clarence Jordan and the Fullers had a goal of building basic structures at little or no cost to the homeowners. Following three years of building homes in Zaire, the Fullers formed Habitat for Humanity International. Today, Habitat has chapters across the country and partners with other organizations and groups.

In January 1984, Fuller visited the Carter home. Jimmy and Rosalynn indicated their interest in being more involved in Habitat for Humanity. Carter asked Fuller to offer suggestions on how they might best help Habitat. Fuller took about two weeks to consult with board members and pray about the issue. He soon wrote the Carters a letter that presented fifteen different ways they might support the nonprofit. Fuller acknowledged that they might only be able to participate in a few of the ways that he had listed. Within a few days, they met again and the Carters indicated their interest in most of the suggested tasks, including Carter working on a one-day build in Americus. The former president arrived early for that project, took part in morning devotionals, and labored all day framing a house.

JIMMY CARTER WORKS ON A HABITAT PROJECT in 2014 in Dallas and Fort Worth. Carter learned self-sufficiency growing up on the farm. He knew how to handle a hammer and nails and had been building structures since boyhood. After his first one-day build, Carter assisted with a project in New York City. He showed up at the build when he happened to be in the city for other business, then decided to return to work on the New York project and brought along a group of volunteers from Georgia. The group received enormous media attention and the project became the model for the Carter Work Weeks that followed. Although working with Habitat seems like a natural progression for the former peanut farmer, many were surprised when he actually showed up at building sites to work. Few people, including leaders at Habitat, expected him to be as active with Habitat as he ended up being.

The Carters donated funds to Habitat in late 1982 and both Carters spoke at the dedication of expanded Habitat office space in Americus that December. Carter joined the board of Habitat and recruited Atlanta mayor Andrew Young for a Habitat filming project which took place in April 1984. Just a few months after getting involved with Habitat, the Carters had helped with build projects and had started generating publicity and recruiting volunteers.[4] Their support of Habitat has continued ever since.

JIMMY AND ROSALYNN CARTER HELP FRAME A HABITAT HOUSE in Memphis in 2015. They began hosting annual weeklong builds where many volunteers gathered at one, two, or even three cities and built several houses in a week. They generally work on U.S. projects one year and then foreign projects the next. Habitat projects appealed to several different aspects of Carter's personality. Being able to see a project from its early stages to completion proved to be satisfying for him as former farmer and engineer. As an elected official, he had helped develop policies and programs that could take months or years to see results, so seeing housing become available to needy people in a short amount of time was gratifying.

Habitat allows Carter to put his religious beliefs into action. His Christian beliefs show up in all his activities. He teaches Sunday school in Plains, where he shares his beliefs with others. He has been involved with various religion classes at Emory, and the chapel is an important part of the Carter Center. At Habitat builds, he found another way to put his Christian beliefs into action. The routine includes morning devotionals and presenting Bibles to homeowners at the end of the project. Jimmy and Rosalynn also viewed the build weeks as vacations, since they took breaks from their routines. Unlike many other aspects of his life, Jimmy has not been in charge of construction builds. He considered himself to be a worker. He does much to help Habitat get publicity, donations, and volunteers, but during build weeks he follows instructions.[5]

THE WEEKLONG CARTER PROJECTS sometimes take place during the summer, a traditional vacation time for many people. This has meant that Jimmy and Rosalynn have celebrated occasional wedding anniversaries during Habitat for Humanity building projects. They spent their fortieth anniversary, July 7, 1986, in Chicago on a build project.

Cofounder Linda Fuller reflected on the importance of their support. "They did a *lot* to help us grow, and it hit the news big-time around the world that a former president of the United States was putting on overalls and swinging a hammer so that a very low-income person was able to have a decent house."[6] Carter and Habitat made at least one concession to his status as a former president of the United States. During a build in the Liberty City section of Miami in 1991, a drive-by shooter missed Carter and instead hit a coworker in his hard hat, causing a flesh wound. Carter said, "The Secret Service asked us not to work on roofs after that. They said we were too exposed."[7]

VOLUNTEERS JOINED THE CARTERS during a meal in Charlotte in 1987. An important part of any Habitat for Humanity project, including Carter Work Projects, are meals, which provide a time to get to know the homeowners and other volunteers. Food is generally provided by partner groups and people eat wherever they can find a seat, including sitting on hay bales. Lunches generally take place at the work site while breakfast for national and international volunteers occurs at the central meeting place, which is often a church or a school cafeteria. Getting to have lunch or dinner with the former president and his wife provides added excitement for others participating in a project. The Carters eat the same food as everyone else.[8]

JIMMY CARTER AND COMEDIAN AND ACTOR BOB HOPE take a break during the 1987 Carter Work Project in Charlotte. Hope entertained audiences for eight decades, including making thousands of active-duty military troops relax and laugh when he performed with the USO (United Service Organizations).

Carter Work Projects have been especially effective in attracting volunteers from all walks of life, including politicians and celebrities. Many, but not all, of them have picked up hammers or screwdrivers and worked at the sites. Talk-show host Oprah Winfrey helped when a build occurred in her hometown of Chicago. Despite wearing a dress, Oprah had a hammer in hand and a tool belt around her waist as fellow workers framed one of the homes.

THE CARTER WORK PROJECTS involve much more than just putting in long hours building houses for worthy recipients. Taking in a local baseball game, as the Carters did in 1986 in Chicago, was one such activity. Though children are not allowed at the work sites, the projects also provide time for entire families to get together, share the experience, and relax after long days of manual labor. Often, adult children will work with their parents at build sites, as Amy and Rosalynn did at the Chicago build.

Local chapters of Habitat for Humanity choose the homeowners. The owners are in need of safer, more secure housing. Their Habitat home may be the first home they have ever owned. Local partners help share instruction about finances, mortgages, and home maintenance. Getting a home is just one step in a process of having a more secure future for the owner and their family.

ROSALYNN CARTER HUGS ABDUL BABAKARKHIL just before the dedication of his new home at the thirty-third Jimmy and Rosalynn Carter Work Project. This Habitat for Humanity build occurred in the greater Memphis area in August 2016. Volunteers who worked on the Babakarkhil home signed his T-shirt. During the week, volunteers built new homes, rehabilitated others, beautified yards and neighborhoods, and modified homes for senior citizens.

Having a traditional southern upbringing, Rosalynn Carter rarely used hammers and nails for anything more difficult than hanging pictures on walls when decorating a house until she got involved with Habitat. For both Carters, participation in the organization has enriched their lives. As he said in *The Craftsmanship of Jimmy Carter*, "This would be a turning point for us, offering unprecedented opportunities to become involved in helping to change the lives of people who had never had the opportunity to live in a decent house."[9]

At one of their early builds, Rosalynn decided to help at the construction site rather than assisting other ladies in preparing meals or fetching water. She intended to help carry materials and clean up, but soon Jimmy showed her how to use a hammer to nail down flooring. All-women Habitat builds started in 1991, though Carter Work Projects have men and women working together on a house. The all-women build projects allow women to step up and help their community and its residents. This is especially meaningful since women and children make up the largest populations of people needing better housing and living in Habitat communities.

HABITAT FOR HUMANITY has work projects going on year round that have yielded more than just houses for needy families. Local conditions sometimes require Habitat to use different building techniques than usual. The Carter Work Project labored in Tijuana and nearby San Diego in 1990. In Mexico, they used an innovative technique of prefabricating panels consisting of Styrofoam sandwiched between sheets of steel mesh. The lightweight sections could easily be carried around construction sites. Workers would attach them with wire ties and then plaster over the section. In south Florida, they built fourteen homes and a daycare in 1991 using similar techniques. Hurricane Andrew hit Miami in August 1992, the costliest American hurricane at that time. Though in Senegal when the hurricane hit, the Carters were relieved to learn that Habitat homes withstood the storm better than many other more expensive homes, thanks to the work of Habitat volunteers.[10]

Carter Work Projects have been held for thirty-five years at sites around the United States and the world. In November 2015, the work project in the Chitwan District of Nepal had to be cancelled because of political unrest in the area. Concern for the safety of those involved in the build plus difficulties in getting most supplies, including fuel, food, and medical goods, to the building site caused Habitat International to cancel the project.[11]

The Carters participated in a one-day build in Memphis that November. That fall, Jimmy Carter also battled melanoma that had spread to his brain and liver.

AT TIMES, POLITICS COMBINES WITH VOLUNTEERING for Habitat for Humanity. On August 19, 1992, Bill Clinton and Al Gore, their wives Hillary and Tipper, and their families joined Carter, Millard Fuller, and others for a build in the Edgewood area of East Atlanta. Volunteers included the homeowner, Michelle Miller, a data processor, and forty employees of Home Depot. The previous month, Clinton, the former governor of Arkansas, and Gore, U.S. Senator from Tennessee, had received the Democratic Party nomination for president and vice president. Clinton and Gore spent most of the five hours at the site working hard, but they did take a few minutes to talk politics with the press as they criticized then president George H. W. Bush, who had mentioned that he might replace some cabinet members if elected to serve a second term. They also enjoyed a cake celebrating the birthdays of Clinton and Tipper Gore that day. Carter complained about the lack of federal spending on housing, declaring, "Since I left the White House, there's been a 92 percent reduction in federal funds to build homes."[12]

Volunteers naturally bring different levels of expertise with them to building sites. Carter commented on the abilities of Clinton and Gore by saying, "They're excellent learners, and they're trying to keep up with their children on the quality of their work."[13] Eleven years later Carter took time out during a build in Anniston to speak to the senior editor of the television show *This Old House*. The editor referenced an interview Carter had done on the *Tonight Show with Jay Leno*. They discussed the fact that Carter could drive a nail in three hits in comparison with film footage from that day in 1992 showing Gore driving a nail. "I think they counted 33 hits. I never saw somebody have such difficulty driving a nail in." Carter then instructed the evening television audience in how to drive a nail.[14] Clinton grew up spending much of each summer on the farm owned by his grandparents and could handle tools with greater ease. During the *This Old House* interview, Carter talked about how Habitat uses different construction techniques at different locations, including using all concrete blocks in the Philippines, steel stud walls and steel screws in New York City, and two-by-four wood in Alabama.

IN 1997, THE CARTERS AND OTHER VOLUNTEERS WORKED IN THE APPALACHIAN MOUNTAINS of eastern Kentucky and Tennessee. The "Hammering in the Hills" event included working on sixty-three homes, and participants had to get up some steep hills to reach some construction sites. Volunteers look forward to these events and often stress the fact that the most important part of the week is the human connections being made, including sharing special moments and laughter. Some volunteers travel together for several years in a row and become good friends in the process, all while making a difference in the world. Jimmy Carter shares this sentiment: "I've worked hard all my life and carpentry is nothing new to me. I'm enjoying it. It's great to meet new friends and do something to help others at the same time."[15]

Volunteers come from all over the United States and the world and include people from all walks of life, including business owners, corporation presidents, teachers, students, and cafeteria and factory workers. Supporters include Democrats, Republicans, and many other political affiliations. Political foes sometimes find common ground when meeting at Habitat work sites. Newt Gingrich, a Georgia Republican and former speaker of the U.S. House of Representatives, often wears a Habitat for Humanity pin on his suit jackets. Participants have noted that the builds often end up being life-altering events for both the family getting a home and the volunteers.[16]

ONE OF THE MOST MOVING MOMENTS of Carter Work Projects comes when homeowners receive Bibles for their new homes. Jimmy Carter and Millard Fuller present a Bible to a homeowner while Rosalynn leans over next to Jimmy. The focus throughout the build stays on the people getting the homes. Manuals developed for build projects contain the names of homeowners and biographical sketches of their families. Homeowners put in several hundred hours of sweat equity working on their home, other Habitat homes, or in Habitat offices, depending on their physical abilities. They also have to pay an affordable low-interest or no-interest mortgage. Carter generally presents Bibles to all homeowners on Carter Work Projects.

JIMMY CARTER PRESENTED THE KEYS to their house to homeowners in Plains, Georgia, in 2000. Rosalynn Carter watched from the porch. The owners also have a plank signed by the various people who worked on the home, including the Carters. Carter admitted in 2018 that working on Habitat houses sometimes brings discomfort, including the weather being too hot, too cold, or too rainy. Nonetheless, he said, "every time we've ever been out as volunteers, whether in this country or around the world, at the end of the Habitat project, we always feel that (Rosalynn) and I got more out of it than we put into it."[17] This was the 100,001st house built by Habitat. The house sat in a cotton field where Carter worked as a boy. The Carter Work Project also labored in 2000 in New York City, where they constructed the 100,000th house, and Jacksonville, Florida.[18]

AT THE START OF A BUSY WEEK in Alabama and Georgia in June 2003, the Carters walked to opening ceremonies of the Carter Work Project in Anniston accompanied by Secret Service agents. The project took place in Alabama and in the Georgia cities of LaGrange and Valdosta. All three places are located within two hundred miles of Plains. In Anniston, the Carters and many of the volunteers stayed in dorms at Jacksonville State University. Volunteers came from across the country plus Canada and other foreign countries. Dr. Kenneth Kaunda, the founding president of Zambia, volunteered later that week on homes in Valdosta with a plan to bring Habitat to his country later that year. Kaunda stressed the importance of working toward one unified world. Habitat for Humanity in Valdosta donated a portion of the funds raised during the Jimmy Carter project to building homes in Zambia.[19] As part of the closing ceremonies in the south Georgia city, Carter and Fuller passed along a symbolic hammer to volunteers from Mexico, site of the 2004 Jimmy Carter Work Project.

MILLARD AND LINDA FULLER, standing to the left of Jimmy Carter, gathered with homeowners and volunteers in LaGrange during the 2003 Jimmy Carter Work Project. The Carters generally make photographs with each of the new homeowners plus the people who worked on that house. During this June build week, devotions occurred each morning at 6:45 and people started working by 7:30 a.m. At each build, Carter holds a press conference at the start of the week as a way to let the general public know about the activities at the site and to share the excitement and importance of the event with the local community. Heavy, monsoon-like rains hit the area early in the project, although summer heat soon arrived to help dry things out. Volunteers had to spread hay at the LaGrange site after more than three inches of rain fell, but everyone continued to work. The wet red clay proved to be beneficial when a volunteer from Tennessee fell as he helped install a prebuilt rafter on one of the structures. The man walked away with bruises despite having the rafter fall on top of him. Had he fallen on hard ground, he might have been badly hurt.

Once the press conference ends, the Carters and their Secret Service team expect the news teams to let them work. Much more work can be done without the distraction of having cameras everywhere, and Habitat leaders want to make sure that volunteer workers, some with little training or prior experience, stay safe at the build sites. Lectures and demonstrations about how to safely build houses take place before every build begins. Carter has said that Habitat for Humanity is "the most practical, tangible way I've ever seen to put Christian principles into action."[20]

HABITAT BUILDS TAKE PLACE WHATEVER THE WEATHER. Heavy rains added chaos in 2003 at the LaGrange build. The building sites are often quite complex, as is evident from the photo made in Valdosta that same year. Over eight hundred volunteers worked on twenty-seven homes there. Entire communities are often constructed during a weeklong build, with much planning and work preceding the build week to make construction possible. The Carter Work Projects have taken place in southern towns and cities one-fourth of the time. Some years, the build happens in one geographic location, while other times the build occurs in two or three cities, states, or even countries. In 2003, the Carters traveled and worked for at least a day in each of three cities, though most volunteers stayed in one location. Volunteers built structures at the Magnolias Campus of Twin Cedars Youth and Family Services, which provides residential and community-based services in LaGrange, Macon, and Columbus, Georgia, and east Alabama. The largest structure is now the Annette Boyd Group Home. Several hundred teenaged girls have stayed in the home through the years. Other volunteers worked on individual homes in the Hillside area, a community which had its roots as housing for textile workers in the Callaway Mills in the early twentieth century. Though no one complained about the rain and mud, project directors and Habitat officials must always balance safety for those involved with the goal of getting houses completed.

DURING THE 2003 BUILD, the Carters traveled mid-week about seventy-five miles southeast to LaGrange, Georgia, to continue the work. During their stay in LaGrange, the Carters and Fullers worked at two different build sites in town and stayed at the home of the president of LaGrange College. Stuart and Kathleen Gulley had initially planned to vacate their home to give the president and Habitat leaders more privacy. Gulley shared this plan with Carter's assistant, who promptly replied, "Let me just tell you, I know that the Carters do not want to feel like they are inconveniencing you and if y'all move out, they won't stay there." The Gulleys quickly agreed to stay in their home as long as their two young and energetic sons could stay elsewhere with their grandmother.[21]

During the project, Stuart Gulley worked at a different location than the Carters. Gulley departed the worksite a little early so he could get cleaned up before meeting the former president. About the time he arrived home, he learned that the Carters had left their work site early as well. The college president had done manual labor all day in the summer heat and humidity and felt as grungy and sweaty as he had ever felt in his life. The Carters arrived and he greeted them, "President and Mrs. Carter, we are so honored to have you here. I have always dreamed of meeting a U.S. President, but never in my dreams did I imagine I would look like this!" President Carter promptly responded, "Never did I imagine I would look like this entering a college president's home."[22]

Before dinner, the Gulleys asked the Carters if they would mind meeting their sons. The Carters assured them that they had hoped to get to meet the boys. They all visited and documented the occasion with a photograph. The adults then walked with a Secret Service escort to a reception for Habitat donors and college supporters at the nearby Sunny Gables Alumni House. Later, the Gulleys realized the Carters and Fullers had left the event. They returned to their home to find them watching JAG, a popular television show with a navy theme. The president had the television remote in hand and the group talked only during commercials.

The next morning, as the Gulleys prepared breakfast, Jimmy Carter came in. Kathleen remembers, "It was such a casual morning visit in the kitchen, with a cup of coffee in hand and fixing eggs, easygoing, very relaxed."[23] Stuart reflected, "The Carters were as down-to-earth, comfortable, and lacking in pretension as anyone I have ever known. They seemed as relaxed as my own parents would be in our home, and they seemed grateful for the hospitality we extended to them."[24]

HABITAT FOR HUMANITY HAS MANY DIFFERENT PARTNERS. Clark Howard, a nationally syndicated consumer expert from Atlanta, did his radio show from Valdosta for several days during the 2003 build and interviewed President Carter. Since 1996, Howard and supporters have helped build over seventy-five Habitat homes, most in the Atlanta area. Howard got involved in Habitat in memory of his father, who grew up in New York City in the Depression. Twice during those years, his family found themselves homeless. Five decades later, the elder Mr. Howard grew upset when six homeless people died during the cold Atlanta winter of 1984. He soon got his synagogue to start a homeless shelter, but Clark pointed out that people needed options beyond temporary housing. The elder Mr. Howard challenged his son to do something about the problem. Clark eventually started volunteering with Habitat on a regular basis. He donates speaking fees to Habitat and encourages his listeners to donate.[25]

JIMMY CARTER PAUSED WITH MILLARD AND LINDA FULLER near a Habitat build site in April 2004. They were in Puebla and Veracruz, Mexico, as part of a "Global Village" trip of Habitat for Humanity. These trips gave participants the opportunity to help build houses and a chance to learn more about the local people and their culture.

In 1990, five women accused Millard Fuller of inappropriate contact. Fuller admitted to hugging the women and kissing them on their cheeks but the women complained about more extensive touching. After several unsettled months, Fuller remained in charge at Habitat, thanks in part to strong support from Jimmy Carter. In 2004, new charges surfaced when a female employee accused him of sexual harassment, but the board found "insufficient proof of inappropriate conduct." In January 2005, the board fired Millard and Linda, citing "a pattern of ongoing public comments and communications by the Fullers that have been divisive and disruptive."[26] The couple soon established the Fuller Center for Housing in Americus. The faith-based center concentrates on providing adequate shelter for all people.

Fuller died on February 3, 2009, of an aneurysm. His burial took place the following day in a simple wooden box on the grounds of Koinonia, near the grave of his mentor and Koinonia founder Clarence Jordan. A month later, President Carter spoke at a memorial service at the Horizon Sanctuary at Ebenezer Baptist Church in Atlanta. The Fuller Center used the memorial service to announce a "Millions for

Millard" campaign to raise funds to provide housing for a million people. Linda Fuller declared, "We didn't want this to be a sad occasion. We want to charge everyone up to continue Millard's work."[27] Following the service, mourners walked to a home nearby that the Fuller Center had helped repair and renovate following damage caused by a tornado that hit Atlanta the previous March.

AFTER HABITAT OFFICIALS FIRED MILLARD
AND LINDA FULLER, Jimmy and Rosalynn Carter continued to support Habitat by giving their time, money, and
prestige to the Carter Work Projects. Habitat for Humanity
survived the transition. A few months after the firing of
Fuller, Carter spoke out against a proposed move of executive
offices to Atlanta. Despite his protests, Habitat announced
in April 2006 that corporate headquarters would move from
Americus, in part to be closer to Hartsfield-Jackson Atlanta
International Airport. One goal of the relocation was to
improve access "to peer organizations, partners, skills, and
services" as well as to Habitat offices around the world. Both
Fuller and Carter opposed moving the headquarters because
they knew that Americus needed the jobs. Fuller feared that
soon the organization would move all of its offices to Atlanta
and that Habitat would become a bureaucracy rather than
a ministry.[28] Carter declared, "I would look on such a decision as a violation of mutual commitments made over the
years, with a damaging effect on Habitat's reputation and
effectiveness."[29]

Habitat officials decided to maintain operational offices
in Americus. About fifty employees moved to Atlanta while
about three hundred stayed in Americus. In 2018, Habitat
officials, employees, and community members formally dedicated their Americus offices in honor of Clarence Jordan,
the "spiritual father" of Habitat. Jordan had established the

Christian farming community of Koinonia Farm nearby in
1942 and he and Millard and Linda Fuller developed the
idea of partnership housing in the late 1960s, which led to
the establishment of Habitat. As Jonathan Reckford, CEO of
Habitat for Humanity, said, "His dedication to his lifelong
ministry has inspired all of us at Habitat to continue working
toward creating a world where everyone has a safe, decent
and affordable place to call home."[30] In 2019, the Atlanta
headquarters moved into larger space in the Marquis Two
Tower in downtown's Peachtree Center.

THE CARTER WORK PROJECT went to Mishawka, Indiana, in 2018. Retired late-night talk show host David Letterman joined the volunteer builders in his home state. Letterman has been involved with Habitat for several years. He attributes his involvement to the Carters and their support of housing for needy people. Over four thousand people attended the opening event at the nearby University of Notre Dame.[31] The previous year, while on a Carter Work Project in Winnipeg, Manitoba, in Canada, Carter suffered from dehydration in the hot sun. Recovery meant a trip to a local hospital, but Carter returned to the work site the next morning and has continued to work on Habitat builds.

THE CARTERS HAVE WORKED WITH HABITAT for over thirty-five years. The Carter Work Project moved on to Nashville, Tennessee, for the 2019 build. Country music stars Garth Brooks and Trisha Yearwood also became major supporters of Habitat after Hurricane Katrina damaged much of New Orleans and surrounding areas in 2005. They made this photograph while still in Indiana in 2018 as they promoted the 2019 event. The country music stars have worked alongside the Carters in the United States and abroad eleven times, including in 2019 in Nashville. Yearwood, a native of Monticello, Georgia, and Brooks work on the home builds, but Brooks has laughingly told reporters, "You don't want to work on a house that Jimmy and Rosalynn Carter are working on, because they will work you to the bone." The reporter remarked on Garth's comment, "At least we think he was joking."[32]

Carter fell and had fourteen stitches the day before the 2019 project started, but he showed up on site the next day and worked all week. Jimmy and Rosalynn Carter have worked with 103,000 volunteers in fourteen countries to help build, renovate, or repair 4,331 homes. Their support of Habitat has brought many thousands of dollars in donations to the organization. Even more significantly, they have also brought worldwide attention to the need for better housing in urban and rural areas in the United States and around the world.

Habitat has also been good for the Carters. The Carter-Habitat connection is so strong that many people think that Jimmy Carter founded Habitat. In reality, the Carters volunteer for Habitat for only one week a year, though they have done additional work serving on the board and contacting possible donors. Certainly, the Carters did not choose to support Habitat because they thought it would be a good publicity move, but both Habitat and Carter have benefitted from the partnership. Author and historian Douglas Brinkley notes, "Habitat jump-started Carter's extraordinary post-presidency. His stock was down when he began working with Habitat. When he picked up that hammer, he started to become a folk hero."[33]

CHAPTER 7

Politics and Awards

SINCE LEAVING POLITICAL OFFICE, Jimmy Carter has at different times joined together with his fellow former presidents of the United States and with former governors of Georgia. The presidents generally gathered either for the opening of a new library or for a funeral of a national political leader. When something is important to him, Carter shares his opinion about policies and events, but otherwise he keeps these thoughts to himself. The former sailor and submariner had the honor of having a U.S. nuclear submarine named for him, the only president to be so recognized.

Since growing up on a farm near Plains, the trajectory of Jimmy Carter's life has taken many unexpected turns. He has received many awards for humanitarian work, including the Nobel Peace Prize in 2002 for his untiring efforts to find peaceful solutions to world problems. Many thought he should have received the Nobel in 1978, the same year that Menachem Begin and Anwar Sadat received the award for their work on the Camp David Accords. Carter became an honorary national park ranger in 2016 in recognition of his work in 1980 putting lands in Alaska under national protection and establishing other national parks. Unexpected recognition includes receiving three Grammy Awards for spoken word albums.

JIMMY CARTER BECAME ACTIVELY INVOLVED IN POLITICS during the 1962 Georgia Senate race. After he lost his bid for reelection as president in 1980, his involvement in politics largely subsided except for trips to Democratic National Conventions and periodic statements to the press. At the July 1988 convention held in Atlanta, he appeared with Georgia governor Joe Frank Harris, standing to his right, and Lieutenant Governor Zell Miller on his left. On the opening day of the convention he spoke to the crowd about nominee Michael Dukakis and his running mate Lloyd Bentsen. Joe Frank Harris led the Georgia delegation and cast a vote for Dukakis, though he did not personally support the New Englander that fall because he considered him to be too liberal.[1]

JIMMY CARTER SERVED AS THE SEVENTY-SIXTH GOVERNOR OF GEORGIA. He joined an elite group of six other Georgians at the state capitol on January 25, 1991. The seven governors who gathered are, left to right, Ernest Vandiver, Zell Miller, who had become governor earlier that month, George Busbee, Carl Sanders, Jimmy Carter, Joe Frank Harris, and Herman Talmadge. All of the men represented the Democratic Party, since state voters did not elect a Republican governor between the Reconstruction days of 1868 and 2002.

The seven men led Georgia for over half a century. They saw their state change from a rural, segregated society into a modern, mostly urban and suburban state. Vandiver served as governor from 1959 to 1963 and died in 2005. Miller, who served from 1991 until 1999, died in 2018. Sanders served from 1963 to 1967, lost to Carter in the 1970 race, and died in 2014. Busbee succeeded Carter, served from 1975 until 1983, and died in 2005. Talmadge served as governor from 1948 to 1955 and died in 2002. Both Miller and Talmadge served in the U.S. Senate after their governorship. The Georgia State University's Georgia Government Documentation Project organized the gathering. They gave each governor a bound volume of transcripts of interviews they had conducted with the governors, starting in 1985.

JIMMY AND ROSALYNN CARTER attended another historic gathering that year, this one in California. On November 4, 1991, President George H. W. Bush and his wife, Barbara, joined four former presidents of the United States and their wives for the opening of the Ronald Reagan Presidential Library. Lady Bird Johnson, widow of Lyndon B. Johnson, joined them (at left) for the official photograph. Others in attendance included John F. Kennedy Jr. and Caroline Kennedy Schlossberg, children of John F. Kennedy, plus offspring of Franklin D. Roosevelt. Lodwrick Cook, director of the Ronald Reagan Presidential Foundation, called this "the largest gathering of American Presidents and Presidential families ever assembled." Indeed, five presidents of the United States had never before been in one place. The last time there had been more living presidents had been during the early Civil War days of 1861 when Lincoln, Van Buren, Tyler, Fillmore, Pierce, and Buchanan had all held the highest office of the land.[2]

These five men had led the country for twenty-two years and all spoke at the library opening. The Carters had arrived in Simi Valley after observing an election in Zambia. Jimmy Carter noted that his Republican colleagues "have another advantage over me. At least all of you have met another Democratic President. I've never had that opportunity yet." He went on to praise Reagan for bringing an end to the Cold War, but he also added the only real criticism of the day by noting continuing problems with homelessness and the need to provide better education and health care for many Americans.[3]

Reagan, the first president to serve two full terms since Dwight Eisenhower served from 1953 until 1961, complimented all the men. He referred to Carter as "a son of the South whose election did more than anything else to restore that great region to its rightful place in the American mainstream and who devoted himself to cleaning the blood of Abraham from the sands of the Middle East." He also mentioned his presidential library and the millions of documents housed inside. "The judgment of history is left to you, the people. I have no fear of that for we have done our best. So I say, come and learn from it."[4]

In 1987, midway through his second term, Reagan expected the library to be located at Stanford University, but that changed when resistance arose within the relatively liberal university community. Instead, officials chose to build the library on a hundred acres of hills where western movies had once been filmed. This was the first presidential library to open under the rules of the Presidential Libraries Act, passed during the Carter administration in 1978.

The five living presidents walk across a courtyard. They are lined up in the order that they served, starting with Richard Nixon on the right, Gerald Ford, Carter, Reagan, and the current president, George H. W. Bush, on the left.

GEORGIANS GATHERED with Democratic presidential nominee and Arkansas governor Bill Clinton at the 1992 Democratic National Convention held at Madison Square Garden in New York City. Atlanta city councilman Bill Campbell and Carter chat to the left of Clinton while Georgia governor Zell Miller and Atlanta mayor Maynard Jackson stand on his right. On July 16, Miller gave the keynote address, noting, "Not all of us can be born rich, handsome, and lucky, and that's why we have a Democratic Party. . . . I am a Democrat because we are the party of hope."[5]

In 1992, Georgia political leaders on the federal, state, and local levels affiliated overwhelmingly with the Democratic Party. In addition to Governor Miller, Jackson and Campbell belonged to the party. Carter had long had close relationships with African Americans in the state. Martin Luther King Sr. provided key support to Carter in the 1976 election as well as during his terms as governor and president. Carter also had a warm connection with Maynard Jackson for years. In 1973, Jackson won election as the first African American mayor of Atlanta or any major southern city. Carter has described their relationship: "As the preeminent Democratic leader in the state, I didn't believe it was my role to get involved in the mayoral race. . . . But I went to the inauguration benefit. . . . Maynard helped me when I ran for president. He went up to states like Pennsylvania and was very influential, and let the Yankees know that I was acceptable as a potential president even though I was from the Deep South. When I was in office, we had a compatible relationship."[6] Jackson served as mayor from 1974 to 1982 and 1990 to 1994. Campbell served as mayor of Atlanta from 1994 to 2002 and then spent time in a federal prison after being convicted of tax evasion.

A loyal Democrat, Carter has continued to not endorse candidates during the primaries. He supported Clinton and Gore during the convention and got them to help with a Habitat for Humanity build in Atlanta that summer. At his inaugural in 1993, Clinton recognized all the celebrities present, including actors and musicians, but failed to mention Jimmy and Rosalynn Carter. Dr. James Laney, the president of Emory University who was appointed as the U.S. ambassador to South Korea in October 1993, noted, "I don't want to say he gave him a cold shoulder, but he did not acknowledge him the way he deserved to be acknowledged, not just as a Democrat but as a former president."[7] Clinton sought to distance himself from the Georgian who won election for only one term.[8] Carter did not attend the 1996 Democratic convention, which saw Clinton nominated for a second term.

JIMMY AND ROSALYNN CARTER visited the Georgia capitol on June 7, 1994. They joined Georgia governor Zell Miller and his wife, Shirley, Lieutenant Governor Pierre Howard, and others at the dedication of the Carter statue. The statue honors the only Georgian ever elected president, showing Carter standing in work clothes with his hands outstretched. Atlanta native Frederick Hart, sculptor of *The Three Servicemen* at the Vietnam Veterans Memorial in Washington, D.C., and other projects, wanted to capture the humanity of Carter. Hart said in 1994 that "I have sculpted him in bronze on a low pedestal, in an informal pose, dressed in khakis with his sleeves rolled up. . . . The gestures of the figure refer to the generosity of Carter's nature, his eagerness to share a vision of justice, and his unpretentious delight in spreading a message of brotherhood."[9] Carter declared that he liked the portrayal. "It was the image that put me in the White House and the governor's office, and I hope I can remain [like that] in the future." The statue is part of a six-ton pink granite form with four granite benches that are inscribed with phrases including author, poet, teacher, and humanitarian, all Carter character traits.[10]

ON JANUARY 11, 1999, Carter greets Governor Zell Miller at the Georgia capitol. That day, Miller became a former governor of Georgia when Roy Barnes was sworn in as the eightieth governor of the state. Elizabeth Harris, wife of Joe Frank Harris, watches in the background. Carter and Miller, a native of the north Georgia mountains, had been friends since serving as colleagues in the Georgia Senate in the early 1960s. After having been a relatively liberal governor, Miller became more conservative while he served in the U.S. Senate from 2000 until 2004. He spoke at the Republican National Convention in New York in 2004 and authored a book, *A National Party No More: The Conscience of a Conservative Democrat*. He argued that the Democratic Party had moved too far left and that the Republican Party better represented the American people. When he died in 2018, three U.S. presidents, Carter, Clinton, and George W. Bush, attended the services.

FORMER GOVERNORS OF GEORGIA converged on the Georgia capitol on January 11, 1999, for the swearing in of Roy Barnes as governor. Shown left to right are Ernest Vandiver, George Busbee, Lester Maddox, Barnes, Zell Miller, Jimmy Carter, Joe Frank Harris, and Carl Sanders. The First Ladies of Georgia also gathered that day. Shirley Miller, Mary Ruth Busbee, Marie Barnes, Rosalynn Carter, Betty Foy Sanders, Elizabeth Harris, and Betty Vandiver stand left to right.

Barnes served from 1999 until 2003. He lost his bid for reelection to Sonny Perdue as part of a shift to the Republican Party by Georgia voters. Barnes had been called "King Roy" by some supporters because of his power as governor and because the former Georgia state senator knew how to make things happen in the Georgia legislature. Many voters criticized actions he took, including leading the change of the Georgia state flag in 2001, which removed the Confederate emblem that had been featured prominently on the flag since 1956. Under Governor Sonny Perdue, the Georgia legislature again changed the flag design to wide red and white stripes with the Georgia state seal and the words "In God We Trust" in a field of blue. Georgia voters approved the design in a vote in March 2004. Barnes received the 2003 John F. Kennedy Library Foundation Profile in Courage Award, thanks largely to his role in removing the Confederate emblem from the Georgia flag.

203

JIMMY AND ROSALYNN CARTER and the Carter Center have accomplished much through the years and have received many awards for their work. In 1999, the Carters and the Carter Center received the inaugural Delta Prize for Global Understanding. UGA president Michael Adams, on the left, and Maurice Worth, chief operating officer of Delta, presented the award to the Carters. The prize is awarded annually to "individuals who by their own initiative have provided opportunities for greater understanding among cultures and nations." Adams presided over the awards banquet at the Ritz-Carlton Buckhead on April 27, 1999.

The University of Georgia administers the prize, which was endowed by Delta Air Lines and the Delta Air Lines Foundation. The prize includes a cash award of ten thousand dollars and a medallion. The recipient also chooses a nonprofit organization to receive a travel allowance from Delta of fifty thousand dollars. Other recipients of the prize have included Desmond Tutu, Mikhail Gorbachev, and Ted Turner. A student selection committee, consisting mostly of University of Georgia Foundation fellows, develops a short list and the Delta Prize Board selects the recipients.[11] The prize has since transitioned into the university naming the recipient as the Delta Visiting Chair. Georgia native and Pulitzer Prize–winning author Alice Walker served as the first chair in 2015.

Carter also received the J. William Fulbright Prize for International Understanding, awarded on his seventieth birthday, October 1, 1994. Nelson Mandela had won the first prize the previous year. The prize was originally supported by the Coca-Cola Foundation, which donated fifty thousand dollars annually for the award winners.[12]

ON AUGUST 9, 1999, U.S. president Bill Clinton presented Jimmy and Rosalynn Carter with the Presidential Medal of Freedom, the highest civilian honor in the country. The president flew to Atlanta to present the award. Clinton spoke about connections between the two southerners. He specifically mentioned that only Arkansas and Georgia gave Carter 65 percent or more of the vote in 1976. He saluted Carter for his strong support of civil rights, going on to note that "Jimmy and Rosalynn Carter have done more good things for more people in more places than any other couple on the face of the Earth."

He listed some of the beneficial things that the Carters have done, including working with Habitat for Humanity, fighting to end hunger and disease around the world, monitoring elections in other countries, seeking the release of political prisoners, and much more. He also talked about having support from Carter as the Clinton Administration tried to preserve democracy in Haiti and on the Korean Peninsula. He recalled programs and actions undertaken during the Carter administration that were still impacting the world in 1999, including the Camp David Accords, SALT II, deregulation, conservation and the Alaska Lands Act, energy conservation, and hiring more women and minorities than any other administration to that point. "He was the first President to put America's commitment to human rights squarely at the heart of our foreign policy." He thanked Rosalynn Carter for her work with mental health and championing children. He closed by stating that "today, we do all we can; a grateful nation says thank you."[13] Carter called the ceremony "one of the most beautiful events of my life."[14]

In reality, Carter and Clinton disagreed over many things through the years. In 1994, Clinton did not seem receptive to comments and actions from Carter about North Korea or Haiti.[15] Carter also criticized the affair with former White House intern Monica Lewinsky which led to the impeachment of Clinton by the U.S. House of Representatives. In 1999, Clinton genuinely wanted to honor Jimmy and Rosalynn Carter, though, perhaps because he knew his own reputation would be helped by appearing with Jimmy and Rosalynn Carter.

THE TELEPHONE RANG at the home of Jimmy and Rosalynn Carter in Plains about 4:30 a.m. on October 11, 2002, with a call originating in Oslo, Norway. A representative of the Nobel Committee shared the long-awaited news that Jimmy Carter had won the Nobel Peace Prize. A record 156 candidates from around the world had been nominated that year, but a former peanut farmer from south Georgia won the award.

Carter had been nominated for a Nobel Peace Prize several times through the years. Many thought he should have also won in 1978 when Anwar Sadat and Menachem Begin shared the award for reaching the Camp David Accords, in negotiations led by Carter, that would lead directly to the 1979 peace treaty between Israel and Egypt. According to some sources, Carter did not receive the nomination that year because of a missed Nobel deadline. His name was rumored to be on the short list for the award in several other years. Rosalynn commented, "He's been nominated a few times. We didn't even think about him getting it this time." The Nobel Committee chair, Gunnar Berge, surprisingly brought politics into the day when he said that the award "should be interpreted as a criticism of the line that the current administration has taken," referring to the George W. Bush administration and its relations with Iraq.[16] Berge shared his opinion that the Bush administration should have tried harder to peacefully resolve the conflict with Iraq. He and others considered the developing Iraq War a disaster for the world.

Just as the Carters had observed election results in the 1970s and 1980 by speaking to the public from downtown Plains, they headed into town for a noon news conference. Carter shared, "I had a feeling of disbelief this morning. I am delighted, humbled, and very grateful that the Nobel committee has given me this award."[17] In the acceptance statement he sent to the committee that day, Carter recognized Rosalynn and the many people who had worked at the Carter Center with them "to promote peace, health, and human rights." He acknowledged that during the two decades of traveling the globe for the Carter Center, his idea of human rights had changed "to include not only the right to live in peace, but also to adequate health care, shelter, food, and to economic opportunity." He closed by stating that the honor inspired them to continue their activities but also that it inspires "suffering people around the world, and I accept it on their behalf."[18]

CARTER ACCEPTED THE NOBEL PEACE PRIZE during a ceremony at the Oslo City Hall on December 10, 2002. On the day of the award announcement, Carter declared that he intended to give most of the $1 million cash prize to continue the work at the Carter Center and would place the plaque and medallion on display next door at the Carter Presidential Library and Museum.[19] He followed two other presidents who had won the award. Theodore Roosevelt received it in 1906 for mediating talks to end the Russo-Japanese War, and Woodrow Wilson received it in 1919 for his efforts leading to the founding of the League of Nations.[20]

In accepting the prize that day, Carter quoted his favorite teacher, Julia Coleman, sharing a saying of hers that he had mentioned in his presidential inaugural address. "We must adjust to changing times but still hold to unchanging principles." He also mentioned fellow Georgian and fellow Nobel Prize winner Martin Luther King Jr. and noted the civil rights movement's important role in the development of the South and his country. He added, "I am not here as a public official, but as a citizen of a troubled world who finds hope in a growing consensus that the generally accepted goals of society are peace, freedom, human rights, environmental quality, the alleviation of suffering, and the rule of law."[21]

ROSALYNN CARTER CHRISTENED the USS *Jimmy Carter* (SSN-23) on June 5, 2004, while the former president watched at a safe distance from the splashing liquid. She gave a blessing for "all who sail in her." Carter declared, "This is a wonderful day for me, and to see my wife break the champagne on undoubtedly the finest, and [most] formidable, ship in the world was a great honor for me. And to have my name on it, I am very grateful."[22] The Electric Boat division of General Dynamics received the contract to build the sub in 1996 as the third and final *Seawolf*-class, nuclear-powered, fast-attack submarine in the United States Navy. Modifications in design and intended use during construction delayed its completion. The ship received its official commission on February 19, 2005.

Fifty-two years earlier, Carter had been a sailor. He remembered, "I once saw Harry Truman [his favorite president] at a distance. He was present when we laid the keel of the first atomic submarine, *Nautilus*, in New London, Connecticut."[23] Carter is the only president to have qualified in submarines. The USS *Jimmy Carter* is only the third to be named for a living person and the only one named for a living president.

The *Jimmy Carter*, at 453 feet long, is a hundred feet longer than the other two *Seawolf*-class submarines. The space gives the sub its most distinguishing characteristic, the Multi-Mission Platform. This allows the sub to have a variety of capabilities, including room for remotely operated vehicles, a dry deck shelter, or an Advanced SEAL Delivery System.[24] The cost was reported to have been $3.2 billion, making the *Carter* one of the most expensive ships in the navy.[25] The Pacific Ocean is the base of operations for the sub. Several news reports have speculated that the submarine has been involved in operations in North Korea. *Popular Mechanics* quotes journalist Ian J. Keddie, saying that "the *Jimmy Carter* represents the USN's most important asset for special operations. The Navy is tight-lipped about the specifics of this but it is likely to have involved intelligence gathering, reconnaissance, or special forces."[26]

On August 11–12, 2005, President and Mrs. Carter met up with the USS *Jimmy Carter* at Kings Bay Naval Submarine Base in Georgia. The Carters met crew members, toured, and spent the night on the submarine. After departing the submarine, Carter saluted the "sideboys," the seamen gathered in parallel rows to honor the former president.

SEVERAL DEMOCRATIC LEADERS gathered in the East Room of the White House on January 19, 2011. Secretary of State Hillary Rodham Clinton, former president Bill Clinton, former First Lady Rosalynn Carter, former president Jimmy Carter, Dr. Jill Biden, and Vice President Joe Biden listen to performers during a state dinner. President Barack Obama and First Lady Michelle Obama hosted Chinese president Hu Jintao. This was their third state dinner. Jimmy Carter has only gone to a few formal events at the White House since he left office. Other guests included Hollywood stars Barbra Streisand and her husband James Brolin and action star Jackie Chan. The menu featured "quintessentially American" selections including apple pie and ice cream for dessert plus jazz music for entertainment.[27]

THE GERALD R. FORD PRESIDENTIAL FOUNDATION

presented their 2017 medal for distinguished public service to Jimmy Carter on May 17, 2017, at the Carter Center. Trustee Carla A. Hills, foundation chairman Red Cavaney, thirty-ninth president of the United States Jimmy Carter, trustee Steven Ford, and foundation executive director Joseph Calvaruso all gathered in Atlanta for the occasion. Carter stated, "As I reflect back on more than 25 different projects that Jerry and I collaborated and shared leadership [on], I can't help but be grateful for the mutual respect and the intense personal friendship that developed during that time together."[28]

Carter and Ford had an intensely combative election during 1976, in which Carter won 297 electoral votes versus 240 for his opponent. The two men became friends over the years. They both represented the United States at the funeral of Anwar Sadat in Egypt and flew home on the same long flight. Afterward, they agreed to cooperate on projects of the Ford Library and the Carter Center. They exchanged visits to each other's institutions. President Ford cochaired Carter Center election-monitoring missions and other programs. Carter received the recognition from the Ford Presidential Foundation for his integrity, character, diligence, patriotism, and judgment.[29] In presenting the award, Steven Ford, son of the former president, mentioned "the current toxic times" and noted that his father and Carter showed "the nation that politics can be handled with dignity, class and respect."[30]

After Ford died on December 26, 2006, Carter eulogized him by using the same words he used at his inaugural: "For myself and for our nation, I want to thank my predecessor for all he has done to heal our land." He added that "We formed a personal bond while lamenting on the difficulty of unexpectedly defeated candidates trying to raise money to build presidential libraries."[31]

JIMMY CARTER HAS WON SEVERAL MAJOR AWARDS
that he never dreamed of winning as a young boy in Plains or even
as a former president when he came back home in 1981. He has
received three Grammy Awards in the Spoken Word Album category
and has been nominated nine times. In 2019, at age ninety-four, he
won for *Faith: A Journey for All*. In 2018 he won his second award
for the audiobook version of his memoir, *A Full Life: Reflections
at Ninety*. He won his first Grammy in 2006 for *Our Endangered
Values: America's Moral Crisis*.[32] Other presidents who have won
Grammys include Barack Obama and Bill Clinton, who have each
won two awards. He also presented the MusiCares Person of the
Year award to Bob Dylan in 2015. Carter enjoyed attending a Dylan
concert in Atlanta in 1974 and quoted the musician in his 1977 presidential address. At the MusiCares ceremony, he said, "There is no
doubt that his words on peace and human rights are much more inci-
sive and much more powerful and much more permanent than those
of any president of the United States."[33] The Recording Academy
presents the Grammy Awards, which recognize achievement in the
music industry, while MusiCares provides assistance to music profes-
sionals in need.

GETTING A NEW HAT TO PLACE ON DISPLAY

in a museum is not a typical award, unless the recognition comes from the National Park Service. National Park Service director Jonathan B. Jarvis, Jimmy Carter, NPS southeast region director Stan Austin, and Jimmy Carter National Historic Site superintendent Barbara Judy gathered in Plains for presentation of an honorary national park ranger award to Carter on April 17, 2016. The recognition is the highest civilian honor awarded by the service. Carter declared, "This is indeed an honor for me. Before I became President I was already deeply committed to the outdoors. I am very proud to have been an integral part of the conservation movement."

The Park Service recognized several of Carter's presidential achievements, including establishing thirty-nine National Park Service units. The Martin Luther King Jr. National Historic Site, the Women's Rights National Historic Park, the Kaloko-Honokahau National Historic Park, and the Boston African American National Historic Site were some of the new sites. Also, the War in the Pacific National Historic Park in Guam expanded the National Park Service across the international dateline. Carter put fifty-six million acres of land in Alaska under national protection with a bill signed on December 1, 1978. The recognition as an honorary park ranger from the park service came as the NPS celebrated its hundredth anniversary in 2016.[34]

FORMER PRESIDENTS, POLITICAL ASSOCIATES, FAMILY, AND FRIENDS
gathered on December 5, 2018, for funeral services for former president George H. W. Bush
at the National Cathedral in Washington, D.C. President Donald J. Trump and First Lady
Melania Trump, former president Barack Obama and First Lady Michelle Obama, former
president Bill Clinton and First Lady Hillary Rodham Clinton, and the Carters watched as
the casket arrived with pallbearers representing each branch of the military. With the passing
of George H. W. Bush, Jimmy Carter became the oldest living former president. During the
funeral service, Bush's son, former president George W. Bush, acknowledged that his father
"showed me what it means to be a president that serves with integrity, leads with courage
and acts with love in his heart for the citizens of our country."[35]

CHAPTER 8

Life in Plains and Georgia

THROUGHOUT THEIR LIVES, Jimmy and Rosalynn Carter have spent much of their "leisure" time in and around the South. They make sure their sons, daughter, grandchildren, and great-grandchildren get together at least once a year for family vacations. They have also worked hard on projects close to their hearts in Plains, such as decorating the bed and breakfast, nurturing a butterfly trail, overseeing development of the Jimmy Carter National Historic Site, and establishing the SAM short line railroad in south Georgia. Carter carved a large cross and collection plates for Maranatha Baptist Church and has regularly taught Sunday school class, creating large boosts in attendance at worship services while sharing the Christian message with visitors from around the world. The Carters have also assisted with projects at Georgia Southwestern State University and Mercer University. Georgia and the South have supported them and the Carters have given much personal attention to the area. In many ways, the Carters have personified part of the speech by president-elect John F. Kennedy in which he paraphrased Luke 12:48 from the Bible on January 9, 1961, and declared, "For of those to whom much is given, much is required."[1]

JIMMY CARTER has always been devoted to his family, regardless of whether he was living in the White House, at the Governor's Mansion in Atlanta, or in Plains. He and Rosalynn have three sons, one daughter, nine grandsons (one deceased), three granddaughters, five great-grandsons, and nine great-granddaughters as of September 2019. Just like many parents and grandparents everywhere, the Carters get together with family whenever they can, including at home, in Atlanta, or on vacations. The family gathered in Fort Myers, Florida, in December 2004.

The importance of families for the future of the nation has always been a core Carter belief. He declared that families provide "a permanent foundation on which our lives can be fashioned."[2] The Carter family often gathers for family dinners at the Carter Center since so many family members live in the Atlanta area. In 2014, they had twenty-two family members living in Atlanta. Jimmy and Rosalynn would typically be in Atlanta one week each month and they try to gather all local family members around the table at least one evening. They also take their family members on vacation the week after Christmas. In 2013, that meant thirty-eight Carter family members gathered. As Carter told his sister-in-law Sybil Carter, "We try to go to very interesting and enjoyable places. . . . Rosalynn and I save up our money every year and pay all the expenses so we have one hundred percent attendance."[3]

A 1976 campaign volunteer, Rita Thompson, who later served as a family assistant, said, "'He relaxes once a year. The week after Christmas.' That's when Carter takes a family trip . . . that he organizes right down to the minutes set aside for 'free time.' To be late for anything on the itinerary is to be left behind, with an exception granted for Rosalynn, whose 57th-birthday present from Carter was a promise to never again nag her about 'tardiness.'"[4]

JIMMY CARTER STAYED CLOSE to siblings Ruth, Gloria, and Billy and to his mother throughout their lives. Miss Lillian was rated as one of the most famous mothers in the world in the late 1970s. Billy, Gloria, and Ruth often made the news during the Carter presidential years. Gloria Carter Spann became one of the first women to be inducted into the Harley Davidson 100,000 miles club.[5] His younger brother endured the scrutiny of the press while also seeming to court its attention. Billy spent years hanging out at the garage he owned in Plains and drinking Billy Beer. The public loved Billy, though the Carter administration suffered great embarrassment because of Billy and his activities.

Billy Carter moved away from southwest Georgia in 1981 and lived and worked in Haleyville, Alabama, and Waycross, Georgia. He learned he had pancreatic cancer in 1987 and died on September 25, 1988. The day after Billy died, his children hung a banner over the Carter warehouse office. The wooden sign had originally been installed in 1970 after Jimmy Carter won election as governor. Billy Carter paid for that sign and its installation as payment on a bet with Jimmy: if Jimmy won, Billy would install a sign, which he did. They updated the sign in 1976 and have kept it touched up since then. Son William "Buddy" and a brother-in-law stapled the painted sheets to the plywood sign. Buddy reflected that they wanted to tell the world that their dad had lived there, too, and "that he wasn't quite the screw-up some people made him out to be . . . because we loved him. If he'd been alive, I think he would have kicked my ass. But it would have been worth it."[6]

JIMMY CARTER has been involved with activities in Plains throughout his life. After moving back to Plains in January 1981, the Carters spent most of the next year at home, writing their memoirs and getting adjusted to life outside the White House.[7] The people of Plains gave them space but also welcomed their involvement in the town. In the post-presidency years, Jimmy and Rosalynn have spent at least one week per month at their house. As they got older, they spent even more time in Plains.

The Carters' involvement in the town extends much further than just speaking at occasional openings. They helped develop the Plains Historic Inn and Antiques Mall. Georgia governor Roy Barnes spoke at the dedication in May 2002. The Plains Mercantile Building, on the right, had been purchased from the estate of cousin Hugh Carter the previous year. They combined the two buildings to create seven hotel rooms and an antiques mall. Decorations in each hotel room reflect a different decade in Jimmy Carter's life from the 1920s to the 1980s. Rosalynn helped decorate the inn and President Carter made a long serving table and a tall cabinet.[8] Guests often stay at the inn, tour sites related to the life of Carter, and then go to church on Sunday to hear President Carter give his Sunday school lesson.

CONGRESSMAN RICHARD RAY joined the Carters and others on February 13, 1988, for the official opening of the Plains Depot as a visitors center. Two Carter projects of his post-presidency garnered significant attention in the 1980s. A major dispute erupted over the proposed Presidential Parkway that would connect the Carter Center and Library to downtown Atlanta and its interstates. The proposed Jimmy Carter National Historic Site in Plains garnered some opposition from individual members of the community, but also generated much excitement in the area.

The Carters and others, especially members of the Plains Historical Preservation Trust, made a major push to have the Plains area declared a national historic site. Discussions with the Park Service started in 1981 and a feasibility study was completed in 1983. Secretary of the Interior James Watt placed a moratorium on establishing any new historic sites. Congress had to

approve legislation creating the national site. Politics came into play since Republicans controlled the presidency and the Senate while the Democrats controlled the House of Representatives.[9]

Some expressed concern about creating a historic site for a living president, recommending instead that a person be dead at least fifty years before a site is established. Part of the Plains project included restoring the high school that Jimmy and Rosalynn had attended. The school had closed in 1979 and members of Congress worried about the high cost of restoration. Congressman Ray, a Georgia Democrat from Perry, shepherded the project through Congress. President Carter, the Park Service, and Congress had to negotiate a plan for the site. President Carter and Plains officials agreed to keep the costs low. On December 23, 1987, President Ronald Reagan signed the act creating the Plains Historic District.

The railroad depot opened on February 13, 1988, as the visitors' center for the historic site. Other components include Plains High, the Carter Boyhood Farm in Archery, and the Carter residence on Woodlawn Avenue. CSX Transportation later donated the depot to the Plains Historical Preservation Trust, which in turn donated the depot to the National Park Service for use as a museum.

The visitors' information center moved into the renovated Plains High School on October 1, 1996, the seventy-second birthday of the former president. Georgia governor Zell Miller and about a thousand people helped dedicate the restored school building. The classical revival design of the school features a monumental portico flanked by single-story wings with another wing to the rear of the building. In 1979, the Georgia legislature declared Plains High School, built circa 1921, to be the state school of Georgia.

JIMMY CARTER HAS TAUGHT SUNDAY SCHOOL

at Maranatha Baptist Church one or two Sundays a month for almost four decades. Special groups often come, including these sailors who are chiefs in training. People come to the church from around the country and the world and sometimes wait in their cars for as much as ten to fifteen hours to get a seat in the sanctuary to hear him teach on Sunday morning.[10]

Carter recalls, "I taught every Sunday in the Naval Academy chapel to the young, junior-aged daughters of the officers and the men assigned permanently in Annapolis. Later, when I was on ships, we didn't have regular services on Easter or sometimes on Christmas if we were at sea, so I would conduct a brief religious service right there between the torpedo tubes of the submarine."[11]

He and Rosalynn joined the newly established Maranatha Baptist Church when they moved back in 1981 and he started teaching periodic Sunday school classes that September. Carter teaches his Sunday school class in the main church sanctuary. If the sanctuary reaches capacity, the overflow crowd goes into the Fellowship Hall where they can watch the sermon on closed-circuit television. Carter generally comes into the Fellowship Hall before the lesson starts and often uses the time to reflect on current events or anniversaries of significant events during his presidential administration. Carter uses the Baptist Church adult lesson guidelines as the basis of his Sunday school lessons.

Jimmy Carter has carved many things since 1981, including the cross hanging in Maranatha Baptist Church and the offering plates. Carter discusses his love of this lifelong hobby at length in *The Craftsmanship of Jimmy Carter*. He notes that "the pleasure does not fade as the years go by; in fact, with age my diminished physical strength has eliminated some of the formerly competing hobbies and made woodworking

even more precious to me." Such projects give Carter time alone, not writing or planning a speech or an event, while also being productive with his hands.[12]

After he left the White House, Carter made furniture for the north Georgia cabin he purchased with John Pope. Later, he began building items and painting pictures to be auctioned in fundraisers for the Carter Center. In 1983, he contributed four ladder-back hickory chairs for auction at the winter meeting of donors. The chairs sold for twenty-one thousand dollars. Over the next twenty-five years, his handcrafted items raised several million dollars for the Carter Center.[13] He has also used his love of woodworking with Habitat for Humanity.

Through the years, the Carters have done much for the church. Carter has made offering plates, a cross for the centerpiece behind the altar, and small pieces of furniture. Rosalynn has helped with a variety of tasks, including teaching youth and assisting with cleaning the church. Carter told Hamilton Jordan in 2002 that he was "chairman" of the grounds committee at the church, which meant that he helped others keep the grass mowed.[14]

AS ONE OF THE MOST FAMOUS SUNDAY SCHOOL TEACHERS in the world, Jimmy Carter, along with his wife, Rosalynn, spends time after church every Sunday that he teaches Sunday school having photographs made with church guests. This has become the easiest place to have a photograph made with the former president. Groups, individuals, couples, and families can have photographs made with the Carters. Here AndrewServes, a group of students from nearby Andrew College in Cuthbert, gathered with the president following a church service.

The one requirement for having a photo made is that the guests must stay and listen to the sermon given by the minister of the church. People who try to come in at the end of the service just to get a photograph are not admitted. Carter has been known to have a very hands-on approach to the growth of the church. One couple moved to Plains from a northern state and joined the church. After a few years, they left Maranatha and joined a church in Americus. Within a few days, they had a visit from the Carters asking why they changed churches.[15]

Tony Lowden, a native of north Philadelphia, became the first African American minister of Maranatha in spring 2019. The previous minister had resigned and Lowden preached one Sunday as a fill-in minister. He had been working with churches and after-school programs in the Macon–Bibb County area when he received a call on his cell phone from an unknown number and did not take the call. Several seconds later, he received a voicemail message. The distinctive southern voice of Jimmy Carter asked Lowden if he would like to be the interim minister and possibly enter in fulltime service to the church. Lowden also serves as the chaplain of the Secret Service of southwest Georgia. The actual congregation is small. One Sunday in August 2019, twenty-seven members attended Sunday service. Many of the members are neighbors or relatives of Jimmy and Rosalynn Carter, including children and grandchildren of Billy and Sybil Carter.

LIKE HIS FOREBEARS, Jimmy Carter has been a Baptist since his early years but he disagrees with the Southern Baptist Convention. Consistently principled, Jimmy and Rosalynn wrote a letter in October 2000 and withdrew from the Southern Baptist Convention. He criticized the group for becoming increasingly conservative, adopting a philosophy against allowing women to become pastors, and calling for wives to be submissive to their husbands. In the letter he declared that he, his father, and his grandfather had been Southern Baptists but he could no longer be part of the group, which included almost sixteen million members at the start of the twenty-first century.

He also disagreed with the Convention for removing references that identify Jesus Christ as "the criterion by which the Bible is to be interpreted." He declared, "I'm familiar with the verses they have quoted about wives being subjugated to their husbands. In my opinion, this is a distortion of the meaning of Scripture. . . . I personally feel the Bible says all people are equal in the eyes of God. I personally feel that women should play an absolutely equal role in service of Christ in the church."[16]

In 2015, Carter talked to Oprah Winfrey about the issue. The human rights activist declared, "I believe that the most serious violation of human rights on Earth is the abuse of women and girls."[17] In a 2009 article, he wrote, "It is simply self-defeating for any community to discriminate against half its population. We need to challenge these self-serving and outdated attitudes and practices."[18] Maranatha Baptist Church remains affiliated with the Southern Baptist Convention but subscribes to the doctrinal statement of the 1963 Baptist Faith and Message. The Carters' stance against

the Convention is largely symbolic since individuals join churches, not the convention. Carter has never been in a leadership role in the Southern Baptist Convention but he has been an extremely influential lay leader. Even after his influence diminished, he brought Southern Baptist leaders together to try to maintain collegiality. When Southern Baptist leadership rejected his proposals, he became a founder of the New Baptist Covenant. This took shape from 2006 to 2008. He has expressed his serious dissatisfaction with the denomination through letters, newspaper articles and editorials, and public statements.

JIMMY CARTER JOINED HIS GRANDSON Jason and Duke University president Richard Brodhead at a Duke program in Atlanta in February 2012. Members of the Carter family played critical roles in Jimmy's election as president. Rosalynn and their sons and daughters-in-law fanned out across the country in 1976 to help secure votes for Jimmy. Despite being so active in politics, the Carter family has not created a political dynasty.

Jason Carter ran on the Democratic ticket for governor of Georgia in 2014. Jason, the son of Jack Carter and Judy Langford, served as a Georgia State Senator from 2010 to 2014 representing a district that included the city of Decatur. During the campaign for governor, Rosalynn Carter addressed a group in Valdosta. She told them, "I love campaigning, I think I'm the only one in our family who really, really enjoys it. It's so exciting to me because I get to meet wonderful people and people who just want good government." She left a Carter Work Project in Texas to return to Georgia early to encourage people to vote for her grandson.[19] Incumbent Republican governor Nathan Deal defeated Carter 52.8 percent to 44.8 percent.[20] Republicans have served as governor of Georgia since January 2003. Jack Carter, father of Jason and the eldest son of Jimmy and Rosalynn, ran unsuccessfully for the U.S. Senate in Nevada in 2006.

JIMMY AND ROSALYNN CARTER have supported several different efforts to attract tourists to Plains, Sumter County, and southwest Georgia. The SAM Shortline Railroad has been a pet project. The railroad opened to travelers in 2002. The train, with vintage 1949 rail cars, runs along the route of the old Savannah, Americus and Montgomery (SAM) Railroad. Jimmy Carter worked to get the railroad for years and rode the train during the dedication ceremony. He and Rosalynn have periodically taken trips on the line, with the trips usually being announced several months in advance. The train typically runs two to three times a week during most of the year.

Railroads had first reached Sumter County in 1854. In 1999–2000, the Georgia Department of Transportation bought 177 miles of the SAM railroad. Today the train makes several stops and generally travels from Cordele to Plains and Americus areas.[21] The main line operates under the auspices of the Heart of Georgia Railway under contract with the Georgia Department of Natural Resources.

THE CARTERS SUPPORT TOURISM and development efforts in Americus and elsewhere in southwest Georgia. On June 15, 2010, Jimmy and Rosalynn Carter joined the owners of the Best Western Plus Windsor Hotel, Mr. and Mrs. Sharad Patel, for the grand reopening of the hotel. Built in 1892, the Victorian structure hosted Franklin Delano Roosevelt in February 1928 when he spoke at an Americus Chamber of Commerce event. He came south from Warm Springs, Georgia, and gave the talk before being elected governor of New York. The hotel closed in the early 1970s. Only a restaurant on the ground floor remained open and the hotel was given to the city. In 1980, Americus government officials had to decide between tearing down the hotel and having a new parking lot in the downtown area or restoring the hotel. They chose to restore the building and the hotel reopened in 1991. The Patels have owned the hotel for over two decades. President and Mrs. Carter have stayed in the Carter Presidential Suite in 2002 and 2010. Carter celebrated his seventy-fifth birthday there and at the nearby Rylander Theatre. Both Carters were honored with a birthday celebration in 2019 followed by a concert at the First Baptist Church of Americus.

JIMMY CARTER HAS BEEN A BASEBALL FAN SINCE HIS YOUTH.
He shared his enthusiasm for the sport with Fidel Castro, leader of Cuba from 1959 until 2011. In May 2002, Carter became the first president of the United States, in or out of the office, to visit Cuba since the communist revolution that put Castro in power. Jimmy and Rosalynn Carter led a Carter Center mission, spending several days in the country trying to improve understanding between the people and governments of the United States and Cuba. Carter gave a speech at the University of Havana that was carried live on television and radio. Immediately afterward, he attended the Cuban all-star game at the Latin American Stadium and joined Castro at the mound to throw out the ceremonial first pitch. This also was carried live on television and radio.[22]

In his youth, duties on the farm during spring sometimes interfered with Carter getting to play baseball. He played in Archery and in pickup games. Farm work meant that he could not try out for the Plains High School baseball team. He has supported the Atlanta Braves since the team moved to Georgia in 1966. His mother cheered the Dodgers because she liked the fact that they drafted Jackie Robinson, the African American native of Cairo, Georgia, who integrated professional baseball in 1947. Governor Carter got to shake Hank Aaron's hand the day he broke the national league record for most home runs. Jimmy and Rosalynn have attended games through the years and have been captured on kiss cams on occasion. Carter threw out the ceremonial first pitch in game six of the World Series in 1995. That night the Braves won the World Series. They played in the series the next year but have not brought the pennant home again. At games, Carter does not want his enjoyment of the event interrupted by the media, so discussions with the press generally happen before or after the game.[23]

Jimmy Carter hosted several concerts by musicians from Georgia and
the South. In the spring of 2016, Carter, a member of the Mercer
University Board of Trustees, congratulated Rock and Roll Hall of
Famer Gregg Allman on receiving an honorary doctorate. Carter
delighted in paying the rock icon back for the support he received
during his presidential campaign. The Allman Brothers Band spent
their early years in Macon. Allman performed and wrote many of the
band's biggest hits. Mercer president William D. Underwood stands to
the right of Carter and Allman.

Carter told the crowd that he was indebted to the band. "When
the Allman brothers, back in 1976, adopted me and began to let the
nation know that I was okay with them, most people said, 'Well, if
he's okay with the Allman Brothers then he must be qualified to be
president.'"[24] Carter drew laughs from the graduation audience while
he referenced lyrics in the song "Don't Stand in My Way" by Gregg
Allman. He assured the audience that the Allman Brothers made
a big difference in his election. Hamilton Jordan had known Phil
Walden of Capricorn Records in Macon since his high school days.
He called on his old friend twenty years later. Jordan later wrote,
"Phil—at the very top of his profession—was responsible for intro-
ducing Jimmy Carter to the music and entertainment industry. . . .
Phil's advocacy of Carter helped to overcome some of the stereotypes
of Carter, the Baptist."[25] Concerts by the Allman Brothers and Willie
Nelson also helped greatly with fundraising for the Carter presiden-
tial campaign in 1975 and 1976.

The university noted that Allman received the award "in recognition of a truly extraordinary accomplishment in creative work."[26]
Allman became only the third musician to receive an honorary doctorate from Mercer. He died a year later at the age of sixty-nine.

ON MAY 2, 2013, Georgia Southwestern State University honored Rosalynn Carter by dedicating a statue of her at the Rosalynn Carter Health and Human Services Complex. Two days later, President Carter introduced his grandson Jason as the commencement speaker. Rosalynn graduated from GSW in 1946 with a two-year degree and Jimmy spent his first year in college there before going to Georgia Tech and the Naval Academy. The library at GSW is named for his father, James Earl Carter. Some 320 students shared their graduation day with Jimmy and Jason Carter.

The complex consists of two buildings and serves as home to the Rosalynn Carter Institute for Caregiving and the GSW Department of Psychology and Sociology. The building houses art classrooms, clinical space for the School of Nursing, the University Health Center, and a display documenting her long commitment to caregiving and advocating for mental health awareness. The ribbon cutting included Chancellor Hank Huckaby of the University System of Georgia and GSW president Dr. Kendall Blanchard. Artists Don Haugen and Teena Stern, a husband-and-wife team out

of Marietta, sculpted the bronze statue. The base of the sculpture is made from keystone blue granite mined in Elberton, Georgia. The statue of Mrs. Carter has her holding a copy of her book *First Lady from Plains* on her lap.

Established in 1988, the Rosalynn Carter Institute for Caregiving supports family, volunteer, and professional caregivers through advocacy, education, research, and service. Each year, the institute recognizes individuals or organizations with the Rosalynn Carter Leadership in Caregiving Award. They also give John and Betty Pope Fellowships and Scholarships to support students pursuing degrees in fields related to caregiving.

JIMMY CARTER SIGHTINGS generate excitement, especially in Georgia and the South. People go to Plains hoping to see him, but spotting him on airplanes, in fast food restaurants, or at performances brings a surprise. In June 2016, Jimmy, Rosalynn, daughter Amy, and one of her sons went to the Atlanta Botanical Gardens, where the president and his grandson are seen enjoying the monumental glass installations of artist Dale Chihuly. The Carters have also been spotted and photographed having lunch at a Chick-fil-A in Columbus and attending a Cirque du Soleil production in Atlanta. Though these occasions appear to have been spontaneous, they usually require careful orchestration by the Secret Service. During the 2016 Christmas holidays, the Carters and several family members visited the Little White House in Warm Springs and then saw the Fantasy in Lights at nearby Callaway Gardens. For both events, staff delayed tours by the general public so that the president, his family, and security could visit with some privacy.[27]

JIMMY CARTER HAD MUCH TO CELEBRATE when he turned ninety-two on October 1, 2016. Just fourteen months earlier, he announced that he had melanoma which had spread to his brain. After receiving a treatment of targeted radiation and a newly developed immunotherapy drug, he happily told his Sunday school class five months later, on March 7, 2016, that doctors had proclaimed him to be cancer free. Given that his parents and siblings all died of cancer, he did not necessarily expect to be around to celebrate his ninety-second birthday. He told an audience at the Carter Center before his birthday that "I'm gonna stay home with my wife. . . . Whenever Rosalynn and I are off somewhere, our main wish is to go back home to Plains, where there are others waiting for us and where we can be together in solitude." Betty Cantrell, recently Miss America, and the David Osborne Trio joined Carter at a birthday celebration at the First Baptist Church of Americus. Cantrell, a native of Warner Robins, won the Miss Georgia pageant before being named Miss America 2016. David Osborne has performed at the White House several times and is known as "Pianist for the Presidents."[28]

IN ADDITION TO PROMOTING HISTORIC SITES in Plains and southwest Georgia, the Carters have helped members of the Plains Historical Preservation Trust revive the Plains Chautauqua programs, beginning in 2008. The weekend events are patterned after tent Chautauquas held by Miss Julia Coleman from the 1920s to 1950s at Plains High School. Carter remembered that "I think that one person that affected my life . . . was Miss Julia Coleman. . . . She was an extraordinary teacher." She "expanded my life in a cultural sense as a child far beyond what would ordinarily be expected in a very isolated rural community."[29] Generally held twice a year, the Chautauquas are similar to ones historically held in New York State and elsewhere. They feature a variety of sessions and speakers, usually around a general theme. The goal is to educate and to highlight Plains history. The program in fall 2016 featured sessions on Rosalynn Carter and butterfly gardening, Franklin D. Roosevelt in Georgia (complete with a trip to the Little White House and the Roosevelt Warm Springs Institute for Rehabilitation and Specialty Hospitals), and a visit and comments by Bill Gates.[30] Organizers sometimes include time for participants to have photographs made with Jimmy and Rosalynn Carter and perhaps to have them sign their latest books.

JIMMY CARTER SIGNED HIS NAME IN WET CONCRETE at Georgia Southwestern for the second time on September 22, 2017. On February 13, 1942, in the midst of World War II, Carter joined three other freshmen in signing a concrete plaque on the driveway of the Wheatley Administration Building. Campus officials chose the young men because they possessed strong leadership skills. Carter attended classes and served as a chemistry lab assistant for Dr. L. R. Towson, a longtime GSW professor who taught physics, chemistry, and astronomy. The etching with the four names remained in the driveway until 2014, when school officials moved the section of concrete for long-term preservation. On the same day, GSW officials dedicated its new Presidential Plaza at the entrance to campus, near the site where Carter had first signed his name in concrete.

GSW president Neal Weaver proclaimed, "I doubt there was anyone there in 1942 that thought we would be here in 2017, or what the impact of one of those individuals would be. You never know how far your impact may reach." Carter told the group, "I'm very grateful for what [the college] did for me, getting me started in my academic life."[31] Carter lived in a dorm during his time at GSW and immersed himself in life on campus. Three years later, Rosalynn commuted to campus each day while living at home.

THE ROSALYNN CARTER BUTTERFLY TRAIL, a free-membership organization, commissioned Jordan Walker to create this painting of Rosalynn Carter as a child, which incorporates monarch butterflies and flowers. This was presented to Mrs. Carter in celebration of her ninety-second birthday in August 2019. The butterfly trail originated from conversations between Rosalynn Carter and her friend and neighbor Annette Wise. Mrs. Carter had learned of the struggling monarch butterfly population and the threatened migration between North America and Mexico. The removal of milkweed plants from farms and fields has been a primary cause of the declining population. Rosalynn sought advice from Annette about the best native plants to use in her garden to attract and feed the monarchs. Soon other neighbors learned of the plan and gradually the butterfly trail grew, one yard and garden at a time. Today, many people and organizations from around the South and the world have become members of the Rosalynn Carter Butterfly Trail. The trail sponsors a spring symposium each year in Plains and brings in speakers.[32]

CHAPTER 9

Legacy

JIMMY CARTER, a product of a small town in the segregated South, started his political career the same way thousands of people across the country do: by serving on local government boards and in civic clubs. He sat on the Sumter County School Board in the 1950s and 1960s when integration became a hot topic in the years after *Brown v. Board of Education*. Then he assumed a seat on a newly created area planning and development commission. In 1965, Carter and other members of the West Central Georgia Area Planning and Development Commission looked at a contract for clearing stumps from Lake Blackshear. Shown are, left to right, Jack Hamilton, Crisp County representative, Justin Allen, a commission employee, Jimmy Carter, representing Sumter County, and Glenn Woodward of the State Planning Bureau. The commissions, which began to be established in Georgia in the early 1960s, served as multicounty and intergovernmental planning and development agencies.

Carter has had several different career paths. For many years, he hoped and prayed to make the navy a career. Then he and Rosalynn, who he had known almost his entire life, moved back with their sons to Georgia in 1953 and he took over the family peanut farm and peanut warehouse business. Like his father Earl and his mother Lillian, he always worked hard. Carter joined the Plains Lions Club, a civic organization, and eventually served as a district governor in Georgia.

In 1962, he ran for and eventually won a seat in the Georgia Senate representing Sumter County. The South had started to slowly move into the modern world. The civil rights movement was beginning to have an impact on politics and society. He later talked about early challenges in the state legislature in the 1960s:

So, this was a time of transition. I never did anything that was courageous about integration, but it was on my conscience and on my mind and that's one of the things that I tried to do when I got to the State Senate. We had a vote in the Senate quite early on the—you might remember the horrible "thirty questions" we used to ask in order to qualify for votes, to vote, registration. If a white person came into the voter registrar's office, they would be given a perfunctory approval. If a black person came in, they would ask him thirty questions that you couldn't answer today, I mean they were fine technicalities on Georgia constitutional law. It was impossible to answer them. So the Senate took the leadership. I made my first speech in the Senate to try to do away with those "thirty questions," and we were successful. There was a national program to outlaw lynching. It seems ridiculous now. This was in the early sixties and the Senate voted almost unanimously to do away with permission for lynching. . . . This was a formative stage of transition.[1]

Carter lost the first time he ran for governor of Georgia in 1966 but won a tough race four years later. In his inaugural address, he announced that the time for racial inequality was over and others began to take note of the south Georgian. He established a commission that had a portrait of Martin Luther King Jr. painted and hung in the capitol. Thirty years later, when he received the Nobel Peace Prize, he mentioned his fellow Georgian and fellow Nobel Prize winner Martin Luther King Jr. He also recognized his own role as a transitional figure between the old segregated South and the modern world. "On a personal note, it is unlikely that my own political career beyond Georgia would ever have been possible without the changes brought about by the civil rights movement in the southern part of our country and throughout our nation."[2]

IN 1976, he won election as president of the United States, the first man from the Deep South elected to the office in 128 years. By 1972, he had set his sights on the presidency, and on January 20, 1977, he was sworn in as the thirty-ninth president. He and Vice President Walter Mondale had several major successes, including the Camp David Accords and the subsequent peace treaty between Egypt and Israel, the Alaska National Interest Lands Conservation Act of 1980, and establishing the U.S. Department of Energy and Department of Education. He also worked to shift control of the Panama Canal to the people of Panama and to protect the environment. During his last years in office, the economy suffered through high inflation and then Iranian students took U.S. citizens as hostages. He lost his bid for reelection to Republican Ronald Reagan.

Jimmy and Rosalynn Carter decided to return to tiny Plains, Georgia. He had an obligation to establish the Jimmy Carter Presidential Library, and this meant fundraising. He soon decided that they would also develop the Carter Center, a nongovernmental organization with a mission to "wage peace, fight disease, [and] build hope."[3] He soon accepted an appointment with Emory University and built his library and the Carter Center near the school. Jimmy and Rosalynn also got involved with Habitat for Humanity and have worked hard ever since to help provide adequate housing to needy people. Within two or three years of returning to the South, many of the future activities of Jimmy and Rosalynn Carter had been set in place.

Dr. James Laney has said that Emory has greatly benefitted from the presence of the Carters. He noted that the legacy of the Carter Center cannot be written for many more years, since the center is involved in so many different things. As for

Carter himself, he reports that "I used to introduce Jimmy Carter as the first president to use the presidency as a stepping stone" to further humanitarian accomplishments. He added, "I think his legacy isn't just at Emory. We share it with the country."[4]

Walter Mondale considers one of the greatest legacies of Jimmy Carter to be "the role of the Carter Administration in transitioning the United States. Carter helped pull our country together. We've always been divided North and South, at great expense to our country. He changed that. There is still a problem, but it is much more manageable than it used to be. Carter took the tension out of our federal relationships. Even though southerners tend to be quite different from the northerners that I knew, we can communicate, we can get along. We are able to understand each other. That is a big victory for our country."[5]

IN THE 1980S, the Carters had time to reconnect with their family and the people of Plains and the South. They joined a fairly new church, Maranatha Baptist Church, which had split off from Plains Baptist. For the next four decades, Carter taught Sunday school there an average of twice a month. Three to four hundred or more people turn out each time to hear him give the lessons and to hear his testimony. In order to assure their seat inside the church, people sometimes start gathering as early as the afternoon before the service—as much as eighteen hours early. Carter has cut grass and built furniture for the church, while Rosalynn has helped clean the building. The Carters do whatever they can to help their church. Thousands of people, including these young Rotary Youth Leadership Academy attendees in 1996, have had their photographs made with the Carters after attending the worship services. Georgia high school students attend RYLA in Americus each summer to learn leadership skills they will carry with them for life. In 1996, these students attended Maranatha Church services on Sunday and then helped renovate a home with Habitat for Humanity in Americus on Monday.

The Carters also worked to establish the Plains Inn, a bed and breakfast in town. They lobbied Congress and the National Park Service to get the Jimmy Carter National Historic Site established in Plains, which includes a renovated Plains High School and a visitors' center. Through the years, the Carters have supported a variety of projects in Plains and Sumter County, including the SAM Shortline excursion railroad.

JIMMY CARTER HAS AUTHORED thirty-two books and given countless interviews through the years. His books about growing up and his early political battles give a better understanding of life in the rural South during much of the twentieth century and about the struggles that whites and blacks faced in trying to be friends and work together during those years. He has written a fictional account of the Revolutionary War and a book of poetry. Other books have focused on American values and the situation in the Middle East and the Holy Land. He has also examined aging, life at ninety, and sharing good times with your spouse (a book that created much tension for the couple while they coauthored it). Rosalynn has authored books about life in Plains and about caring for those with mental illness. Through their books alone, they are leaving an extensive legacy of documenting life and values in the world.

ANDY YOUNG visited with Jimmy Carter and Pastor Tony Lowden at Maranatha Baptist Church in August 2019. Lowden, who has memorabilia from the 1976 election just behind him, became the pastor earlier that year. Young and Carter have been friends since the early 1970s. Young served as a minister in Congregational churches in south Georgia in the 1950s and first came to national attention as executive director of the Southern Christian Leadership Conference and as an aide to Martin Luther King Jr. during the civil rights protests of the 1960s.[6] Carter appointed Young as ambassador to the United Nations, a position he resigned from in 1979 because of issues with Israel and Palestine. Through it all, the men have remained friends. Similarly, Carter has remained friends with Walter Mondale, his vice president, and with Dr. James Laney, who recruited him to Emory University in 1982. Carter sets an example of the importance and value of keeping close personal connections through the years.

JIMMY AND ROSALYNN CARTER leave the podium at a Habitat for Humanity event in Biloxi, Mississippi, in 2008. Married for seventy-three years in 2019, the Carters hold the record for the longest marriage of a presidential couple. Even more important is the fact that theirs has been a true partnership. They have both grown in the marriage. She transitioned from being a shy housewife and mother to a business partner and then to a woman who spoke at political rallies and conferences about issues of concern. She has fought hard to help ease the stigma of having mental illness and to recognize the strength needed to be a caregiver to the elderly or those with disabilities. She has also learned how to swing a hammer and work at Habitat building sites. Her activities at Carter Work Projects helped lead to the creation of Women Build projects by Habitat and to greater recognition that women and children most often suffer from inadequate housing. The Carters have been the best-known volunteers of Habitat for Humanity for over thirty-five years. They have worked on many homes in the United States and fourteen foreign countries. They have also inspired many other people to volunteer for Habitat and other causes.

THE CARTER CENTER began to operate in its new building on the grounds next to the Jimmy Carter Presidential Library and Museum in 1986. Through the years, the Carters and Carter Center staff have monitored elections and worked for greater democracy and better government in the world. They have also fought disease and worked to improve life for people in more than eighty countries around the globe.

In 2015, Carter announced to the world that he had been diagnosed with melanoma and would begin treatment. His parents and siblings had all died from cancer and many feared the worst. Before the year ended, he reported that doctors considered him to be cancer free. Though melanoma typically occurs on the skin, the cancer can show up elsewhere in the body. For Carter, cancer was found on his liver. He underwent surgery followed by radiation treatments that targeted four small lesions found on his brain. Throughout his treatment, Carter generally felt well and continued most of his planned activities.

Attorney and former state senator Jason Carter, grandson of Jimmy and Rosalynn, became chairman of the Board of Trustees of the Carter Center in November 2015, after having served on the board for six years. Jason stated, "I am honored to have this opportunity to help further the mission of the Carter Center to wage peace, fight disease, and build hope. Millions of people in the poorest nations have better lives and hope for a better future because of the effective, action-oriented work of The Carter Center."[7]

In 2018, with the death of President George H. W. Bush, Jimmy Carter became the oldest living former president. Carter has an important legacy as a champion of human rights and of bringing human rights into political consideration. The 2002 Nobel Peace Prize recognized Carter for his devotion to improving human rights.

Through all these activities and much more, Jimmy Carter has created a legacy of an active man. He and Rosalynn could have retired anywhere they wanted, but they chose to come back home, back to the South which nurtured them. The proud southerners have continued to work for the betterment of their area.

NOTES

Introduction

1. *1980 Census of Population*, vol. 1, "Georgia," https://www2.census.gov/library/publications/decennial/1980/volume-1/georgia/1980a_gaabc-01.pdf.
2. Rosalynn Carter, *First Lady from Plains*, 10.
3. Jimmy Carter, *Remarkable Mother*, 21–22.
4. "Jimmy Carter Genealogical Information," Jimmy Carter Presidential Library and Museum, https://www.jimmycarterlibrary.gov/about_us/genealogical_information; Jeff Carter, *Ancestors of Jimmy and Rosalynn Carter*, 57–60, 89–91.
5. Rosalynn Carter, *First Lady from Plains*, 1.
6. Archery, Georgia, historical marker, Georgia Historical Markers, http://www.georgiaplanning.com/hm/ViewMarker.aspx?DCA_ID=2514.
7. Jimmy Carter, *Why Not the Best?*, 29–30.
8. Jimmy Carter, interview with Gary M. Fink.
9. Plains Historical Preservation Trust, *History of Plains, Georgia*, 74.
10. Rosalynn Carter, *First Lady from Plains*, 13.
11. Georgia School of Technology was renamed Georgia Institute of Technology in 1948.
12. Jimmy Carter, *Full Life*, 67.
13. Jimmy Carter gives an in-depth look at that election in *Turning Point*.
14. See Bourne, *Jimmy Carter*, 149–53.
15. Mazlish and Diamond, *Jimmy Carter*, 147.
16. B. Drummond Ayres Jr., "1976 Surprise: Carter Is Running Well," *New York Times*, December 26, 1975, https://www.nytimes.com/1975/12/26/archives/1976-surprise-carter-is-running-well-carter-is-running-well-for.html.
17. Miller, *National Party No More*, 208–9.
18. Jimmy Carter, "Inaugural Address, January 12, 1971," Jimmy Carter Presidential Library and Museum, https://www.jimmycarterlibrary.gov/assets/documents/inaugural_address_gov.pdf, 1–2.
19. For more information, see Woodward and Bernstein, *Final Days*.
20. Eizenstat, *President Carter*, 26–27.
21. Fink, "Jimmy Carter (b. 1924)," *New Georgia Encyclopedia*, last edited August 10, 2018, https://www.georgiaencyclopedia.org/articles/government-politics/jimmy-carter-b-1924.
22. Jimmy Carter, *Keeping Faith*, 573–74.
23. Ibid., 574.
24. Mark K. Updegrove, "An Intimate Chat with Jimmy and Rosalynn Carter," *Parade*, November 2, 2013, https://parade.com/220733/markupdegrove/an-intimate-chat-with-jimmy-and-rosalynn-carter/.
25. Jimmy Carter, *Keeping Faith*, 581–82.
26. Lewis Grizzard, "For Fans, 'This One is Forever,'" *Atlanta Constitution*, January 2, 1981.

27. Maxine Reese, interview with Ed Bearss, National Park Service (NPS), December 17, 1985.

28. Betty and John Pope, interview with Jim Small, NPS, June 28, 1989.

29. Jimmy Carter, *Keeping Faith*, 575.

30. Jimmy Carter, *Beyond the White House*, 4.

31. Gulley, *Academic President as Moral Leader*, 174–76.

32. Slavicek, *Jimmy Carter*, 12.

33. "Carter Work Project," Habitat for Humanity, https://www.habitat.org/volunteer/build-events/carter-work-project.

Chapter 1. Early Years

1. Jimmy Carter, interview with Ed Bearss, National Park Service (NPS), May 11, 1988.

2. Jimmy Carter, *Faith*, 71–72. In 1994, the home of Annie Mae Rhodes flooded during Tropical Storm Alberto. Within a few days, relief volunteers learned that Annie Mae had once worked for the Carters. She did not want to bother Jimmy Carter, who was in Japan, but the volunteers wrote him about the problem. Carter and other Habitat for Humanity volunteers soon built a new home for Annie Mae and her brother.

3. Jimmy Carter, *An Hour before Daylight*, 31.

4. Jimmy Carter, NPS interview.

5. Archery, Georgia, Historical Marker, Georgia Historical Markers, http://www.georgiaplanning.com/hm/ViewMarker.aspx?DCA_ID=2514.

6. Jimmy Carter, NPS interview.

7. Jimmy Carter, *An Hour before Daylight*, 70.

8. Jimmy Carter, *Why Not the Best?*, 7; ellipsis in original.

9. Jimmy Carter, NPS interview.

10. Jimmy Carter, NPS recording, February 4, 2015, https://www.nps.gov/media/video/view.htm?id=603FCF81-1DD8-B71C-073B49D6D258049B.

11. Carter, *An Hour before Daylight*, 92.

12. Ibid., 100–101.

13. Jimmy Carter, NPS interview.

14. Carter, *An Hour before Daylight*, 189.

15. Jimmy Carter, NPS interview.

16. Jimmy Carter, *An Hour before Daylight*, 189–90.

17. Steven H. Hochman, interview with the author, April 22, 2019.

18. Tartan and Hayes, *Miss Lillian and Friends*, 243.

19. Jimmy Carter, NPS interview.

20. Jimmy Carter, *Why Not the Best?*, 27–29.

21. Jimmy Carter, *An Hour before Daylight*, 146–48.

22. Jimmy Carter, *Why Not the Best?*, 18.

23. Jimmy Carter, NPS interview.

24. Jimmy Carter, NPS interview.

25. Carter used this quote at his presidential inaugural address in 1977 and his Nobel Peace Prize lecture in 2002. See https://www.jimmycarterlibrary.gov/assets/documents/speeches/inaugadd.phtml; and https://www.jimmycarterlibrary.gov/about_us/nobel_peace_prize_lecture.

26. Jimmy Carter, NPS interview.

27. Joiner, *History of Public Education in Georgia*, 335.

28. Jimmy and Rosalynn Carter, NPS interviews; Jimmy Carter, *An Hour before Daylight*, 217.

29. Jonathan Alter, "The Carters' Platinum Anniversary," *New Yorker*, August 1, 2016, https://www.newyorker.com/magazine/2016/08/01/the-carters-platinum-anniversary.

30. Rosalynn Carter, NPS interview.

31. Ibid.

32. Jimmy Carter, Omicron Delta Kappa interview, Georgia Tech, March 30, 1984.

33. Jimmy Carter, NPS interview.

34. Jimmy Carter, Omicron Delta Kappa interview.

35. "In Memoriam," *Blue Print*, Georgia Tech Yearbook, 1943.

36. Haugabook, *Remembering Plains*, 63.

37. Rosalynn Carter, *First Lady from Plains*, 15, 18.

38. "Jimmy Carter's Naval Service," Jimmy Carter Presidential Library and Museum, https://www.jimmycarterlibrary.gov/about_us/naval_service.

39. Jimmy Carter, NPS interview.

40. Jimmy Carter, *Why Not the Best?*, 57–58.

41. Plains Historical Preservation Trust, *History of Plains, Georgia*, 315.
42. Jimmy Carter, *Why Not the Best?*, 58.
43. Carter, NPS interview.
44. Jimmy Carter, interview with Gary M. Fink.
45. Hugh Carter, *Cousin Beedie and Cousin Hot*, 91; Collins, *Search for Jimmy Carter*, 51.
46. The Plains Historical Preservation Trust now has its office in this unit while the rest of the complex still serves as public housing.
47. Jimmy and Rosalynn Carter, NPS interview.
48. Jimmy Carter, interview with Gary M. Fink.
49. *Brown v. Board of Education*, 347 U.S. 483 (1954).
50. Jimmy Carter, NPS interview.
51. Jimmy Carter, interview with Gary M. Fink.
52. Jimmy Carter, NPS interview.
53. Collins, *Search for Jimmy Carter*, 52.
54. Haugabook, *Remembering Plains*, 24.
55. John William "Jack" Carter, interview with Martin Elzy, Carter Library Oral History Project, June 25, 2003.

Chapter 2. Georgia Politics

1. Michael, *Jimmy Carter as Educational Policymaker*, 11.
2. Sara Rimer, "Enjoying the Ex-Presidency? Never Been Better," *New York Times*, February 16, 2000, https://www.nytimes.com/2000/02/16/jobs/enjoying-the-ex-presidency-never-been-better.html.
3. Rosalynn Carter, *First Lady from Plains*, 44-45.
4. Jimmy Carter, interview with Gary M. Fink.
5. Jimmy Carter, Town Hall Meeting, The Carter Presidency: Lessons for the 21st Century, January 20, 2007.
6. Jimmy Carter, *Turning Point*, 180-82.
7. Jimmy Carter, interview with Gary M. Fink.
8. Jimmy Carter, interview, Omicron Delta Kappa Collection.
9. Balmer, *Redeemer*, 21–22.
10. Jimmy Carter, *Faith*, 96.
11. Glad, *Jimmy Carter*, 111.
12. Hargrove, *Jimmy Carter as President*, 5.
13. Hal Gulliver, "On Remembering Pinkie Masters," *Atlanta Constitution*, November 16, 1977.
14. Dash Coleman, "Jimmy Carter Plaque Back in Savannah's Pinkie Masters on St. Patrick's Day," *Savannah Morning News*, March 17, 2017, https://www.savannahnow.com/news/st-patricks-day/2017-03-17/jimmy-carter-plaque-back-savannah-s-pinkie-masters-st-patrick-s-day.
15. Stapleton, *Brother Billy*, 101.
16. James F. Cook, "Carl Sanders (1925–2014)," *New Georgia Encyclopedia*, last edited July 13, 2018, https://www.georgiaencyclopedia.org/articles/government-politics/carl-sanders-b-1925.
17. Gary M. Fink, "Jimmy Carter (b. 1924)," *New Georgia Encyclopedia*, last edited August 10, 2018, https://www.georgiaencyclopedia.org/articles/government-politics/jimmy-carter-b-1924.
18. "Carter Sharecropper Houses Are Opened for Inspectors," *Atlanta Constitution*, September 17, 1970.
19. Morris Shelton, "No Land Baron or Slaver, Carter Says," *Atlanta Journal*, September 20, 1970.
20. Rosalynn Carter, *First Lady from Plains*, 66–67.
21. Stapleton, *Brother Billy*, 101.
22. Carl E. Sanders, interview with George W. Justice, August 17, 2004, Oral History Documentary Series of Richard B. Russell Library, Atlanta, Georgia.
23. Miller, *National Party No More*, 208–9.
24. Sanders, Oral History Documentary Series.
25. Hugh Carter, interview with Ed Bearss, National Park Service (NPS), December 18, 1985; and Hugh Carter, *Cousin Beedie and Cousin Hot*, 126–27.
26. "Establishment Takes a Licking," *Valdosta Daily Times*, September 24, 1970.
27. Rosalynn Carter, *First Lady from Plains*, 70.
28. Jimmy Carter, "Inaugural Address, January 12, 1971," Jimmy Carter Presidential Library and Museum, https://www

.jimmycarterlibrary.gov/assets/documents/inaugural_address_gov
.pdf, 1–2.

29. Eizenstat, *President Carter*, 29.

30. The design house Mary Matise for Jimmae made the dress
for the First Lady. Rosalynn purchased the gown through Jason's
in Americus. "Rosalynn Carter: First Partner," The First Ladies
at the Smithsonian (online exhibition), National Museum of
American History, Behring Center, http://americanhistory.si.edu
/first-ladies/rosalynn-carter.

31. Jimmy Carter, NPS interview.

32. Eizenstat, *President Carter*, 36.

33. Dave Gilson, "Politicians Kissing Babies: A Short History,"
Mother Jones, January 17, 2012, https://www.motherjones.com
/media/2012/01/politicians-kissing-babies-brief-history.

34. Sam Hopkins and Duane Riner, "Wallace Gets Ovations,"
Atlanta Constitution, February 25, 1972.

35. Hamilton Jordan, Memo to Jimmy Carter, 1972, Governor
Carter's Personal Working Files, 1970–1974, Carter Family
Papers, Jimmy Carter Presidential Library and Museum.

36. Tom Johnson, "Into the Ring, and Just about Out," *New York
Times*, March 28, 1976, 15E.

37. Presidential Correspondence with George C. Wallace, Jimmy
Carter Presidential Library and Museum.

38. Hamilton Jordan, Memo to Jimmy Carter, 1972, Governor
Carter's Personal Working Files.

39. Lance, *Truth of the Matter*, 62.

40. Bo Emerson, "Carter Library Exhibit Tells Story of Georgia's
Film Industry," *Atlanta Journal-Constitution*, May 6, 2019; and
Craig Dominey, "Film Industry in Georgia," *New Georgia
Encyclopedia*, last edited July 9, 2018, https://www
.georgiaencyclopedia.org/articles/arts-culture/film-industry
-georgia.

41. Preface to Brown and Smith, *Flint River*, 15.

42. "Flint River," Georgia River Network, https://garivers.org
/flint-river.

43. Jimmy Carter, *Why Not the Best?*, 117.

44. John Pennington, "The Pine Mountain Battle," *Atlanta
Constitution*, March 19, 1972; "Saving Pine Mountain," *Atlanta
Constitution*, January 22, 1973.

45. Graham, *Just as I Am*, 493.

46. Gibbs and Duffy, *Preacher and the Presidents*, 244; bracketed
text in original.

47. Jimmy Carter, *Faith*, 42.

48. Graham, *Just as I Am*, 493.

49. Gibbs and Duffy, *Preacher and the Presidents*, 249.

50. Gary M. Fink, *Prelude to the Presidency*, 56.

51. "Look at Reorganization Plan Promised Soon," *Atlanta
Constitution*, July 1, 1971, 10a.

52. Jimmy Carter, *Why Not the Best?*, 118.

53. Georgia Historical Records Advisory Council, "2019 Awards,"
[24], https://www.georgiaarchives.org/documents/ghrac/2019
_Awards.pdf.

54. Jen Christensen, "Besting Ruth, Beating Hate," CNN.com,
https://www.cnn.com/interactive/2014/04/us/hank-aaron
-anniversary.

55. Bourne, *Jimmy Carter*, 241.

56. Jimmy Carter, Georgia Law Day address at the University
of Georgia, May 4, 1974, https://www.americanrhetoric.com
/speeches/jimmycarterlawday1974.htm.

57. Bourne, *Jimmy Carter*, 242.

58. Jimmy Carter, *Full Life*, 109.

59. Quoted in Balmer, *Redeemer*, 47–48.

60. Jimmy Carter, *Turning Point*, 63.

61. Hefley and Hefley, *Church That Produced a President*,
198–99.

62. Carter, NPS interview. The issue of blacks being members of
traditionally white churches had been a big one in Americus and
had spread to Plains. See Auchmutey, *Class of '65*.

63. Hugh Carter, *Cousin Beedie and Cousin Hot*, 310–25; Quiros,
God with Us, 183–96.

64. Hugh Carter, *Cousin Beedie and Cousin Hot*, 320–24.

65. Schram, *Running for President*, 54.

1. Jimmy Carter, interview with Ed Bearss, National Park Service (NPS), May 11, 1988, 104–5.
2. "Text of Carter's Address in Washington," *Atlanta Constitution*, December 13, 1974.
3. Jimmy Carter, *Why Not the Best?*, 137.
4. Maxine Reese, NPS interview, December 17, 1985.
5. John and Betty Pope, NPS interview, June 28, 1989.
6. Lee Kinnamon, "History Of The Historic SAM Shortline Railroad," Historic SAM Shortline Railroad, https://samshortline .com/history.
7. Hugh Carter, NPS interview, December 18, 1988.
8. Maxine Reese, NPS interview, December 17, 1985.
9. John and Betty Pope, NPS interview, June 28, 1989.
10. Maxine Reese, NPS interview, December 17, 1985.
11. Padgett, *Jimmy Carter*, xi; Beth Alston, "Leila S. Case—1976: Vivid Memory of History in the Making," *Americus Times-Recorder*, March 8, 2016, https://www.americustimesrecorder .com/2016/03/08/leila-s-case-1976-vivid-memory-of-history -in-the-making.
12. John and Betty Pope, NPS interview, June 28, 1989.
13. Rudy Hayes, NPS interview with Jim Small, June 27, 1989.
14. Bourne, *Jimmy Carter*, 270.
15. John and Betty Pope, NPS interview, June 28, 1989.
16. Hugh Carter, *Cousin Beedie and Cousin Hot*, 216.
17. B. Drummond Ayres Jr., "Billy Carter Loses," *New York Times*, December 7, 1976, https://www.nytimes.com /1976/12/07/archives/billy-carter-loses-blames-antidrinking-vote .html.
18. Leonard Blanton, NPS interviews, December 21, 1985.
19. Ayres, "Billy Carter Loses."
20. Eizenstat, *President Carter*, 42.
21. Bartley, *Jimmy Carter and the Politics of the New South*, 11.
22. "1976 Democratic Party Presidential Primaries," Wikipedia, March 18, 2020, https://en.wikipedia.org/wiki/1976_Democratic _Party_presidential_primaries; Walton, *Native Son Presidential Candidate*, 79.
23. Mondale, *Good Fight*, 157.
24. Ibid., 157–58.
25. Walter Mondale, interview with the author, August 22, 2019.
26. Mondale, *Good Fight*, 164.
27. Walter Mondale, interview with the author, August 22, 2019.
28. Richard Moe, roundtable discussion "The Carter Reforms of the Vice Presidency," The Carter Presidency: Lessons for the 21st Century, January 19, 2007.
29. Chip Carter, quoted in exhibit at Jimmy Carter Presidential Library and Museum, viewed October 17, 2019.
30. Barbara Charline Jordan, "1976 Democratic National Convention Keynote Address," July 12,1976, American Rhetoric, last updated February 13, 2017, https://www.americanrhetoric .com/speeches/barbarajordan1976dnc.html.
31. Bill Kirby, "LBJ's Unfortunate Augusta Visit," *Augusta Chronicle*, October 25, 2014, http://www.lbjlibrary.org/press /lbj-in-the-news/lbjs-unfortunate-augusta-visit.
32. Jimmy Carter, Town Hall Meeting, The Carter Presidency: Lessons for the 21st Century, January 20, 2007.
33. Schram, *Running for President*, 271–73.
34. Douglas E. Kneeland, "Dole Sees Carter at Southern 500," *New York Times*, September 7, 1976, https://www.nytimes .com/1976/09/07/archives/dole-sees-carter-at-southern-500.html.
35. Eizenstat, *President Carter*, 80.
36. Lance, *Truth of the Matter*, 88–89; emphasis in original.
37. Robert Lamb and Fay S. Joyce, "Carter Playboy Talk Starts 'Em Buzzing," *Atlanta Constitution*, September 22, 1976, https://www.ajc.com/news/state—regional-govt—politics /the-time-jimmy-carter-was-interviewed-playboy-about-lust /qYHZQip6pyQF2rB8kxOk4K.
38. Hyatt, *Carters of Plains*, 146.
39. Isaacs, *Jimmy Carter's Peanut Brigade*, 101.
40. Walton, *Native Son Presidential Candidate*, 130; "Jimmy Carter Doing Damage Control for 'Ethnic Purity' Remarks,"

NBC Today Show, NBC, April 9, 1976, NBC Learn, https://archives.nbclearn.com/portal/site/k-12/browse/?cuecard=33592.

41. Rosalynn Carter, *First Lady from Plains*, 70.

42. Ibid., 149–50.

43. Bourne, *Jimmy Carter*, 355.

44. Rosalynn Carter, *First Lady From Plains*, 150.

45. Maxine Reese, NPS interview, December 17, 1985.

46. John and Betty Pope, NPS interview.

47. Walter Mondale, interview with the author, August 22, 2019.

48. Mazlish and Diamond, *Jimmy Carter*, 231.

49. Bethany Nagle, "The Inauguration of Jimmy Carter," White House Historical Association, January 13, 2017, https://www.whitehousehistory.org/the-inauguration-of-jimmy-carter.

50. James Reston, "Revival Meeting," *New York Times*, January 21, 1977.

51. Sally Quinn, "Just Folks," *Atlanta Constitution*, January 21, 1977.

52. Allen and Polmar, *Rickover*, 84–87.

53. Rosalynn Carter, *First Lady from Plains*, 191.

54. Jimmy Carter, NPS interview.

55. Bill Ganzel, "Afghan Boycott," Wessels Living History Farm, https://livinghistoryfarm.org/farminginthe70s/money_06.html.

56. Lance, *Truth of the Matter*, 38.

57. Ibid., 98.

58. Eizenstat, *President Carter*, 134.

59. Walter Mondale, interview with the author, August 22, 2019.

60. Eizenstat, *President Carter*, 134.

61. Eizenstat, *President Carter*, 107.

62. Rosalynn Carter, *Equal Partner in the White House*, 129.

63. Rosalynn Carter, Luncheon Keynote Speech, The Carter Presidency: Lessons for the 21st Century, January 20, 2007.

64. Walter Mondale, interview with the author, August 22, 2019.

65. Jimmy Carter, NPS interview.

66. Jimmy Carter, Omicron Delta Kappa interview.

67. Daily Diary of the President, November 17, 1977, Jimmy Carter Presidential Library and Museum.

68. "Landscapes & Gardens," White House Historical Association, https://www.whitehousehistory.org/landscapes-gardens; "Fall Garden Tours" brochure, October 2012.

69. "Nixon Leaves Exile as Honor to HHH," and "Farewell to Humphrey," *Atlanta Constitution*, January 16, 1978.

70. Andrew Glass, "Willie Nelson Performed for President Jimmy Carter, Sept. 13, 1980," Politico, September 13, 2012, https://www.politico.com/story/2012/09/this-day-in-politics-081124.

71. Scott Kaufman, *Rosalynn Carter*, 105.

72. Ibid., 106.

73. Eizenstat, *President Carter*, 112.

74. Sheryl Vogt, email to author, March 29, 2019.

75. Carole Cadwalladr, "Jimmy Carter: 'We Never Dropped a Bomb. We Never Fired a Bullet. We Never Went to War,'" *Guardian*, September 10, 2011, https://www.theguardian.com/world/2011/sep/11/president-jimmy-carter-interview.

76. Scott Kaufman, *Rosalynn Carter*, 54–60.

77. Rosalynn Carter, Luncheon Keynote Speech, The Carter Presidency: Lessons for the 21st Century, January 20, 2007.

78. Jimmy Carter, *Full Life*, 181.

79. Ernest Dumas, "Bill Clinton (1946–)," CALS Encyclopedia of Arkansas, last updated May 31, 2018, https://encyclopediaofarkansas.net/entries/bill-clinton-95.

80. Brinkley, *Unfinished Presidency*, 353.

81. Steven Hochman, email to author, February 14, 2020.

82. Douglas Brinkley, "Clintons and Carters Don't Mix," *New York Times*, August 28, 1996, https://www.nytimes.com/1996/08/28/opinion/clintons-and-carters-don-t-mix.html.

83. Frances Romero, "A Brief History of Martin Luther King Jr. Day," *Time*, January 18, 2010, http://content.time.com/time/nation/article/0,8599,1872501,00.html.

84. "Text of President Carter's Speech on Martin Luther King, Jr.," *Atlanta Constitution*, January 15, 1979.

85. "The Fall of Andy Young," *Time*, August 27, 1979, http://content.time.com/time/magazine/article/0,9171,920547,00

.html. For more information about this complicated episode, see Eizenstat, President Carter, 845–53.

86. Ann Woolner, "Carter here today for MLK event," *Atlanta Constitution*, January 14, 1979.

87. Eizenstat, *President Carter*, 530.

88. Carter, *Faith*, 116–17.

89. Eizenstat, *President Carter*, 529–30.

90. James Laney, interview with the author, July 17, 2019.

91. Patrick J. Lyons, "Griffin Bell, Ex-Attorney General, Dies at 90." *New York Times*, January 5, 2009, https://www.nytimes.com/2009/01/06/washington/06bell.html.

92. Sharon Bailey, "Carter to Meet Energy Experts," *Atlanta Constitution*, August 29, 1979.

93. Eizenstat, *President Carter*, 238.

94. Jimmy Carter, Omicron Delta Kappa interview.

95. Ibid., 237–39.

96. Sam Donaldson, *Hold On, Mr. President!*, 79–80.

97. Billy Carter and Sybil Carter, *Billy*, 100–101.

98. Rosalynn Carter, Luncheon Keynote Speech, The Carter Presidency: Lessons for the 21st Century, January 20, 2007.

99. Kathryn Cade, interview with Emily Soapes, January 7, 1981, Exit Interview Project, Jimmy Carter Presidential Library and Museum.

100. Rosalynn Carter, *Helping Someone with Mental Health Illness*, 15.

101. William "Buddy" Carter, *Billy Carter*, 178.

102. Bourne, *Jimmy Carter*, 461.

103. Bourne, *Jimmy Carter*, 462.

104. Walter Mondale, interview with the author, August 22, 2019.

105. Rosalynn Carter, *First Lady of Plains*, 347.

106. Jimmy Carter, *Keeping Faith*, 567.

107. Walter Mondale, interview with the author, August 22, 2019.

108. John and Betty Pope, NPS interview, June 28, 1989.

109. Hugh Carter, NPS interview, December 18, 1985.

110. Ibid., 570.

111. Rosalynn Carter, *First Lady from Plains*, 378.

112. Walter Mondale, interview with the author, August 22, 2019.

113. Sam Hopkins, "The Hostage Deal: 'Carter at His Best,'" *Atlanta Constitution*, January 22, 1981.

114. Jimmy Carter, *Keeping Faith*, 14.

115. "Many of His Achievements Overlooked, Pres. Carter Says," *Americus Times-Recorder*, January 5, 1981.

Chapter 4. Post-presidency Begins

1. Rosalynn Carter, *First Lady from Plains*, 377–78.

2. Ibid., 379.

3. Maxine Reese, National Park Service (NPS) interview.

4. Bill Shipp, "A Footnote to Carter's Homecoming," *Atlanta Constitution*, January 22, 1981.

5. Lewis Grizzard, "Jimmy Earl, a Tired, Drained Man," *Atlanta Constitution*, January 21, 1981.

6. "Jimmy Carter House," Historic American Buildings Survey, National Park Service, 1989, https://cdn.loc.gov/master/pnp/habshaer/ga/ga0400/ga0438/data/ga0438data.pdf.

7. Jimmy Carter, *Faith*, 113.

8. Ibid.

9. Rosalynn Carter, NPS interviews.

10. Kevin Sullivan and Mary Jordan, "The Un-Celebrity President," *Washington Post*, August 17, 2018.

11. Jimmy and Rosalynn Carter, NPS interviews.

12. Craig Fehrman, "First Lady Lit," *New York Times*, May 21, 2010, Sunday Book Review, https://www.nytimes.com/2010/05/2/books/review/Fehrman-t.html.

13. Jimmy Carter, *Sharing Good Times*, 161–62.

14. Jimmy Carter, NPS interview.

15. Jimmy Carter, *Sharing Good Times*, 156.

16. Jimmy and Rosalynn Carter, NPS interviews.

17. Jimmy Carter, NPS interview.

18. Rosalynn Carter, *First Lady from Plains*, 378.

19. Rosalynn Carter, NPS interview,

20. Jimmy Carter, NPS interview.

21. Tracy Thompson, "Sadat Pays Neighborly Visit," *Atlanta Constitution*, August 10, 1981; Leslie Phillips, UPI Archives, August 9, 1981.
22. Jimmy Carter, *Negotiation*, 4.
23. Ibid.
24. Jordan survived several bouts of cancer before dying on May 20, 2008.
25. Committee on the Judiciary, United States Senate, *Inquiry into the Matter of Billy Carter and Libya, Hearings before the Subcommittee to Investigate the Activities of Individuals Representing the Interests of Foreign Governments*, August–October 1980, 504, https://babel.hathitrust.org/cgi/pt?id=mdp .39015083099211.
26. Greg McDonald, "Billy Selling Land to Pay IRS Debt," *Atlanta Constitution*, February 15, 1981.
27. Collins, *Search for Jimmy Carter*, 41.
28. "Commissioner Thomas 'Tommy' Irvin, 1969–2011," Georgia Department of Agriculture, http://agr.georgia.gov/tommy-irvin .aspx.
29. Statement released after Thomas Irvin's death, quoted in Russ Bynum, "Tommy Irvin, Longtime Georgia Agriculture Chief, Dies at 88," Associated Press, September 15, 2017, https://apnews.com/bced609a99b8445e92914f320122db4f.
30. J. Merritt Melancon, "Former President Carter Joins Agricultural Hall of Fame," *UGA Today*, November 12, 2018, https://news.uga.edu/president-jimmy-carter.
31. Jimmy Carter, *Keeping Faith*, 596.
32. Max Cleland, interview by Bob Short, May 5, 2009.

Chapter 5. The Carter Center and Emory University
....

1. Jimmy Carter, *Beyond the White House*, 4.
2. Steele Holman, "Carter Museum Gaining Plains Citizens' Backing," *Atlanta Constitution*, January 27, 1981.
3. Jimmy Carter, "Introduction," *Atlanta*, 11.
4. Ken Willis, "Carter Library Is Proposed as Part of Great Park Plan," *Atlanta Constitution*, October 13, 1979.
5. Kimber Williams, "Presidential Leadership Lessons," *Emory News Center*, February 19, 2019, https://news.emory.edu /features/2019/02/presidential-lessons/index.html.
6. James Laney, interview with the author, July 17, 2019.
7. Jimmy Carter, "Foreword," in Laney, *Education of the Heart*, vii.
8. Gulley, *Academic President as Moral Leader*, 135.
9. Ibid., 135–36.
10. James Laney, interview with the author, July 17, 2019.
11. Gail Epstein, "Carter Lobbying for Young's Park Plan," *Atlanta Constitution*, July 10, 1982.
12. James Laney, interview with the author, July 17, 2019.
13. Ibid.
14. Jimmy Carter, "Committee of Scholars Describe the Future without Me," in *Beyond the White House*, 9.
15. James T. Laney Papers, Carter Center Strategic Planning, Box 31, Emory University Archives.
16. Jim Auchmutey, "25 Years of the Carter Center," *Atlanta Journal-Constitution*, October 1, 2007.
17. Metro Digest, Local News, *Atlanta Journal-Constitution*, March 19, 1986.
18. James Laney, interview with the author, July 17, 2019.
19. Jimmy Carter, *Beyond the White House*, 9–11.
20. Brinkley, *Unfinished Presidency*, 211.
21. Slavicek, *Jimmy Carter*, 85.
22. James Laney, interview with the author, July 17, 2019.
23. Jimmy Carter, *Beyond the White House*, 5.
24. "Carter Center Dedicated," *Carter Center News*, Summer 1987, 1.
25. Jimmy Carter, *Beyond the White House*, 7–8.
26. Mrs. Carter and Susan K. Golant wrote *Helping Yourself Help Others* in 1994 and *Helping Someone with Mental Illness* n 1998. Carter, Golant, and Kathryn E. Cade wrote *Within Our Reach* in 2010.
27. Carter Center, *2018 Annual Report*, 27.
28. Rosalynn Carter, *Within Our Reach*, 10.
29. James Laney, interview with the author, July 17, 2019.

30. Emory University, press release, April 15, 1999, http://www .emory.edu/WELCOME/journcontents/archive/univ/tutugen.html.
31. Peter Applebome, "Unofficially, Era of Carter Is Still Here," *New York Times*, May 11, 1989.
32. "Carter Center Celebrates Opening of New Pavilion and Chapel," *Carter Center News*, Fall 1993, https://www .cartercenter.org/documents/1150.pdf.
33. Jimmy Carter, interview with Gary Pomerantz.
34. Emory University History and Traditions, "Timeline: 1833–Present," http://www.emoryhistory.emory.edu/facts-figures/dates /timeline.html#tab4.
35. Jeff Kunerth, "Ex-Soviet Chief on Lecture Trail," *Orlando Sentinel*, May 12, 1992, https://www.orlandosentinel.com/news /os-xpm-1992-05-12-9205120294-story.html.
36. James Laney, interview with the author, July 17, 2019; and Jimmy Carter, *Beyond the White House*, 235.
37. Jill Vejnoska, "Even Carter Can't Defeat Urban Woes," *Atlanta Journal-Constitution*, October 12, 2002.
38. Jimmy Carter, "Introduction," *Atlanta*, 17.
39. Ibid., 241.
40. Ibid., 242.
41. Brinkley, *Unfinished Presidency*, 363.
42. Vejnoska, "Even Carter Can't Defeat Urban Woes."
43. Jimmy Carter, *Beyond the White House*, 244–45.
44. Jimmy Carter Presidential Library and Museum, "Carter Presidential Museum Is All New," news release, January 19, 2010, https:// www.jimmycarterlibrary.gov/assets/documents/news/10-02.pdf.
45. "A Unique Collaboration, Emory University + the Carter Center," Carter Center, YouTube video, https://www.youtube .com/watch?v=Z_dW3rq0P2U.
46. Meredith Hobbs, "Carter: It's Time for U.S. to Abolish the Death Penalty," Southern Center for Human Rights, November 14, 2013, https://www.schr.org/resources /carter_its_time_for_us_to_abolish_the_death_penalty.
47. Jimmy Carter, *A Call to Action*, 37–40.
48. "State by State," Death Penalty Information Center, https:// deathpenaltyinfo.org/state-and-federal-info/state_by_state.
49. "Intern Insights," Carter Center, September 2, 2016, https:// www.cartercenter.org/news/features/cc/intern-insights.html.
50. "Jimmy Carter Speaks to Students at 31st Carter Town Hall," September 13, 2012, http://news.emory.edu/stories/2012/09/mm _carter_town_hall/index.html.
51. "President Carter Granted Tenure at Emory," Conversations with Claire, Emory University, https://news.emory.edu/features /2019/06/conversations-with-claire-carter-tenure.
52. James Laney, interview with the author, July 17, 2019.
53. Steven H. Hochman, email to author, February 19, 2020.

Chapter 6. Habitat for Humanity

1. Jimmy Carter, *Craftsmanship of Jimmy Carter*, 25.
2. Fuller, *No More Shacks!*, 76.
3. Vikas Shah MBE, "How to Change the World," Thought Economics, June 15, 2019, https://thoughteconomics.com/how-to -change-the-world.
4. Fuller, *No More Shacks!*, 75–83.
5. Brinkley, *Unfinished Presidency*, 156–57.
6. Vikas Shah MBE, "How to Change the World."
7. Jim Auchmutey, "The Carters' 25 Years with Habitat," *Atlanta Journal-Constitution*, May 16, 2008.
8. Jeff Hansen, "Birmingham Habitat Project," *Birmingham News*, April 13, 2010, http://blog.al.com/spotnews/2010/04/former _president_jimmy_carter_2.html.
9. Jimmy Carter, *Craftsmanship of Jimmy Carter*, 25.
10. Ibid., 32.
11. Habitat for Humanity, "Carter Work Project in Nepal Canceled Due to Shortage of Fuel and Essential Supplies in the Country," press release, October 5, 2015, https://www.habitat.org /ap/about/newsroom/2015-10-8-Carter-Work-Project-in-Nepal -canceled-due-to-shortage-of-fuel-and-essential-supplies-in-the -country.
12. Steve Glasser, "Clinton and Gore Help Carter Build House," UPI, August 19, 1992, https://www.upi.com/Archives/1992/08/19 /Clinton-and-Gore-help-Carter-build-house/8269714196800/.

13. Ibid.

14. Alexandra Bandon, "An Interview with Jimmy Carter," ThisOldHouse.com, https://www.thisoldhouse.com/ideas/interview-jimmy-carter; and "Memorable Moments with Jay Leno and the Tonight Show," https://www.wplucey.com/2009/05/memorable-moments-with-jay-leno-and-the-tonight-show.html.

15. Fuller, *No More Shacks!*, 89.

16. Charlene Stevenson, "My Thoughts," Charlene's Web Page, http://www.charlenestevenson.com/files/jcwp05-43.gif.

17. Jill Vejnoska, "Jimmy & Rosalynn Carter's 35-Year Habitat History," *Atlanta Constitution*, August 30, 2018, https://www.ajc.com/news/jimmy-rosalynn-carter-year-habitat-history-told-mostly-through-photos/ELK4WsgwSQuywdY1CzCwxK.

18. Jimmy Carter, *Craftsmanship of Jimmy Carter*, 32–34.

19. Jessica Pope, "JCWP comes to a close," *Valdosta Daily Times*, June 2003.

20. Balmer, *Redeemer*, 163.

21. Stuart and Kathleen Gulley, interview with the author, July 10, 2019.

22. Stuart Gulley, "A President in the House," *LaGrange Daily News*, June 14, 2003.

23. Stuart and Kathleen Gulley, interview with the author, July 10, 2019.

24. Gulley, "A President in the House."

25. Clark Howard, "How I Got Involved in Habitat," Clark.com, https://clark.com/story/clark-howard-habitat-for-humanity-history.

26. Mark Bixler, "Ex-Habitat Chief Builds from the Ground Up," *Atlanta Journal-Constitution*, May 24, 2006.

27. Jim Auchmutey, "Faith & Values—Farewell to Fuller," *Atlanta Journal-Constitution*, March 14, 2009.

28. "Habitat for Humanity International Moving Headquarters," *Daily Citizen-News*, Dalton, Georgia, April 20, 2006, https://www.dailycitizen.news/news/habitat-for-humanity-international-moving-headquarters-to-atlanta/article_edf7c258-399f-5f63-81fe-a32c74a8e067.html.

29. Mark Bixler, "Carter Opposes Move by Habitat," *Atlanta Journal-Constitution*, August 25, 2005.

30. Habitat for Humanity, "Habitat for Humanity Dedicates Primary Americus Headquarters Building in Honor of Clarence Jordan," June 6, 2018, Habitat for Humanity Pressroom, https://www.habitat.org/newsroom/2018/habitat-humanity-dedicates-primary-americus-headquarters-building-honor-clarence.

31. "David Letterman, Jimmy Carter Launch Habitat for Humanity Indiana Project," *Chicago Sun-Times*, August 27, 2018, https://chicago.suntimes.com/2018/8/27/18403560/david-letterman-jimmy-carter-launch-habitat-for-humanity-indiana-project.

32. Vejnoska, "Jimmy and Rosalynn Carter's 35-year Habitat History."

33. Auchmutey, "The Carters' 25 Years with Habitat."

Chapter 7. Politics and Awards

1. "July 20," Today in Georgia History, https://www.todayingeorgiahistory.org/content/democratic-national-convention.

2. Robert Reinhold, "4 Presidents Join Reagan in Dedicating His Library," *New York Times*, November 5, 1991, https://www.nytimes.com/1991/11/05/us/4-presidents-join-reagan-in-dedicating-his-library.html.

3. Ibid.

4. Reagan Foundation, "Opening Ceremonies at the Ronald Reagan Presidential Library, 11/4/91," YouTube video, posted October 4, 2012, https://www.youtube.com/watch?time_continue=4683&v=ysqbx_EDxVM.

5. "Governor Zell Miller 1992 Democratic National Convention Keynote Address," July 13, 1992, C-SPAN, https://www.c-span.org/video/?27051-1/governor-zell-miller-1992-democratic-national-convention-keynote-address.

6. Jimmy Carter, interview with Gary M. Pomerantz, March 18, 1993.

7. James Laney, interview with the author, July 17, 2019.

8. Douglas Brinkley, "Clintons and Carters Don't Mix," *New York Times*, August 28, 1996, https://www.nytimes.com/1996/08/28/opinion/clintons-and-carters-don-t-mix.html.

9. Frederick Hart, "Celebrating the 25th Anniversary of the James Earl Carter Presidential Statue," Frederick Hart's website, January 10, 2019, https://frederickhart.wordpress.com/2019/01/10/celebrating-the-25th-anniversary-of-the-james-earl-carter-presidential-statue. Ellipsis in original.

10. "Statue of a Casual Jimmy Carter Is Formally Unveiled in Georgia," *Los Angeles Times*, June 8, 1994, https://www.latimes.com/archives/la-xpm-1994-06-08-mn-1697-story.html.

11. Betty J. Craige, "Delta Prize for Global Understanding," *New Georgia Encyclopedia*, last edited July 23, 2018, https://www.georgiaencyclopedia.org/articles/education/delta-prize-global-understanding.

12. Carter Center, "President Carter Receives Second Annual Fulbright Prize," press release, September 1, 1994, https://www.cartercenter.org/news/documents/doc215.html.

13. William J. Clinton, "Remarks at a Ceremony Presenting the Presidential Medal of Freedom to Former President Jimmy Carter and Rosalynn Carter in Atlanta," August 9, 1999, https://www.govinfo.gov/content/pkg/PPP-1999-book2/pdf/PPP-1999-book2-doc-pg1421.pdf.

14. Mark Bixler, "Carters 'a Force for Good' Everywhere," *Atlanta Constitution*, August 10, 1999.

15. James Laney interview with the author, July 17, 2019.

16. Moni Basu, "Carter Wins Nobel Peace Prize," *Atlanta Journal-Constitution*, October 12, 2002, https://www.ajc.com/news/local/carter-wins-nobel-peace-prize/n3Bc2AQdKobUauu1RJwwPJ/.

17. Ibid.

18. Jimmy Carter, "Nobel Acceptance Statement from President Carter," October 11, 2002, Carter Center, https://www.cartercenter.org/news/documents/doc1084.html.

19. Basu, "Carter Wins Nobel Peace Prize."

20. Bridget Johnson, "How Many U.S. Presidents Have Won the Nobel Peace Prize: Find Out Which of Our Commanders in Chief Held the Honor," ThoughtCo, July 16, 2019, https://www.thoughtco.com/which-presidents-won-nobel-peace-prize-3555573.

21. Jimmy Carter, "2002 Nobel Peace Prize Lecture," December 9, 2002, Carter Center, https://www.cartercenter.org/news/documents/doc1233.html.

22. Steven Feller, "PCU Jimmy Carter Christened at Electric Boat," America's Navy, June 9, 2004, https://www.navy.mil/submit/display.asp?story_id=13696.

23. Jimmy Carter, *Why Not the Best?*, 137.

24. Feller, "PCU Jimmy Carter Christened at Electric Boat."

25. "SSN 23 Jimmy Carter," Deagal.com, http://www.deagel.com/Fighting-Ships/SSN-23-Jimmy-Carter_a000493002.aspx.

26. Kyle Mizokami, "Why a U.S. Navy Spy Submarine Is Flying the Jolly Roger," *Popular Mechanics*, September 14, 2017, https://www.popularmechanics.com/military/weapons/news/a28209/navy-spy-sub-jolly-roger-uss-jimmy-carter.

27. "State Dinner for Chinese President All-American," CBS News, January 19, 2011, https://www.cbsnews.com/news/state-dinner-for-chinese-president-all-american.

28. "Jimmy Carter Honored by Former Opponent Gerald R. Ford's Foundation," mlive.com, June 5, 2017, https://www.mlive.com/news/grand-rapids/2017/06/jimmy_carter_honored_by_former.html.

29. "Medal for Distinguished Public Service 2017," Gerald R. Ford Presidential Foundation, June 5, 2017, https://geraldrfordfoundation.org/medal-distinguished-publi-service-2017.

30. Jill Vejnoska, "Jimmy Carter Wins Award from Former Political Rival Gerald Ford's Foundation," *Atlanta Journal-Constitution*, June 5, 2017.

31. Jimmy Carter, "President Jimmy Carter's Eulogy for President Ford," January 3, 2007, Gerald R. Ford Presidential Library and Museum, https://www.fordlibrarymuseum.gov/grf/Funeral/Carter.asp.

32. "2006 Grammy Winners: 49th Annual Grammy Awards," https://www.grammy.com/grammys/awards/49th-annual-grammy-awards-2006.

33. "Bob Dylan: 2015 MusiCares Person of the Year," GRAMMYs, https://www.youtube.com/watch?v=scjD7h6v2Zc.

34. National Park Service, "President Carter Made Honorary Park Ranger," April 17, 2016, https://www.nps.gov/ever/learn/news/president-carter-made-honorary-national-park-ranger.htm.

35. John Wagner and Felicia Sonmez, "George H. W. Bush Funeral," *Washington Post*, December 5, 2018, https://www.washingtonpost.com/politics/the-state-funeral-for-george-hw-bush-mourners-to-include-all-living-us-presidents/2018/12/05/952dcc72-f87f-11e8-8d64-4e79db33382f_story.html.

Chapter 8. Life in Plains and Georgia

1. *Respectfully Quoted: A Dictionary of Quotations Requested from the Congressional Research Service* (Washington D.C.: Library of Congress, 1989), quoted at Bartleby.com, https://www.bartleby.com/73/1604.html.

2. Flippen, *Jimmy Carter*, 346.

3. Jimmy Carter, interview of Jimmy Carter by Sybil Carter, February 21, 2014, First Person Project, Richard B. Russell Library for Political Research and Studies, http://ohms.libs.uga.edu/viewer.php?cachefile=russell/RBRL324FPP-0042.xml.

4. Nicholas Dawidoff, "The Riddle of Jimmy Carter," *Rolling Stone*, February 2, 2011, http://www.rollingstone.com/politics/news/the-riddle-of-jimmy-carter-20110201.

5. Elliott Minor, "Motorcyclists Will Lead Procession of Jimmy Carter's Sister," *San Bernardino County Sun*, March 6, 1990.

6. William "Buddy" Carter, *Billy Carter*, 8.

7. Jimmy Carter, *Full Life*, 230, 232.

8. Ibid., 54–55; and Jimmy Carter, *Handicrafts of Jimmy Carter*, 24.

9. Plains Historical Preservation Trust, *History of Plains, Georgia*, 149–53.

10. The author attended Sunday services on August 25, 2019. The earliest attendees arrived by 5:30 p.m. or so the day before the service. Arriving at 12:45 a.m., we ended up being in the overflow area until space was found in the church. People arriving by 6:00 a.m. ended up being turned away. Sunday school started at 10:00 a.m. President Carter does not teach Sunday school when he has health problems.

11. Ariail and Heckler-Feltz, *Carpenter's Apprentice*, 118–19.

12. Jimmy Carter, *Craftsmanship of Jimmy Carter*, 2.

13. Ibid., 43.

14. Plains Historical Preservation Trust, *History of Plains, Georgia*, 72–74; and Hamilton Jordan, proposal for a biography of Jimmy Carter, June 2003, 4.

15. Discussions with the author at Plains Chautauqua, August 2019.

16. Gayle White, "Carter Cuts Ties to 'Rigid' Southern Baptists," *Atlanta Journal-Constitution*, October 20, 2000.

17. President Jimmy Carter on 'the Most Serious Violation of Human Rights on Earth,'" interview September 28, 2015, Oprah.com, http://www.oprah.com/own-super-soul-sunday/jimmy-carter-on-leaving-the-southern-baptist-convention-video.

18. Jimmy Carter, "The Words of God Do Not Justify Cruelty to Women," *Observer*, July 12, 2009, available at https://www.cartercenter.org/news/editorials_speeches/observer_071209.html.

19. Joe Adgie, "Former First Lady Returns," *Valdosta Daily Times*, October 10, 2014.

20. "2014 Georgia Governor Election Results," Politico, November 15, 2014, https://www.politico.com/2014-election/results/map/governor/georgia/#.WodUiPZFyM8.

21. Lee Kinnamon, "History of the Historic SAM Shortline Railroad," Historic SAM Shortline Railroad, https://samshortline.com/history-historic-sam-shortline-railroad.

22. Jennifer Lynn McCoy, "Jimmy Carter in Cuba," *Conversation*, August 14, 2015, http://theconversation.com/jimmy-carter-in-cuba-46109.

23. Jeff Denberg, "Sellout! But Jimmy and Lillian Had Tickets," *Atlanta Journal-Constitution*, July 31, 1982.

24. "Former President Jimmy Carter Addresses Mercer Graduates," *Macon Telegraph*, January 29, 2018, https://www.macon.com/news/local/article77677157.html.

25. Jordan, *Boy from Georgia*, 105.

26. "Carter, Allman at Mercer Graduation," *Macon Telegraph*, https://www.macon.com/news/local/article77679512.html; and Jill Vejnoska, "Jimmy Carter Helps Give Gregg Allman Honorary

Degree," *Atlanta Journal-Constitution*, May 17, 2016, https://www.ajc.com/entertainment/music/jimmy-carter-helps-give-gregg-allman-honorary-degree/2QVSkLijeokzHOwY6LwBNL.

27. Jeff Brown interview, July 18, 2018. Brown served in the Georgia legislature from 1994 to 2006 as a Republican. He and his family were surprised in December 2016 when they seemed to be traveling the same route as the Carter family as they visited Warm Springs and Callaway Gardens.

28. Jill Vejnoska, "Jimmy Carter Is Turning 92," *Atlanta Journal-Constitution*, September 30, 2016, https://www.ajc.com/news/jimmy-carter-turning/XjC4NdQHMJckHkBcdukvuJ.

29. Jimmy and Rosalynn Carter, National Park Service interviews.

30. I had the honor of addressing attendees and talking about my book *A President in Our Midst: Franklin Delano Roosevelt in Georgia*. I spoke on the opening night, right after President Carter addressed the group.

31. "President Carter Leaves Mark on GSW at Plaza Dedication Ceremony," Georgia Southwestern State University, September 25, 2017, https://www.gsw.edu/news/index/1747-president-carter-leaves-mark-on-gsw-at-plaza-dedication-ceremony.

32. Rosalyn Carter Butterfly Trail website, https://rosalynncarterbutterflytrail.org.

Chapter 9. Legacy

1. Jimmy Carter, interview with Gary M. Fink.

2. Jimmy Carter, "2002 Nobel Peace Prize Lecture," December 9, 2002, https://www.cartercenter.org/news/documents/doc1233.html.

3. "Our Mission," Carter Center, https://www.cartercenter.org/about/index.html.

4. James Laney, interview with the author, July 17, 2019.

5. Walter Mondale, interview with the author, August 22, 2019.

6. J. Todd Moye, "Andrew Young (b. 1932)," *New Georgia Encyclopedia*, last edited August 10, 2018, https://www.georgiaencyclopedia.org/articles/government-politics/andrew-young-b-1932.

7. "Jason Carter to Chair Carter Center Board," *Carter Center News*, Fall 2015, 3.

SELECTED BIBLIOGRAPHY

Oral Histories

Carter, Jimmy. Interview by Gary M. Fink, February 17, 1987. Series A, Georgia Governors, Georgia Government Documentation Project, Special Collections and Archives, Georgia State University Library.

———. Interview March 30, 1984. Omicron Delta Kappa Collection (MS127), Archives and Special Collections, Library, Georgia Institute of Technology.

———. Interview by Gary Pomerantz, March 18, 1993. Interview transcript, Gary M. Pomerantz Papers, Emory University.

Carter, Jimmy, Jeff Carter, and Jody Powell. Miller Center interviews, 1982.

Cleland, Max. Interview by Bob Short, May 5, 2009. Reflections on Georgia Politics Oral History Collection, ROGP 079, Richard B. Russell Library for Political Research and Studies, University of Georgia Libraries.

Gulley, Stuart, and Kathleen Gulley. Interview with the author, July 10, 2019.

Hochman, Steven H. Interview with the author, April 22, 2019.

Laney, James, Dr. Interview with the author, July 17, 2019.

Mondale, Walter. Interview with the author, August 22, 2019.

National Park Service (Plains, Georgia) interviews, 1985–89. Various interviewees identifies in notes. Transcripts at Carter Library.

Manuscript and Photograph Collections

Emory University Special Collections
Georgia Archives
Georgia State University Special Collections
Hargrett Library
Jimmy Carter Library
Library of Congress
Richard B. Russell Library
Special Collections, Georgia Tech
Troup County Archives

Publications

Allen, Thomas B., and Norman Polmar. *Rickover: Father of the Nuclear Navy*. Washington, D.C.: Potomac Books, 2007.

Ariail, Dan, and Cheryl Heckler-Feltz. *The Carpenter's Apprentice: The Spiritual Biography of Jimmy Carter*. Grand Rapids, Mich.: Zondervan, 1996.

Auchmutey, Jim. *The Class of '65: A Student, a Divided Town, and the Long Road to Forgiveness. New York: PublicAffairs, 2015.*

Balmer, Randall. *Redeemer: The Life of Jimmy Carter*. New York: Basic Books, 2014.

Bartley, Numan V. *Jimmy Carter and the Politics of the New South*. St. Louis, Mo.: Forum Press, 1979.

Bell, Griffin B., with Ronald J. Ostrow. *Taking Care of the Law*. New York: William Morrow, 1982.

Black, Earl, and Merle Black. *The Vital South: How Presidents Are Elected*. Cambridge, Mass.: Harvard University Press, 1992.

Bourne, Peter G. *Jimmy Carter: A Comprehensive Biography from Plains to Post-presidency*. New York: Scribner, 1997.

Brinkley, Douglas. *The Unfinished Presidency: Jimmy Carter's Journey beyond the White House*. New York: Viking, 1998.

Brown, Fred, and Sherri M. L. Smith. *The Flint River: A Recreational Guidebook*. Atlanta, Ga.: CI Publishing, 2001.

Carlson, Jody. *George C. Wallace and the Politics of Powerlessness: The Wallace Campaigns for the Presidency, 1964–1976*. New Brunswick, N.J.: Transaction Books, 1981.

Carter, Billy, and Sybil Carter, with Ken Estes. *Billy: Billy Carter's Reflections on His Struggle with Fame, Alcoholism and Cancer*. Newport, R.I.: Edgehill, 1990.

Carter, Hugh, as told to Frances Spatz Leighton. *Cousin Beedie and Cousin Hot: My Life with the Carter Family of Plains, Georgia*. Englewood Cliffs, N.J.: Prentice-Hall, 1978.

Carter, Jeff. *Ancestors of Jimmy and Rosalynn Carter*. Jefferson, N.C.: McFarland, 2012.

Carter, Jimmy. *Addresses of Jimmy Carter (James Earl Carter), Governor of Georgia: 1971–1975*. Compiled by Frank Daniel. Atlanta, Ga.: B. W. Fortson, Secretary of State, 1975. Distributed by the Georgia Department of Archives and History.

———. *Atlanta: The Right Kind of Courage*. Memphis, Tenn.: Towery, 2000.

———. *Beyond the White House: Waging Peace, Fighting Disease, Building Hope*. New York: Simon & Schuster, 2007.

———. *A Call to Action: Women, Religion, Violence, and Power*. New York: Simon & Schuster, 2014.

———. *The Craftsmanship of Jimmy Carter*. Macon, Ga.: Mercer University Press, 2018.

———. *Faith: A Journey for All*. New York: Simon & Schuster, 2018.

———. *A Full Life: Reflections at Ninety*. New York: Simon & Schuster, 2015.

———. *An Hour before Daylight: Memories of a Rural Boyhood*. New York: Simon & Schuster, 2001.

———. *Keeping Faith: Memoirs of a President*. New York: Bantam Books, 1982.

———. *Negotiation: The Alternative to Hostility*. Macon, Ga.: Mercer University Press, 1984.

———. *A Remarkable Mother*. New York: Simon & Schuster, 2008.

———. *Sharing Good Times*. New York: Simon & Schuster, 2004.

———. *Turning Point: A Candidate, a State, and a Nation Come of Age*. New York: Times Books, 1992.

———. *Why Not the Best?: The First Fifty Years*. Introduction by Douglas Brinkley. Fayetteville: University of Arkansas Press, 1996.

Carter, Rosalynn. *First Lady from Plains*. 1984. Reprint, Fayetteville: University of Arkansas Press, 1994.

Carter, Rosalynn, with Susan K. Golant, *Helping Someone with Mental Illness: A Compassionate Guide for Family, Friends, and Caregivers*. New York: Random House, 1998.

Carter, Rosalynn, with Susan K. Golant and Kathryn E. Cade. *Within Our Reach: Ending the Mental Health Crisis*. Emmaus, Pa.: Rodale, 2010.

Carter, William "Buddy." *Billy Carter: A Journey through the Shadows*. Atlanta, Ga.: Longstreet, 1999.

Collins, Tom. *The Search for Jimmy Carter*. Waco, Tex.: Word Books, 1976.

Cox, Jack F., with the Sumter Historic Preservation Society. *History of Sumter County, Georgia*. Roswell, Ga.: W. H. Wolfe Associates, 1983.

Donaldson, Sam. *Hold On, Mr. President!* New York: Random House, 1987.

Dumbrell, John. *The Carter Presidency: A Re-evaluation*. Manchester, UK: Manchester University Press, 1993.

Eizenstat, Stuart E. *President Carter: The White House Years*. New York: St. Martin's, 2018.

Fink, Gary M. *Prelude to the Presidency: The Political Character and Legislative Leadership Style of Governor Jimmy Carter*. Westport, Conn.: Greenwood, 1980.

Flippen, J. Brooks. *Jimmy Carter, the Politics of Family, and the Rise of the Religious Right*. Athens: University of Georgia Press, 2011.

Fuller, Millard, with Diane Scott. *No More Shacks! The Daring Vision of Habitat for Humanity*. Waco, Tex.: Word Books, 1986.

Gaillard, Frye. *Prophet from Plains: Jimmy Carter and His Legacy*. Athens: University of Georgia Press, 2007.

Gerhardt, Michael J. *The Forgotten Presidents: Their Untold Constitutional Legacy*. New York: Oxford University Press, 2013.

Gibbs, Nancy, and Michael Duffy. *The Preacher and the Presidents: Billy Graham in the White House*. New York: Center Street, 2007.

Glad, Betty. *Jimmy Carter: In Search of the Great White House*. New York: W. W. Norton, 1980.

Godbold, E. Stanly, Jr. *Jimmy and Rosalynn Carter: The Georgia Years, 1924–1974*. New York: Oxford University Press, 2010.

Graham, Billy. *Just as I Am: The Autobiography of Billy Graham*. New York: HarperCollins, 1997.

Gulley, F. Stuart. *The Academic President as Moral Leader: James T. Laney at Emory University, 1977–1993*. Macon, Ga.: Mercer University Press, 2001.

Gulliver, Hal. *A Friendly Tongue*. Macon, Ga.: Mercer University Press, 1984.

Haas, Garland A. *Jimmy Carter and the Politics of Frustration*. Jefferson, N.C.: McFarland, 1992

Hargrove, Erwin C. *Jimmy Carter as President: Leadership and Politics of the Public Good*. Baton Rouge: Louisiana State University Press, 1988..

Haugabook, Allene T. *Remembering Plains in the 1930s, 1940s, 1950s, and a Little Beyond*. N.p.: printed by the author, 1996.

Hayward, Steven F. *The Real Jimmy Carter*. Washington, D.C.: Regnery, 2004.

Hawkins, Ken. *Jimmy Carter: Photographs 1970–2010*. [Lake Oswego, Ore.]: Stumptown Visuals, 2016.

Hefley, James C., and Marti Hefley. *The Church That Produced a President*. New York: Wyden Books, 1977.

Hyatt, Richard. *The Carters of Plains*. Huntsville, Ala.: Strode, 1977.

Isaacs, Harold. *Jimmy Carter's Peanut Brigade*. Dallas, Tex.: Taylor, 1977.

Joiner, Oscar H., gen. ed. *A History of Public Education in Georgia, 1734–1976*. Columbia, S.C.: R. L. Bryan, 1979.

Jones, Charles O. *The Trusteeship Presidency: Jimmy Carter and the United States Congress*. Baton Rouge: Louisiana State University Press, 1988.

Jordan, Hamilton. *A Boy from Georgia: Coming of Age in the Segregated South*. Athens: University of Georgia Press, 2015.

———. *Crisis: The Last Year of the Carter Presidency*. New York: Putnam, 1982.

Kaufman, Burton I. *The Presidency of James Earl Carter, Jr.* Lawrence: University Press of Kansas, 1993.

Kaufman, Scott. *Rosalynn Carter: Equal Partner in the White House*. Lawrence: University Press of Kansas, 2007.

Kessler, Ronald. *In the President's Secret Service*. New York: Three Rivers, 2010.

Lance, Bert. *The Truth of the Matter: My Life in and out of Politics*. New York: Summit Books, 1991.

Laney, James T. *The Education of the Heart: Selected Speeches of James T. Laney*. Edited by Gary S. Hauk and Sandra J. Still. Atlanta, Ga.: Emory University, 1994.

Lesher, Stephan. *George Wallace: American Populist*. Reading, Mass.: Addison-Wesley, 1994.

Mazlish, Bruce, and Edwin Diamond. *Jimmy Carter: A Character Portrait*. New York: Simon and Schuster, 1979.

Meyer, Peter. *James Earl Carter: The Man and the Myth*. Kansas City, Mo.: Sheed Andrews and McMeel, 1978.

Michael, Deanna L., *Jimmy Carter as Educational Policymaker: Equal Opportunity and Efficiency*. Albany: State University of New York Press, 2009.

Miller, Zell. *A National Party No More: The Conscience of a Conservative Democrat*. Macon, Ga.: Stroud and Hall, 2003.

Mondale, Walter F. *The Good Fight: A Life in Liberal Politics*. New York: Scribner, 2010.

Morris, Kenneth E. *Jimmy Carter: American Moralist*. Athens: University of Georgia Press, 1996.

Neyland, James. *The Carter Family Scrapbook: An Intimate Close-Up of America's First Family*. New York: Grosset & Dunlap, 1977.

Padgett, Dorothy. *Jimmy Carter: Elected President with Pocket Change and Peanuts*. Macon, Ga.: Mercer University Press, 2016.

Plains Historical Preservation Trust. *History of Plains, Georgia*. Fernandina Beach, Fla.: Wolfe, 2003.

Powell, Jody. *The Other Side of the Story*. New York: William Morrow, 1984.

Public Papers of the Presidents of the United States: Jimmy Carter, 1977–1981. Washington, D.C.: Government Printing Office, 1977–82.

Quiros, Ansley L. *God with Us: Lived Theology and the Freedom Struggle in Americus, Georgia, 1942–1976*. Chapel Hill: University of North Carolina Press, 2018.

Schram, Martin. *Running for President, 1976: The Carter Campaign*. New York: Stein and Day, 1977.

Short, Bob. *Everything Is Pickrick: The Life of Lester Maddox*. Macon, Ga.: Mercer University Press, 1999.

Slavicek, Louise Chipley. *Jimmy Carter*, Philadelphia: Chelsea House, 2003.

Stapleton, Ruth Carter. *Brother Billy*. New York: Harper & Row, 1978.

St. John, Jeffrey. *Jimmy Carter's Betrayal of the South*. Ottawa, Ill.: Green Hill, 1976.

Tartan, Beth, and Rudy Hayes. *Miss Lillian and Friends: The Plains, Georgia, Family Philosophy and Recipe Book*. New York: A & W, 1977.

Thompson, Kenneth W., ed., *The Carter Presidency: Fourteen Intimate Perspectives of Jimmy Carter*. Lanham, Md.: University Press of America, 1990.

Troester, Rod. *Jimmy Carter as Peacemaker: A Post-presidential Biography*. Westport, Conn.: Praeger, 1996.

Veale, Frank H., Jr. *Carter: A Son of Georgia*. Cairo, Ga.: published by the author, 1977.

Walton, Hanes, Jr. *The Native Son Presidential Candidate: The Carter Vote in Georgia*. New York: Praeger, 1992.

Whipple, Chris. *The Gatekeepers: How the White House Chiefs of Staff Define Every Presidency*. New York: Crown, 2017.

Woodward, Bob, and Carl Bernstein. *The Final Days*. New York: Simon & Schuster, 2005.

Wooten, James T. *Dasher: The Roots and the Rising of Jimmy Carter*. New York: Summit Books, 1978.

Young, Andrew. *A Way Out of No Way*. Nashville, Tenn.: Thomas Nelson, 1994.

Zelizer, Julian E. *Jimmy Carter: The 39th President, 1977–81*. New York: Times Books, 2010.

Websites

. . . .

"Carter Work Project." Habitat for Humanity website. https://www.habitat.org/volunteer/build-events/carter-work-project

Conference

. . . .

The Carter Presidency: Lessons for the 21st Century. Conference commemorating the thirtieth anniversary of the inauguration of President Jimmy Carter, University of Georgia, Athens, Georgia, January 19–21, 2007. Videos available at https://www.c-span.org/video/?196200-6/carter-presidency-town-hall-meeting (Jimmy Carter, Town Hall Meeting); https://www.c-span.org/video/?196200-4/luncheon-keynote-speech (Rosalynn Carter, Luncheon Keynote Speech); and https://www.c-span.org/video/?196199-1/vice-presidency-carter-administration (Richard Moe, roundtable discussion "The Carter Reforms of the Vice Presidency").

Newspapers and Magazines

. . . .

Americus Times-Recorder
Atlanta Journal-Constitution
Columbus Ledger-Enquirer
New Yorker
New York Times
Time
Valdosta Daily Times
Washington Post

PHOTO CREDITS

50   Photo by David Lewis, Carter Family Papers, Jimmy Carter Library.

51   WSB Radio Records, Popular Music and Culture Collection, Special Collections and Archives, Georgia State University Library.

52   Photo by Audley Tucker, Democratic Party Collection, Richard B. Russell Library for Political Research and Studies, University of Georgia Libraries.

53   Democratic Party Collection, Richard B. Russell Library for Political Research and Studies, University of Georgia Libraries.

54   Georgia Archives.

55L   Photo by Audley Tucker, Democratic Party Collection, Richard B. Russell Library for Political Research and Studies, University of Georgia Libraries.

55R   Democratic Party Collection, Richard B. Russell Library for Political Research and Studies, University of Georgia Libraries.

56   Photo by Audley Tucker, Democratic Party Collection, Richard B. Russell Library for Political Research and Studies, University of Georgia Libraries.

57   Photo by Red Holsclaw, Emory University Photograph Collection, Stuart A. Rose Manuscript, Archives, and Rare Book Library, Emory University.

58   Carter Family Papers, Jimmy Carter Library.

59   Zell B. Miller Papers, Richard B. Russell Library for Political Research and Studies, University of Georgia Libraries.

60L   Georgia Archives, Governmental Records Prints, grp01-01.

60R   Carter Family Papers, Jimmy Carter Library.

61   Callaway Gardens and Troup County Archives, MS080.b08.f17.10.

62   Georgia Archives, Vanishing Georgia, ful0088.

63   Georgia Archives, Vanishing Georgia, ben341.

64   Photo courtesy of Mr. and Mrs. Beauchamp Carr.

65   Georgia Capitol Museum.

66L&R Photo by Ron Sherman.

67   Jimmy Carter Library, Wikimedia Commons.

69   Photo by Thomas J. O'Halloran, Library of Congress.

70   Jimmy Carter Library, Wikimedia Commons.

72   Georgia Capitol Museum.

74   Library of Congress.

76   Georgia Archives, Vanishing Georgia, sum099.

77   Georgia Archives, Vanishing Georgia, stw5.

78   Photo by Warren K. Leffler, Library of Congress.

80   Photo by Warren K. Leffler, Library of Congress.

81   Courtesy of the Little White House.

82   Photo by Thomas J. O'Halloran, Library of Congress.

83   Photo by Ashmore Photographs, Millard Grimes Papers, Hargrett Rare Book and Manuscript Library, University of Georgia Libraries.

84   Georgia Archives, Vanishing Georgia, sum131.

85   Jimmy Carter Library, Wikimedia Commons.

87   Jimmy Carter Library, Wikimedia Commons.

88   Jimmy Carter Library, Wikimedia Commons.

89   Jimmy Carter Library, Wikimedia Commons.

90   Georgia Archives, Vanishing Georgia. sum97.

91   Jimmy Carter Library, Wikimedia Commons.

93   Jimmy Carter Library, Wikimedia Commons.

94   Photo by Kightlighter, Jimmy Carter Library.

95   Photo by Schumacher, Jimmy Carter Library.

96   Jimmy Carter Library, Wikimedia Commons.

97   Jimmy Carter Library, Wikimedia Commons.

98   William Tapley Bennett Jr. Papers, Richard B. Russell Library for Political Research and Studies, University of Georgia Library.

99   Jimmy Carter Library, Wikimedia Commons.

100   Jimmy Carter Library, Wikimedia Commons.

101   Jimmy Carter Library, Wikimedia Commons.

103   Jimmy Carter Library, Wikimedia Commons.

104   Jimmy Carter Library.

105   Jimmy Carter Library.

106   Jimmy Carter Library.

107   John P. Culver Jr. Photograph Collection, Georgia Tech Archives and Special Collections.

108   Jimmy Carter Library, Wikimedia Commons.

109   Jimmy Carter Library, Wikimedia Commons.

110   Photo by Audley Tucker, Democratic Party Collection, Richard B. Russell Library for Political Research and Studies, University of Georgia Libraries.

112   Photo by Fackelman, Jimmy Carter Library.

113   Department of Defense Photographs, National Archives and Records Administration.

117   Jimmy Carter Library, Wikimedia Commons.

118   Zell Miller Papers, Richard B. Russell Library for Political Research and Studies, University of Georgia Libraries.

119T&B   Library of Congress.

121   Photo by Fackelman, Jimmy Carter Library.

122T&B   Photo by author.

123   Photo by Fitz-Patrick, Jimmy Carter Library.

124   Floyd Jillson Collection, Kenan Research Center at the Atlanta History Center.

127   Democratic Party Collection, Richard B. Russell Library for Political Research and Studies, University of Georgia Libraries.

128   Photo by Audley Tucker, Democratic Party Collection, Richard B. Russell Library for Political Research and Studies, University of Georgia Libraries.

129   Miller Center, University of Virginia.

130   Zell Miller Papers, Richard B. Russell Library for Political Research and Studies, University of Georgia Libraries.

131   John A. Sibley Papers, Stuart A. Rose Manuscript, Archives, and Rare Book Library, Emory University.

132T&B   Jimmy Carter Library, Wikimedia Commons.

133   Tommy Irvin Democratic Party Papers, Richard B. Russell Library for Political Research and Studies, University of Georgia Libraries.

134   Max Cleland Collection, Richard B. Russell Library for Political Research and Studies, University of Georgia Libraries.

137   Courtesy of the Carter Center.

138   Stuart A. Rose Manuscript, Archives, and Rare Book Library, Emory University.

140   Stuart A. Rose Manuscript, Archives, and Rare Book Library, Emory University.

141   Stuart A. Rose Manuscript, Archives, and Rare Book Library, Emory University.

142   Democratic Party Collection, Richard B. Russell Library for Political Research and Studies, University of Georgia Libraries.

143   Democratic Party Collection, Richard B. Russell Library for Political Research and Studies, University of Georgia Libraries.

144   Democratic Party Collection, Richard B. Russell Library for Political Research and Studies, University of Georgia Libraries.

145   Ronald Reagan Library.

147   Courtesy of the Carter Center.

148   Stuart A. Rose Manuscript, Archives, and Rare Book Library, Emory University.

149   Photo by W. A. Bridges Jr., courtesy of the Carter Center.

150   Louise Blemant Suggs Papers, Richard B. Russell Library for Political Research and Studies, University of Georgia Libraries.

151   Photo by Billy Howard, courtesy of the Carter Center.

152   Stuart A. Rose Manuscript, Archives, and Rare Book Library, Emory University.

153   Courtesy of the Carter Center.

154   Courtesy of the Carter Center.

155   Courtesy of the Carter Center.

156   Courtesy of the Carter Center.

157   Courtesy of the Carter Center.

158   Courtesy of the Carter Center.

159   Photo by Michael A. Schwarz, Constitution Project at the Project on Government Oversight.

160   Courtesy of the Carter Center.

163   Emory University social media (Facebook).

167TL   Habitat for Humanity International Records, Series 2, photographs, ms 3786, Hargrett Rare Book and Manuscript Library, University of Georgia Libraries.

167BL   Habitat for Humanity International.

167R   Millard and Linda Fuller Papers, Series V, photographs, ms 3770, Hargrett Rare Book and Manuscript Library, University of Georgia Libraries.

169   Habitat for Humanity International.

170   Habitat for Humanity International.

171   Millard and Linda Fuller Papers, Series V, photographs, ms 3770, Hargrett Rare Book and Manuscript Library, University of Georgia Libraries.

172   Millard and Linda Fuller Papers, Series V, photographs, ms 3770, Hargrett Rare Book and Manuscript Library, University of Georgia Libraries.

173L   Millard and Linda Fuller Papers, Series V, photographs, ms 3786, Hargrett Rare Book and Manuscript Library, University of Georgia Libraries.

173R   Millard and Linda Fuller Papers, Series V, photographs, ms 3770, Hargrett Rare Book and Manuscript Library, University of Georgia Libraries.

174T&B   Millard and Linda Fuller Papers, Series V, photographs, ms 3770, Hargrett Rare Book and Manuscript Library, University of Georgia Libraries.

175   Habitat for Humanity International.

176   Millard and Linda Fuller Papers, Series V, photographs, ms 3770, Hargrett Rare Book and Manuscript Library, University of Georgia Libraries.

178   Habitat for Humanity International Records, Series 2, photographs, ms 3786, Hargrett Rare Book and Manuscript Library, University of Georgia Libraries.

180   Habitat for Humanity International.

181   Habitat for Humanity International Records, Series 2, photographs, ms 3786, Hargrett Rare Book and Manuscript Library, University of Georgia Libraries.

182   Habitat for Humanity International.

183   Habitat for Humanity International Records, Series 2, photographs, ms 3786, Hargrett Rare Book and Manuscript Library, University of Georgia Libraries.

184   Habitat for Humanity International Records, Series 2, photographs, ms 3786, Hargrett Rare Book and Manuscript Library, University of Georgia Libraries.

186T&B   Habitat for Humanity International Records, Series 2, photographs, ms 3786, Hargrett Rare Book and Manuscript Library, University of Georgia Libraries.

187   Courtesy of Dr. and Mrs. Stuart Gulley.

188   Habitat for Humanity International Records, Series 2, photographs, ms 3786, Hargrett Rare Book and Manuscript Library, University of Georgia Libraries.

189   Millard and Linda Fuller Papers, Series V, photographs, ms 3770, Hargrett Rare Book and Manuscript Library, University of Georgia Libraries.

190   Photo by author.

191   Habitat for Humanity International.

192   Habitat for Humanity International.

196   Zell Miller Papers, Richard B. Russell Library for Political Research and Studies, University of Georgia Libraries.

197   Georgia Archives, RG 1-18-92, ah01856.

198   National Archives and Records Administration, Wikimedia Commons.

199   George H. W. Bush Presidential Library and Museum.

200   Zell Miller Papers, Richard B. Russell Library for Political Research and Studies, University of Georgia Libraries.

201L   Photo by Greg B. Minchew.

201R   Zell Miller Papers, Richard B. Russell Library for Political Research and Studies, University of Georgia Libraries.

202   Zell Miller Papers, Richard B. Russell Library for Political Research and Studies, University of Georgia Libraries.

203   Photo by Laura Heath, Zell Miller Papers, Richard B. Russell Library for Political Research and Studies, University of Georgia Libraries.

204   Photo by Laura Heath, Zell Miller Papers, Richard B. Russell Library for Political Research and Studies, University of Georgia Libraries.

205   University of Georgia Division of Marketing and Communications.

206   Courtesy of the Carter Center.

207   Photo by Steffan Hacker, Habitat for Humanity International Records, Series 2, photographs, ms 3786, Hargrett Rare Book and Manuscript Library, University of Georgia Libraries.

208   Courtesy of the Carter Center.

211L   Photo by Journalist 3rd Class Steven Feller, U.S. Navy, Wikimedia Commons.

211R	Photo by Journalist 1st Class Jennifer Spinner, U.S. Navy, Wikimedia Commons.
212	Photo by Pete Souza, Wikimedia Commons.
213	Gerald R. Ford Presidential Foundation.
214	Shutterstock.
215	National Park Service.
216	Photo by Andrea Hanks, Official White House Photograph.
219	Courtesy of the Carter Center.
220	Friends of Jimmy Carter Historic District.
221	Library of Congress.
222	Photo by Lewis Jones, Richard Ray papers, Richard B. Russell Library for Political Research and Studies, University of Georgia Libraries.
223	Photo by the author.
224	Photo by the author.
225L, TR&BR	Photo by the author.
226	AndrewServes, Andrew College.
227	Library of Congress.
228L	News and Communications, Duke University.
228R	Habitat for Humanity International Records, Series 2, photographs, ms 3786, Hargrett Rare Book and Manuscript Library, University of Georgia Libraries.
229	Courtesy of Best Western Plus Windsor Hotel.
230L	Photo by A. Poyo, courtesy of the Carter Center.
230TR	Atlanta Braves Kiss Cam.
230BR	Photo by Mitch Kincaid.
232	Mercer University.
233	Chris Fenn, Georgia Southwestern State University.
234	Chris Fenn, Georgia Southwestern State University.
235	Photo by Bo Shell, Atlanta Botanical Gardens. Artwork © 2020 Chihuly Studio / Artists Rights Society (ARS), New York.
236L	Betty Cantrell.
236R	Diane Hollis Harrell.
237L&R	Chris Fenn, Georgia Southwestern State University.
238	Courtesy of Rosalynn Carter Butterfly Trail™.
240	Georgia Archives, Vanishing Georgia, sum83.
242	Jimmy Carter Library, Wikimedia Commons.
243	Courtesy of Matthew Graham.
244	Emory University social media.
245	Photo by Jill Stuckey, Maranatha Baptist Church.
246	Habitat for Humanity International.
248	Courtesy of the Carter Center.

INDEX